I0821585

Guerrilla Warfare in Civil War Kentucky

Guerrilla Warfare in Civil War Kentucky

Gerald W. Fischer

Acclaim Press
MORLEY, MISSOURI

P.O. Box 238
Morley, MO 63767
(573) 472-9800
www.acclaimpress.com

Book Design: Devon Burroughs
Cover Design: M. Frene Melton

Library of Congress Control Number: 2014917277
ISBN-13: 978-1-938905-80-3
ISBN-10: 1-938905-80-6

Second Printing 2015
Printed in the United States of America
10 9 8 7 6 5 4 3 2

Cover photo: A group of "Morgan's Men" while prisoners of war in Western Penitentiary, Pennsylvania. Pictured (l to r): Captain William E. Curry, 8th Kentucky Cavalry; Lieutenant Andrew J. Church, 8th Kentucky Cavalry; Lieutenant Leeland Hathaway, 14th Kentucky Cavalry; Lieutenant Henry D. Brown, 10th Kentucky Cavalry; Lieutenant William Hays, 20th Kentucky Cavalry. All were captured with John Hunt Morgan in Ohio, 1863. This image is part of the Hunt-Morgan House Deposit of photographs, 1860-1949, housed at the University of Kentucky Special Collections and Digital Programs.

Contents

Introduction

When I was a child, I was brought up in an environment where history was not a thing of the past, but was part of everyday life. My Grandfather Fischer was born in 1891, and told stories about living in a log cabin in Alabama where his parents, both from Germany, homesteaded, and told him stories of the Civil War. He remembered Ku Klux Klan activities when he was a boy, and faced a machine gun during the 1927 railroad strike in Decatur, Alabama.

Stories were told about a cousin of ours who stole a steamboat loaded with contraband liquor in 1921 from Decatur, Alabama, and steamed it to Chattanooga, Tennessee, where he sold the liquor and the steamboat. My Grandfather Bryant was born in 1886, and as a boy had been captured by Ojibwa Indians in Minnesota. He rafted crops down the Kentucky River from Irvine, Kentucky, to Frankfort because the roads were so bad.

I grew up listening to them recount the stories, as if they had just recently happened. My father, Henry C. Fischer Jr., was in the U.S. Navy during WWII and sailed on the Battleships *Nevada* and *Iowa*. He was stationed on Okinawa. My Uncle Fred Fischer was on Guam. Each year when we took vacations, my parents mapped out AAA Triptiks that included Civil War battlefields, museums, and other historical sites. We camped out on these vacations that took us south to Monterey, Mexico, throughout the eastern seaboard, the southwest, and in every corner of Kentucky. Even when we enjoyed outdoor sports, such as fishing, there were oftentimes historic markers near our fishing holes, in Jefferson, Shelby and Spencer Counties, that told about the exploits of Edwin Terrell, William Clarke Quantrill, Dr. John Knight, Sue Mundy and others. Whenever we passed a new or heretofore-unseen historic marker, Dad would stop and back up the car to read it and see what had happened to commemorate this place. History was something we, my brother and I, lived with daily because of the interests of our family.

After high school I entered the University of Louisville, where I majored in History and Anthropology. Obtaining an Associate degree in Anthropology and a Bachelor of Liberal Studies degree in History and Anthropology, I studied archaeology, anthropology, and World, European, and American History. I enjoyed Kentucky History and the Civil War above others. I became an archaeologist of sorts, a member, and later an officer of the Louisville Archaeological Society. I was fortunate to present archaeological papers at the University of Louisville, Eastern Kentucky University, and Western Kentucky University. Writing excited me. I wrote sections of various archaeological reports, and in 1968 I had my first article published.

During this period I became one of Dr. Joseph E. Grainger's student assistants and co-supervised the Mill Creek Station archaeological excavation. Later I was assistant supervisor on the South Western Jefferson County Floodwall Survey for the Army Corps of Engineers as contracted with the University of Louisville. I often spoke at schools and society meetings about the prehistory of the area. I moved with my day job to Florida, and thence to Phoenix Arizona, where, after surviving a heart attack, I determined to return to Kentucky. On my return to Kentucky I decided to teach, enrolling in Spalding University, where in 2002 I completed a Master of Arts Degree in Teaching.

I made a trip back to Kentucky in the spring of 1993 and I met 74-year-old James Wakefield who guided my wife, mother, and me to visit the Quantrill capture site. He told me of little known unpublished stories and family anecdotes of the Wakefield's. He knew stories of Jesse and Frank James, as well as Bad Ed Terrell and Quantrill's Raiders. His family once owned the farm where Terrell captured Quantrill.

I came back to Kentucky, settling in Meade County in January of 1997, and began working as a Catholic school teacher for St. Simon and Jude School, a job from which I retired in 2007. In 2006 I wrote a story about Sue Mundy's Capture in Meade County, Kentucky, as told to me by Mr. Mark Henderson, the great-great-grandson of John Cox. He had a totally different story about the capture of Mundy from the one commonly accepted. Ten years later, I asked Mark if I could write his version of the events. He provided me with several interviews and copies of his family's papers. This article, published in the *Meade County Messenger* in 2006, was my first foray into writing since the 1970's. In 2007 I was very fortunate to meet 97-year-old Hobart Coomes, when a friend told me of a Confederate Raid that occurred about three miles from my house. Hobart told me the story of the raid and he, too, had a different version from what has been previously written. He died two months after our interview.

I have met and interviewed a number of people in Kentucky (Meade, Shelby, and Spencer Counties in particular) familiar with the old stories. I have met and discussed these topics with many historians and authors, but what I have found equally important are those historians like Bill Whalen, Rice Dugan, Steve Straney, Herb Pollock, Larry and Peggy Greenwell, Shirley Brown, Dan Redenius, James Wakefield, Frances and Jess Scott, and Alice Bondurant Scott; I have found it a humbling experience to sit and talk with these most knowledgeable historians. Discussing events with them taught me that no matter how much I have learned about this subject, I will never be able to equal their collective knowledge. Investigating history is an addiction, and to that end, I have become a historic field trip junky.

I have tromped through the fields, woods, and cemeteries to gather the information for this book, and have personally taken many of the photographs. I am fortunate to have been provided many others by friends who share my interests. Where I think it appropriate, I have included footnotes that sometimes quote the facts of others in their words, but more often are references where readers can find verification or corroboration about what I write. Most of the material for this book comes from old newspaper accounts, abstracts, church histories, and other lesser-known historical documents.

Three newspaper abstract compilations deserve special mention: Mr. Steven Wright has compiled a five-volumes set of abstracts that have proved to be a real boon for any serious researcher. Carolyn Wimp has several volumes of abstracts that pertain to Meade, Breckenridge and associated counties that are excellent. Lastly, the Shelby County Library in Shelbyville, Kentucky, has several wonderfully compiled abstracts from newspapers that served that area. I have included reference to these works in the bibliography (References) section.

I will readily admit that my stories do not always comport with other written histories. They are, however, from sources that were written when memories were fresher, and from family stories that have been passed down through time. Whether the stories I have written are in agreement with others or not, they add facts and details that make them interesting and, to me at least, become richer and more alive. Some of the stories in this book are taken from articles I have previously researched and written, and most of them contain up-dated facts and information not contained in the original pieces. Considerable material in this book has not previously been published, in detail. Whenever possible, I have noted where the stories I tell differ from the accounts of others.

I have written this book for three reasons: Firstly, I believe as does Virgil Carrington Jones that the guerrilla warriors, *Partisan Rangers,* usually only a footnote in history without much credit given to them, prolonged the Civil War by perhaps a year. They disrupted supply lines and communications, causing troops to be withdrawn from the front lines or diverted in order to quell the guerrilla activity. They persecuted Unionists, killed soldiers sent home on leave, burned trains, trestles, and stations and raised hell in general. This terrified many of the Unionists. Secondly, I write this to memorialize in one document my research and the facts and details I have uncovered. Lastly, I have written this book to share some my enjoyment in the discovery of little known events that fill gaps in previously written histories, and telling the little stories of Kentucky's Civil War.

This book is dedicated to
Stephen K. Fischer

Guerrilla Warfare in Civil War Kentucky

Chapter 1

Time and Place

For the purposes of this book, the "Heartland of Kentucky" is defined as the central and west central area of Kentucky that includes much of two major regions—the Bluegrass and the Pennyroyal. To the north and west of the heartland, the Ohio River forms the physical and political boundary of Kentucky. The two regions are divided between the southwestern Bluegrass, at its eastern juncture with the Pennyroyal Region, by the high knobs of the Muldraugh Escarpment. The Pennyroyal is a karst region underlain with Mississippian Limestone plateaus. Caves and sinkholes are present in the hills, and exposures of chert are found at the bedding plains. Clear flowing springs and spring fed creeks are abundant in the area.[1]

The chert deposits and clear natural springs and creeks were important to the earliest human inhabitants of the county, the Native Americans. It was from the flint-like chert deposits that their finely made knives, arrow and spear points were shaped. The earliest Native Americans to inhabit Kentucky were the Paleo-Indians that hunted the migrating mega fauna of the Rancholobrian that existed until the end of the Pleistocene.[2]

Over time, the large animals such as mammoth, dire wolf, saber-toothed cat and others became extinct, and as the glaciers retreated and the climate changed these nomadic wanderers became more restricted in their range, and gathering activities assumed greater importance than hunting, resulting in a more sedentary lifestyle. Approximately 5,000 years before present rude horticulture was developed that later became intensive agriculture, giving rise to the manufacture of ceramics (pottery), walled villages, ceremonial plazas, and truncated ceremonial mounds. Small triangular projectile points, shell tempered decorated pottery, incised shell ornaments, and game stones typify the artifact complex. These last native peoples were called Mississippian[3] and they evolved or devolved into the historic Native Americans found by the early settlers, Cherokee, Shawnee, Mingo, Wyandotte and others.

The Bluegrass Region was the first area of Kentucky to be settled by white immigrants. The region is the geologic result of a large basin of underlying Ordovician limestone. On all sides save the north, which is bordered by the Ohio River, the Knobs surround and border the Bluegrass. Three major river systems provide the drainage to the area, the Salt, the Licking, and the Kentucky. These rivers are deeply channeled and steep sided with narrow river bottoms. The Salt River at its confluence with the Ohio River in West Point, Kentucky, became of significant importance because of its juncture with the Mulldraugh Escarpment, the two navigable rivers, and the confluence of the Pond Creek drainage. Before the pioneer settlement of the 1770's, hardwood forests covered the Bluegrass Region. Forests of Ash, Beech, Hickories, Oaks, Maples, Red Cedar, and Walnut abounded.

The Pennyroyal, a rolling plateau, dominates west central Kentucky. It is also a karst region with sinkholes and underground streams riddling the underlying limestone formations. Tall grass prairie was the common native upland cover and hardwood forests filled the stream valleys. Early pioneers called the Pennyroyal the "Barrens". This did not mean the region was actually barren, only that there were few trees. Finley called the region the Green River Plains and noted that it was fertile land with excellent herbage. The native cover is a mixed forest of beech, yellow poplar, sugar maple and other deciduous and evergreen trees.[4]

The eastern knobs of the Pennyroyal and western border of the Bluegrass Region are the dissected rim of the Pennyroyal called Muldraugh Hills. These knobs range up to 900' above mean sea level. They are steep sided, forested, and have little flat land on their summits. At the time of discovery, wildlife found in both regions was not much different than that found today. The first explorers encountered white tail deer, black bear, wolf, mountain lion, elk, wild turkey, fox, raccoon, opossum, grey and fox squirrels, cottontail rabbits, ducks, geese, quail, dove, and passenger pigeons (now extinct). Various aquatic species and fishes such as black bass, bluegill, catfish, crappie, white bass, mussels, crayfish, bullfrogs and various turtles, other reptiles and amphibians, inhabited the creeks and the Ohio River into which they flowed.

Kentucky was truly a hunter's paradise. With the exception of wolf, black bear, elk, mountain lion, and passenger pigeons, the wildlife indigenous to the area remain today as discovered by the first European explorers.

The first white explorers, perhaps Spanish, French, or Welsh as anecdotal myths and legends relate, found thousands of acres of grassy plains and the forests of hardwoods we see today. Under-canopy growth along the woodland borders such as blackberry, raspberry, pawpaw, hazelnut, sumac, wild strawberry, grapes and cherries provided sustenance to the first human inhabitants and later to the white settlers, but it was the Ohio River, with its drainage and geologic formations, that created the rich environment for plant and animal life to abound. Later, these natural attributes supported the industries that continue to sustain the population even until today.

In 1774, James Harrod and a party of men established the first permanent settlement in Kentucky, called at that time Harrod's Town but now known as Harrodsburg. The next year, after several previous trips to the area, Daniel Boone led a group of settlers across the Cumberland Gap to a place on the Kentucky River and founded Fort Boonesborough. The first recorded exploration in the Pennyroyal Region was in the summer of 1774, when Daniel Boone and Michael Stoner explored the area of Otter Creek in Meade County. Daniel and his equally resourceful brother Squire Boone made many trips throughout the Bluegrass and Pennyroyal Regions. The names of the early settlers into Harrod's Town and Boonesborough are commonly found throughout the Bluegrass and Pennyroyal, as the settlers moved westward into the interior of the state searching for free land. Boone, Bryant, Breckenridge, Brown, Bullitt, Coomes, Floyd, Finley, Gist, Greer, Henderson, Horn, Logan, Lincoln, Seivers, Speed, and Woolfolk are just some of the commonly found names.

The portion of the two combined regions I call the "Heartland" consists of 26 contiguous counties: Anderson, Breckenridge, Bullitt, Butler, Davies, Edmondson, Franklin, Grayson, Green, Hancock, Hardin, Hart, Henry, Jefferson, Larue, Marion, Meade, Mercer, Nelson, Ohio, Oldham, Shelby, Spencer, Taylor, Washington, and Woodford. The geographic center of Kentucky lies in north central Marion County, which is truly the heart of the state. To be sure, there was guerrilla activity in all areas of Kentucky, but the 26 heartland counties, previously named, experienced some of the most intense and desperate guerrilla activity found anywhere in the state.

The Political Situation in Kentucky in 1861

Kentucky in 1861 had every intention of remaining neutral. It did not want to secede from the Union, but neither did it wish to furnish troops to invade either the south or north. Politically, Kentucky faced a dilemma. April 12th, 1861, the Confederate Army fired on Fort Sumter, South Carolina. War had begun. On May 16, 1861, the Kentucky committee on Federal Relations met and issued the following resolutions:

> *"Considering the deplorable condition of the country and for which the State of Kentucky is in no way responsible, and looking to the best means of preserving the internal peace and securing the lives, and liberty, and property of the citizens of the State; therefore", "Resolved by the House of Representatives, that this State and the citizens thereof should take no part in this war now being waged, except as mediators and friends to the belligerent parties; and that Kentucky should, during the contest, occupy the position of strict neutrality." "Resolved, that the act of the governor in refusing to furnish troops or military forces upon the call of the executive authority of the United States under existing circumstances is approved."*[5]

In a letter to Lieutenant W. Nelson, U.S.N. in Cincinnati, Ohio, from the Adjutant-General's Office Washington, D.C., dated July 1, 1861.

> *Sir: Your services having been placed at the disposal of the war department for the performance of a special duty, the Secretary of War directs me to communicate to you the following instructions: It being the fixed purpose of the general government to maintain the Constitution and execute the laws of the Union and to protect all loyal citizens in their constitutional rights, the Secretary directs that you muster into the service of the United States five regiments of infantry and one of cavalry in East Tennessee, to receive pay when called into active service by this department. You will designate the regimental and company officers, having due respect for the preferences of the regiments and companies, and send their names to this office for commissions. The ordinance bureau will*

forward to Cincinnati, Ohio 10,000 stand of arms and acountriments, six pieces of field artillery, two smooth and two rifle bore cannon and two mountain howitzers and ample supplies of ammunition to be carried through Kentucky into East Tennessee, in such manner as you may direct, for distribution among the men so mustered into service and organized as Home Guards. You will also at the same time muster into service or designate some suitable person to do so in southeast Kentucky three regiments of infantry, to be commanded and officered in the same manner as herein provided for the Tennessee Regiments. All the regiments aforesaid will be raised for service in East and West Tennessee and adjacent counties in East Kentucky. Blank muster rolls and the usual instructions to mustering officers will be sent to you from this office, and in carrying out this order you are authorized to employ such service and use such means as you may deem expedient and proper for its faithful execution. You will likewise report frequently to this office as you progress with your work.

I am sir, etc

L. Thomas, Adjutant-General[6]

Kentucky neutrality was being ignored. The north was invading Kentucky in spite of Kentucky's vow to remain neutral.

Kentucky Governor McGoffin, when he realized that Union forces were being assembled in Kentucky, on or about August 20th appointed George W. Johnson, of Scott County as a commissioner and wrote a letter to Jefferson Davis, hand delivered to Davis by Johnson questioning whether Kentucky's neutrality would be honored. One reason for the concern beyond the commission and mustering of troops and officers in the state by the Union was the massing of Confederate troops along the southern border of Kentucky by the Confederate Government. Davis wrote back to McGoffin, that the Confederate States Government would respect Kentucky's neutrality, and that the massing of troops along the border in Tennessee was to drive out the Union forces making incursions into the Confederacy. He further added that:

"... if the door be opened on the one side to aggression of one of the belligerent parties upon the other it ought not to be shut to the assailed when they seek to enter it for the purposes of self-defense.

I do not, however, for a moment believe that your gallant State will suffer its soil to be used for the purpose of giving an advantage to those who violate its neutrality and disregard its rights over those who respect them both.

In conclusion I tender to your Excellency the assurance of my high consideration and regard, and am, sir, Very respectfully yours, etc."

Jefferson Davis[7]

This declaration certainly did little to reassure McGoffin, and the letter convinced him that war within the borders of Kentucky was not only possible but also likely. McGoffin wrote letters to Lincoln that were not similarly published, but the sentiments of Lincoln's response was that the forces being raised by Lt. Nelson consisted exclusively of Kentuckians and were raised at the urging of Kentucky citizens. Lincoln stated, "*Taking all means to form a judgment, I do not believe it is the popular wish of Kentucky that this force shall be removed beyond her limits, and with this impression I must decline to remove it.*" The stage seemed set for war in the Commonwealth.[8]

The peace convention called by the Southern Rights leaders was held at Frankfort, Kentucky, on the 9th and 10th of September, 1861, but resulted only in the adoption of the resolutions deploring the unnatural war, advocating strict neutrality, favoring the dispersing of federal camps in the state, and expressing readiness when that was done to assist in enforcing the removal of the Tennesseans from Kentucky borders. The legislature directed the governor to order the withdrawal of the Tennessee troops from Kentucky soil. Brigadier General George H. Thompson assumed command of Camp Dick Robinson and Lieutenant Nelson was congratulated for doing such good work distributing arms to the Union men of Kentucky and organizing the troops at Camp Dick Robinson.

Within a few weeks, Lt. Nelson was assigned a command in eastern Kentucky as Brigadier General. Still, no overt acts of war had occurred within the political limits of Kentucky. No recruiting camps were established within Kentucky borders save those organized by Nelson. Many Kentuckians had joined the Union or Confederate military, but there was an abstinence of action on both sides that would violate Kentucky's neutrality. The Peace Commission of September 9th and 10th had Southern Rights leaders that were outspoken, and were exasperating to the Union leaders who looked for a pretext to take extreme measures. Without grounds for arrests, the Union men made them anyway. The first arrest was ex-Gov. Charles S. Morehead and Col. R. T. Durrett, who on the 18th of September were dragged from their beds without warrant or charge against them and were carried across the Ohio River into Indiana and thence east where they were imprisoned in Fort Warren, in Boston Harbor. The next day, under the false pretext that the southern men were going to take Lexington, but having the view to arresting the ex-Vice President John C. Breckenridge and other prominent southern men at their homes, Col. Thomas Bramlette with his regiment, then at Camp Dick Robinson, marched to Lexington and took charge of that place at midnight. Breckenridge, General William Preston, George W. Johnson, George B. Hodge, and William E. Simms, all Southern Rights men notified of their impending arrests, left at the same time and avoided apprehension.[9] Thus the people of Kentucky found that their fellow citizens, and indeed outspoken leaders advancing neutrality, were arrested without warrants or charges, and were imprisoned or forced to leave their homes. The arrests and abductions were in fact a violation of neutrality.

Chapter 2

Partisan Rangers Act

In May of 1861, a military minded man in Forest Depot, Bedford County, Virginia set down on paper an idea that was to grow like a rolling snowball. He was R.C. W. Radford, late captain of the first U.S. Dragoons, and his missive was directed to Robert E. Lee, newly resigned from the Union Army to command military and naval forces of his native Virginia. In it was an offer to raise and mount a company of 1,000 active men for Ranger or irregular service if the Confederate government would furnish them with long-range guns and pistols.[10] Lee forwarded the letter to Jubal A. Early where it was kept filed, probably in Early's saddlebags, although Early did make a note recommending Radford command troops in a five county area. The *Richmond Dispatch* was writing editorials at the same time urging Virginia men to form into companies of irregular soldiers to promulgate guerrilla war. It was suggested they arm themselves with smooth bore fowling pieces loaded with buckshot.[11] The possibility of guerrilla warfare becoming a reality was being given serious consideration in the press and by the Confederate Government. Already Kentucky Union Home Guards were being organized as militia units stationed in cities and towns across the state in order protect federal facilities and interests.

Further west, beginning in 1855, Missouri and Kansas experienced war on their borders that was in every sense a guerrilla war. Small bands of armed men pro-and anti- slavery, sometimes in uniform although many times not, would brutally attack each other in order to promote one political view or the other. The border states of Missouri, Kentucky, Maryland, and Delaware, were important to the Union, not only as a buffer between the Confederate States and a barrier to its potential invasion of the North by Confederate forces, but also as a source of raw materials, manufacturing, and tax revenue. These needs, equally necessary to both sides, made each strive to influence the sentiments of the border-states' citizenry to their way of thinking. If the border-states joined the Confederacy, the Union would be in greater jeopardy of losing the conflict, as the United States became financially and materially weaker and the South became proportionally stronger. Thus, the protracted warfare between Kansas and Missouri that escalated when Civil War was declared, as well as the divided and pro-southern sentiments in Maryland, Kentucky, and Delaware, made a fertile environment to promote the growth of guerrilla war on the border allowing it to blossom and bloom. On April 21, 1862, the Confederate Government finally passed the Partisan Ranger Act.

The Partisan Ranger Act was composed of three sections and was intended as a stimulus for recruitment of irregulars for service into the Confederate Army during the Civil War. It reads as follows:

> *Section 1. The Congress of the Confederate States of America do enact, that the President be, and he is hereby authorized to commission such officers as he may deem proper with authority to form bands of partisan rangers, in companies, battalions, or regiments, to be composed of such members as the President may approve.*
>
> *Section 2. Be it further enacted, that such partisan rangers, after being regularly received in the service, shall be entitled to the same pay, rations, and quarters during the term of service, and be subject to the same regulations as other soldiers.*
>
> *Section 3. Be it further enacted, that for any arms and munitions of war captured from the enemy by any, body of partisan rangers and delivered to any quartermaster at such place or places as may be designated by a commanding General, the rangers shall be paid their full value in such manner as the Secretary of War may prescribe.*

These provisions seemed to be followed in the beginning of the war, but the payment of soldiers was not always prompt or possible. In practice, especially late in the war, many of the Partisan Rangers were authorized by other soldiers who were given battlefield commissions, or sent north by the Confederacy, into Kentucky to raise guerrilla forces. Adam Rankin Johnson and his Breckenridge Guards, Lee Sypert, and maybe Thomas Dupoyster who might have gotten his orders from

John Hunt Morgan, and Billy Shacklett were all such commissioned recruiters. As the war continued, the legitimacy of some of the Partisan Rangers became murky and clouded.

Chapter 3

Guerrilla Warfare on the Border

The border states of Kentucky and Missouri were particularly ripe for the initiation of guerrilla warfare. Missouri had for six years before the Civil War experienced a shooting war on its border with Kansas. Kentucky, Maryland, Delaware, and Missouri were divergent in sentiments for the belligerent parties. Slavery was a factor when determining whether one was pro-southern or not. Although 19.5 percent or 225,483 slaves were included in the Kentucky population of 1860, most Kentuckians did not own slaves.[12] Kentucky considered itself culturally linked to the southern states, since it was at one time a part of the Old Dominion, but it held very friendly ties with Ohio, Indiana, and other northern states.

In the 1860 census of Meade County, 8,898 people are listed in the total population. Of these there were 1,232 black slaves and 468 mulatto slaves, 13 free blacks and nine free mulattos. The 1,700 slaves in Meade County were owned by 372 slave owners. Edward Rhodes, the Postmaster of Payneville during the war, owned seven slaves while the Richardson family owned perhaps 10 times that many. The average slave owner probably owned no more than three slaves, and likely fewer. Because families were larger in those times one in three Meade County people likely owned other people.

Estimates of Kentuckians who fought for the Union are between 90,000 and 100,000 men, while those that fought for the Confederacy are estimated between 25,000 and 40,000. One reason for the disparity in the numbers was the conscription act that was passed in the United States, allowing for men to be drafted. There was a Confederate draft, however, Kentucky was held by Union forces throughout most of the war, so no Confederate enforcement of the draft took place. Kentucky saw an invasion of Confederate troops in 1862. Simon Bolivar Buckner occupied Bowling Green. General Zollicoffer moved through Cumberland Gap and occupied parts of Eastern Kentucky, and Johnston held a thin line across Kentucky from Columbus to Bowling Green. Grant occupied Paducah, and Louisville and other towns along the Ohio River soon were occupied by Federal forces.

On September 11th the Kentucky House of Representatives by a vote of 71-26 instructed the governor to order the Confederates to withdraw from the state. Then on a vote of 29-68 it defeated a motion asking both sides to withdraw. The senate approved the Confederate-only withdrawal. Some Kentuckians were embarrassed and disappointed at the support of the Union, and on October 29-30 a convention met behind Confederate lines in Russellville, the result of which was the setting of a date for a sovereignty convention to be held on November 18-20 due to the Frankfort Government having been replaced by a military despotism. The delegates at this convention severed their connection with the United States and formed a provisional government until such time as a convention could be held to provide a regular one. This government would consist of a governor and a council of 10 members and such judges and other officials as might be needed; Bowling Green was made the capital.

One of the first acts of the provisional government was to request admission into the Confederate States of America. In spite of the irregular procedure the Confederacy admitted Kentucky on December 10th, 1861. Kentucky became a star on the Confederate flag.[13] Promptly, southern-leaning Governor Beriah McGoffin resigned due to his disagreement with the highly irregular procedure employed to circumvent the actions of the State legislature.

In January of 1862, George Thomas defeated General Felix Zollicoffer at the battle of Mill Springs. In February of the same year, Ulysses Grant and Admiral Andrew Foote's gunboats captured Forts Henry and Donelson on the Kentucky/Tennessee border. The Confederate line of General Johnston crumbled, and the army had to withdraw to Corinth, Mississippi.[14] Other Confederate and Union forces invaded and fought battles at Munfordville, Elizabethtown, Perryville, Brandenburg, and skirmishes around Louisville.

The year 1862 was in real terms the beginning of the Civil War in Kentucky. When the first fighting took place, many soldiers in the Union Army found themselves to be in a unique position where they had to rethink their allegiance. As arms came into Kentucky, some of the Union soldiers, Home Guards, or others that were issued such arms, or put in charge of their distribution, switched sides. In the fall of 1861 a Captain Gorsuch, living with his wife and children in New Albany, Indiana, while stationed across the Ohio River, in Louisville, was charged with embezzling arms from the Union Army. On September 9th, the *Louisville Daily Journal* wrote: "The charge against Capt. Gorsuch - charged with embezzlement of State arms. An argument that Louisville's City Court had no jurisdiction over was quashed. Gorsuch gave bail in the sum of $800, his father, Mr. A.P. Gorsuch, H.F. Simrall, and Jeff Brown was sureties."[15]

In May of 1861, the *Louisville Daily Journal* reported that J.G. Gorsuch had been assigned the Company of Newcomb Grays and had to go into camp at Camp Shelby, near Shepherdsville. Ten companies composed the first regiment of the (Union) Kentucky State Guard.[16] These men were supplied with arms that arrived from Cincinnati, Ohio, at the time they went into camp, on or about May 27, 1861.

June 5, 1861, the *Louisville Daily Journal* reported that James Gorsuch was departing for the new encampment at Muldraugh's Hill, on the L&N Railroad named Camp Daviess. It was reported, the Armstrong Guards, Captain Gorsuch, "will leave for the encampment today."[17] Between May 27, 1861, and September 5th of the same year, Gorsuch became a Rebel. The *Louisville Daily Journal* on September 5, 1861, reported: "Captain James G. Gorsuch, the commander of the Armstrong Rifles, a company belonging to the State Guard, left Portland yesterday morning, with 60 guns and accoutrements, all arms belonging to the company, attended by 12 men of his company. They took possession of the steamer *Masonic Gem,* which lay at Portland, and embarked for some point below. We are well aware that an order for the return of arms would not be obeyed."[18] By September 6, 1861, Gorsuch and his associate, Captain Mitchell Pete, were being referred to as Confederates. September 6, 1861, the *Louisville Daily Journal* wrote: "A Portland gentleman, who saw most of the proceedings of Capt. Mitchell Pete, Capt. Gorsuch, and his Confederates in the stealing of the State arms: The guns were kept in the coffee-house of Fred Duckwall. Near midnight, a wagon having driven up in front of the door, Capt. Pete stepped out and blew a horn three times, and a minute afterwards, the loud rattle of arms as they were being tossed into the wagon was heard. The guns were driven to the river, where the marauders, or a portion of them, went on board the *Masonic Gem*, and broke into the Captain's state room, from which they stole a valuable revolver. They broke into other rooms, stealing bedding. The whole of the plunder was put on board the yawl of the *John Raine*, and taken down river."[19]

Apparently stealing arms issued to the Union from Cincinnati, Ohio, was wide spread or was being adopted by other secessionists around the state. Arms were also stolen from Mayfield, Kentucky, and other areas in the state that caused Governor Magoffin to issue a proclamation that all stolen arms were to be turned over to county judges of their respective counties, although he later decided that he had no power to make such an arrangement. On September 9th, bail was made for James Gorsuch. In the September 16th issue of the *Louisville Daily Journal* the following story was reported: "We are informed that the freight train going south over the L&N Railroad yesterday was detained beyond its usual time by Blanton Duncan, James G. Gorsuch, John D. Pope, Mitchell La Pielle, Phil. Victor, and a party of sixty or seventy secessionists, who compelled the engineer to remain long enough to enable them to ship sixty guns from that point for the Confederacy. They had been seized at Elizabethtown, it appears by Maj. A. L. Symmes and placed in the jail for safe keeping, but the party broke open the jail and took possession, sending them to Camp Boone."[20]

"On October 25, 1861, the Jefferson County Grand Jury returned an indictment against James Gorsuch for stealing arms."[21] The last mention of Gorsuch in the *Louisville Daily Journal* while he was alive was printed April 5, 1862. It read: "It will be remembered that Capt. Jim Gorsuch, of Portland, was arrested, examined, and held to bail sometime last summer on the charge of misapplying the arms of the State in sending a number of guns south. It is alleged that he was aided by a man named Charles McCaffey, who returned home a few days ago, from the South. He was arrested."[22]

Sometime in the fall of 1861 or late winter of 1862, James Gorsuch became attached to William K. Shacklett and his Meade County Confederates. A Mr. J. (John) Boling, a frequent writer to the *Meade County Messenger* and a historian that lived through the Civil War, on Wednesday April 1, 1908, wrote a story for the *Messenger*. In the story that covered several different incidents of guerrilla activity in Meade County, he told of the Battle of Meadeville, referred to variously as the

Battle of the Sheep Shed, or the Raid on Billy Shacklett. A week later, on April 8, 1908, Mr. A.J. Thompson, a witness to part of the battle, wrote another story about the same fight and in an attempt to correct some details, added material not included in the Boling article. Both men agree on most of the salient points of the battle, but differ in the details.

In January of 2010, I wrote a two-part story of the Battle of the Sheep Shed for the Meade County *News Standard* newspaper. I included material from both articles, and explored the overgrown and dilapidated Meadeville Cemetery. About this same time I met two historians named Frances and Jess Scott, who chronicled the old times in Stith Valley on their website, stithvalley.com. In 2010, after a devastating 2009 ice storm that caused major damage in Meade County, we traversed the woods of Meadeville to locate the Schumate Schoolhouse, the scene of some of the fighting, and aftermath of the battle.

As happens to historians, just when you think you have all the facts and the complete story, new information emerges that changes what was first thought. Such is the case with this story. Before relating the Battle of the Sheep Shed, some differing facts between the Boling and Thompson articles, and the reports in the *Louisville Daily Journal* should be clarified. Both Boling and Thompson refer to Union Capt. Joseph Herr. The name and rank as reported in the *Louisville Daily Journal* on May 1st, is "Capt. Christopher C. Hare." Hare's Company G, 34th Ky., Mtd. Inf. was attached to the 25th Mich. Inf.[23] I suspect both Thompson and Boling were pronouncing and writing the Captain's name phonetically.

A gunrunner named Gossett or Gossip is mentioned by both men. It is reported he was the first man to run guns from Kentucky to the Confederacy. James G. Gorsuch likely made his way with the arms from the jailbreak at Elizabethtown to the Meadeville Big Springs area where Billy Shacklett was recruiting for the Confederacy. There is another disagreement between Boling and Thompson on the escape of Jess Taylor, who survived the battle. Boling states that William (Billy) Shacklett was the Captain of the Brandenburg Union Home Guard, and Thompson does not dispute the fact. Shacklett left Brandenburg in July of 1862 and enlisted in the Confederate Army in Big Springs, Kentucky, about five miles from Meadeville. Boling stated that although he didn't know it at the time, Shacklett had turned Confederate and was scouting in Meade County preparatory to going south. Shacklett was training the men he recruited in the Meadeville-Hill Grove area. He and his men had a sham battle in front of a Mr. Lon Moorman's house. The cavalry charged the infantry, who reserved half their fire for close range. When the cavalry were at close range, Shacklett's men gave them the reserve fire. Some of the horses threw their riders. There was a great excitement for a while, and the sham battle came very near terminating in a real one. Shacklett's company used to drill in one field where Mr. Ditto's house now stands. Mr. John Sealy beat the kettle drum and John Cain played the fife.

In relating the battle, based on the two articles written by Thompson and Boling and reported by the *Louisville Daily Journal*, I will use Gorsuch's correct name (Boling refers to him as Gossett, and Thompson calls him Gossip), and give both versions of the Jess Taylor escape and the death of Billy Shacklett. Boling states Shacklett was killed in the initial gun battle by Hare, while Thompson states he died later. There is a dispute about Tobin and Hedges being killed or even being at the battle however, both versions of the story will be relayed. When the facts are not in dispute, I will include additional details from both men, and apply dates and times based on the four reports of the battle. These *Messenger* articles are lengthy, but can be found in Meade County Newspaper Abstracts, 1906-1908, compiled by Carolyn Wimp, (Vine Grove, Kentucky, published by Ancestral Trails, Historical Society, 2007) Pages 193-194 and 200-203.

The Battle of the Sheep Shed

On April 28, 1863, a pretty spring day, Captain Hare, his orderly Amos Griffin and 100 mounted infantry, and two Negroes riding mules and leading two mules loaded with kettles and equipment, rode into Brandenburg that afternoon. They bivouacked that night at the Meade County Courthouse, and started off early the morning of April 29, 1863. Hare, according to Boling, had written orders to kill Billy Shacklett. As Hare's men came into Meadeville, Shacklett's men were lodging under a large rock called the Sheep Shed. Sheep were kept penned and sheltered there on occasion.

The Confederates caught unaware, saw Hare's men charge them and they broke in all directions. A desperate running fight ensued. Hare's men first came upon Gorsuch, who tried to jump a small cliff and was pinned against a tree by his horse. He was the first to die. One of Hare's men, to make sure Gorsuch was dead, placed his pistol under his nose and fired a bullet through his head. The barrel was so close to his face that Gorsuch's moustache caught fire. After that they ran upon John Wimp, and after Wimp emptied his revolvers, he raised his hands and surrendered. While Wimp was standing as a prisoner, orderly Amos Griffin came up behind Wimp and shot him through the head. The bullet exited under the left eye. This was close to the Shumate School and the path the children used to travel. It lay on a little hill near the W.W. Barne's house, and blood ran to the bottom of the hill. Dan Morgan Shacklett saw this when he was captured.

They next found Billy Shacklett, and he began shooting at them from behind a big Red Oak tree. When the Mounted Union Infantry returned fire he was wounded. Approaching the tree behind which he was firing, they shot him several times more. After Shacklett had been shot through the eye and body, he dragged himself to a tree, leaning against it for support and with a pistol in each hand, the fatally wounded man continued to fight. Captain Hare dashed up to him and demanded his surrender, but the desperate fighting man refused. Hare shot him two or three times more according to Boling, and he fell dead. Thompson states that Billy Shacklett was thought to be dead, but though unconscious he yet lived. Three of Hare's men put their foot on Shacklett's stomach and tore his heavy tick leather gun belt from his body. Before he died later that night, he said those men hurt him worse than the bullets. Later, Billy Shacklett crawled through the woods and leaves about 50 yards toward the Barne's house, 600 yards distant.

Captain Hare said afterwards he regretted killing Shacklett, for he was the bravest man he had ever seen. According to Boling, five men, Billie Shacklett, John Wimp, Tom Tobin, Jim Gorsuch, and Dick Hedges were killed. Jess Taylor checked his horse, as he was being chased and fell in the road feigning death, and after Hare's men rode by he made his way back to a sinkhole nearby and hid. Thompson states that Hare's men never saw Taylor. He crawled under a rock and Hare's men passed on by, not seeing him. Thompson states that Tobin, Hedges, and Duke were not there with the Confederates. He does say that Hedges was killed near Garnettsville or hung in Louisville at a later date. A. J. Thompson was one of the school children in class at the time of the battle, and he helped locate the dead. Susan Willett was the teacher.

A man named Jarrett or Garrett tried to hide 60 feet in front of the school, and was found. When spotted, he took off his gun belt and held his guns up, stating, "I surrender, Captain". After he surrendered he stood up, placed his back against a tree and began cursing his captors. Boling states he was drunk. They brought him up to the schoolhouse, where Susan Willett gave him a drink of water from a gourd dipper. One of the soldiers said, "Drink it, it will be the last drink you ever get". And it was. At that time the soldiers had Dan Morgan Shacklett bound and captured. All of the students saw him. He was quiet and would not say a word. Boling states that going back to Louisville, Hare had a prisoner named Duke that cursed his captors. A soldier asked Hare if he could shoot him and shut him up. Hare consented, and he was shot to death near Garnettsville. This could have been Jarrett or Garret.

After the battle, Captain Hare went back to Meadeville and told Thomas Shumate and others to go up and collect the dead. They found Gorsuch first, put him in the wagon, and proceeded on the death hunt. Thompson, a student, said that the school children met the party soon after Gorsuch was placed in the wagon. Next they came to John Wimp and he was put in the wagon. Billy Shacklett was found where he had crawled from the place he was shot, and tender hands carried him to the nearest house, that of Mrs. Barnes. That night at approximately 11:00 p.m. he died, but not before his wife Anne and their daughter Juliet arrived to see him.

I think a there is a strong case that Gorsuch, if he was alive when he was shot, John Wimp, Dan Morgan Shacklett, and Jarrett or Garrett, and, or Duke, were murdered. If you count Dan Morgan Shacklett, Billy Shacklett, Jerrett or Garrett, Duke, Wimp, Hedges, and Tobin, the tally comes to eight killed. The *Louisville Daily Journal* on May 2, 1863 reported that seven notorious guerrillas were killed in Hare's raid. Gorsuch, Dan Morgan Shacklett, John Wymp (sic), and John Garrett of Bullitt County were listed.[24] But we know that Billy Shacklett was killed. While it's anyone's guess, I suspect Tobin or a man named Duke was/were also casualties. Interestingly, a Meade County bicentennial history was published that states nine men were killed outright in the raid and one died later from fatal wounds.[25] The Federals killed between seven and 10 Confederates in the battle.

Chapter 4

Meadeville, Kentucky – A Guerrilla Stronghold

Meadeville, from 1850 to 1857, was named Good Springs, but even before that time the region was known as Hill Grove. Hill Grove and Meadeville are synonymous in geographical area today; although the town of Meadeville is now only a memory, Meadeville and the Hill Grove country share a common location.

Meade County was originally discovered by Squire and Daniel Boone during the late 1770's. Squire explored Hill Grove and named it Black Oak Grove in 1783.[26] Early settlers to this area were Shacklett, Preston, Willett, Wimp, Wells and others who renamed the area Hill Grove. The first settlement was on what was known as the high ground of Hill Grove, and sits on a knob that provided a lookout for marauding Indians. Upon this knob lies the first Hill Grove Cemetery that has grave stones marked from 1814. The first settler in the area was a man named Allen, and he is the first man buried in the old graveyard.[27] (According to Laura Young Brown and Marie Coleman, written in "The History of Meade County, Kentucky, 1824-1991", the first settler in the area was Benjamin Allen, likely the first man buried there.)

Of all the early settlers, Benjamin Shacklett, known as Ben Wooly was probably the most prominent. Immigrating from Pennsylvania with the Shackletts came well-educated John Wimp, likely the grandfather of the man killed in the battle of the Sheep Shed. He was a Mason initiated in Europe. Wimp frequently spoke of having met General Washington in the Lodge at Fairfax, Virginia, and had a Masonic Medal he greatly prized, having brought it from the old country, which was tied about his neck and buried with him as he requested, in the old Hill Grove Cemetery.[28] General Benjamin Shacklett became a Captain in the army in 1811, and was promoted to major in the War of 1812 by General Wilcox. He was always called General as a sign of respect, although he may not have attained that rank.

When Meade County was named a county in 1823, he was appointed the first sheriff, and served for several years before he died at his home in Hill Grove, in 1838. He was 98-years-old when he died. The early settlements in the area were usually cabins of logs sometimes with a stockade. The roofs of the cabins were slanted and sloped toward the inside of the stockade to reduce the risk of fire arrows shot by Indians. Indian attacks were periodic occurrences and defending one's home was a shooting affair. In those days hogs ran free and were rounded up each fall. Their ears were notched so that one family could tell their animals from those of their neighbors. These notches were registered with the local government in an effort to reduce disputes. These settlers were free men and women that had wrested the land from the Indians, and they were fiercely independent. Their allegiance was to their God, neighbors, county, commonwealth and lastly the federal government, pretty much in that order.

Simeon Buchanan was a soldier during the War of 1812 from 1812-1815, and was ordained a Baptist minister in 1822. His ordination was in Hardin County, Kentucky, and he moved to Hill Grove that same year. "After Ohio," now Wolf Creek, Kentucky was established as a town in 1821 and it had the oldest Baptist Church in Meade County, which also served the area of Hill Grove. The first church in Hill Grove was the New Hope Baptist Church, and it was established in the area that was to become Meadeville, on June 29, 1822, with 14 members. The Hill Grove Church served the communities of Ekron, Stith Valley, Guston, Buck Grove, and Garrett. The original congregation met in the homes and barns of the members until in 1827, when land was bought for a church. A split in the church and a fire caused the original church to be relocated.

There are five cemeteries in the Hill Grove area. The first is the old High Ground of Hill Grove; the second is the Meadeville Cemetery that has stones dating from 1830. The third and fourth are located at the present church of Hill Grove built in 1897. The older of the two is directly behind the church, but was abandoned due to high water problems. Directly across the road and at a higher elevation is the newest Hill Grove Cemetery. At the springs a mile or so south, there is a fifth small family cemetery in the yard of the only dwelling left at the old stagecoach stop.

The Hill Grove region included the town of Meadeville. At Meadeville there was a large flowing spring that provided water to the citizens, Shumate School, and a town that built up around the springs. There were parallel roads a mile or two on each side of the Meadeville Road: Stith Valley Road to the east and Stringtown Road to the west. At Meadeville the crossroad went west to Smith School House, near Stringtown Road, and east through the Board and Barnes places to the Stith Valley Road, at the W.A. Stith farm. The Shumate School was located between the Hill Grove Road, and the Stith farm, on the crossroad. According to written material supplied to me by Peggy Greenwell, copied from "The History of Meade Co., Kentucky, 1824-1991" by Laura Brown and Marie Coleman, Good Spring in 1850 became Meadeville in 1851 and then Hill Grove in 1864.

At Meadeville the stagecoach made a stop to change horses, to allow the weary to rest, and to pick up mail and passengers. There was a saloon, store, hotel, stage station, blacksmith shop, and several dwellings. Mr. Mason operated the hotel and stage station. The Meadeville post office name was changed to the Hill Grove post office in 1862, but was discontinued in 1906. (Anecdotal evidence states that there were two Good Springs causing the mail to be confused, resulting in the first name change.) Note: there is a dispute of two years between the various chroniclers as to when Meadeville came into being, when it changed to Hill Grove, and when it was no longer a town. No matter when that happened to be, the area of Hill Grove was highly Confederate in its sympathies, so much so that it caused a change in the Shacklett name. After the war, those Shackletts favoring the Union added an E to their spelling of the name. Some say it was the other way around. Either way, the name was changed.

Meadeville and the area of Hill Grove became the central area for guerrilla activity in Meade County, especially from 1863-1865. Guerrilla leaders later launched raids from the region and used it as a safe house location to remount and regroup. For this to have happened there had to be strong southern support by the local population. The most noted guerrilla captains to use Hill Grove as a base when operating in Meade County were Captain Bill Marion (real name Stanley Young) and Captain Thomas Carlin Dupoyster with his second in command, Captain John Bryant. It is chronicled in old newspaper stories that Hayes, Horsely, Webster (likely Mose Webster, Marion's sometimes second in command), Hedges, and Williams operated in Meade County, and were at different times in Hill Grove. Marion was a close associate of Marcellous Jerome Clarke, better known as Sue Mundy, who was captured in Meade County about four miles from Hill Grove. It seems likely to me that Mundy and his other associates like One Arm Sam Berry, and Henry Clay (Billy) Magruder with whom Mundy and Henry Medkiff or Metcalf were captured, may have also used the location to hide and launch raids. Sam Berry traveled to the area with a 15-man gang in late 1865, after the war was ended. It is known that Magruder visited Meade County, and according to his confession he stayed several weeks with the Richardson's near Payneville after he had eluded Union troops when John Hunt Morgan was captured. And, he probably stayed occasionally with relatives by marriage in the Cox family and upon whose farm he and his associates were finally captured.

On Wednesday, January 8, 1908, John C. Boling wrote a story entitled "Guerrilla Times in and around Brandenburg."[29] The retelling that was written by Boling, differs in part from what the noted historian Thomas Shelby Watson, in his scholarly work "Confederate Guerrilla Sue Mundy", has chronicled. The compiler of the abstract in which Boling's article is compiled, notes that a section from it was torn off, and at places letters are missing from words that seem to me easily identified. I will place the word that seems most likely correct and that does not change the context of the article, or that has been ascertained from other sources, in italics so the reader will be able to identify them.

Some years before the beginning of the Civil War, there lived in Harrison County, *Indiana*, not many miles from Brandenburg, Kentucky, a man named Marsh, and *St. Claire* Young. Marsh, being a brother-in-law of *Young*. One day Young and his family *were* spending the day with Marsh. A dispute arose at the dinner table, the termination of which was the killing of Young by Marsh with a carving knife. Stanley Young a son of the elder Young, being a small boy at the time was present at the table and witness to the tragedy. As his father lay dead, bathed in his own blood, the young son registered a vow that if he lived to be a man and the opportunity ever presented itself; he would avenge his father's death by taking the life of his Uncle Marsh, who had made him an orphan. Time went on, and the revengeful hand of Stanley Young accomplished its purpose at Brandenburg in 1859. Circuit Court was in session and Marsh was attending court. Marsh was standing in front of Ashcraft's Hotel, which stood where Woodson's

Grainery now stands. There was a large signpost standing at the corner of the pavement in front of the hotel. Dr. Owings, the father of Bob and Stewart Owings, was leaning against the post and Marsh was standing in front of him talking. There was an upper porch which came out directly above him. Out upon this porch stealthily came Stanley Young, now a grown man. He quickly laid his pistol upon the railing of the porch and fired. The bullet striking Marsh in the top of the head and he fell dead upon the pavement. Stanley Young, the assassin, and keeper of a youthful vow, ran back through the hotel, up the hill by the old courthouse and disappeared. He was never seen in Brandenburg or vicinity again, at least not under the name of Young, but that he did return in a few years to wage guerrilla warfare, under the name of Captain Marion, is a pretty *well* fact. He, together with Capt. Bryant, Horsely, Webster, Hays, Dr. Royster (sic) (Dupoyster) and others pursued their career of bushwhacking and guerrilla warfare in Meade County until the close of the war. A coterie of dangerous men, most of which had more or less *erred* before the war....

Note: William Marsh's tombstone in Laconia, Indiana states he died May 26, 1858, instead of 1859 as Boling writes. We know from the 1850 census that St. Clair Young was a farmer of some wealth, $2,000.00, residing in Harrison County, Indiana. He was married to Amelia, age 50, and he had his children listed as, William 21, Sandley (sic) 19, Robert 16, James 14, Amelia 11, Matilda 3, and Nancy Thompson 18. In 1858 Stanley Young would have been 27 years of age when he killed his Uncle Marsh. The killing of St. Clair Young in 1850 would have made Stanley 19 years of age. For nine years Stanley had his hate for his uncle fester inside him, fueling his desire for revenge.

The summer of '64 came. The guerrilla Captains: Webster, Williams, Horsley, Hays, Marion, *erstwhile* Young, combined their forces into one guard (grand?) army to attack the Home Guards in Brandenburg. They came in near the town into the woods between Jailer Bondurant's place on the Hardinsburg Road, and the Capt. Anderson Cemetery, and began firing on the courthouse on East Hill. The soldiers from town slipped out under cover of the woods and fences and rebuked them. Marion rode a white horse and made a very soldierly and leader-like appearance during the skirmish. The horse was shot and ran with his rider through the woods and fell dead in the woods near Wm. Fulton's place on the Hill Grove Road.[30] We lose track of Marion for a while….

Captain Bill Marion

Marion was actually Stanley Young of Nelson County, Kentucky. The Young family had relocated from Nelson County to Harrison County, Indiana. Stanley Young was born in 1831, the son of St. Clair Young and Amelia Hammond. Watson writes St. Claire Young was gunned down at the table,[31] while Boling states he was stabbed to death (either way he was dead), and according to both men, Young was caught and served time in Prison.

Note: In the rewrite of his book Watson states that Young was not apprehended and served no sentence for killing Marsh.[32] *The term of imprisonment if there was one, must have been short, four years or less because Marion was very active in 1864. The crime occurring in 1858 any sentence seems light for cold-blooded murder. Marion would have been over 30 when he began his guerrilla career. Suffice it to say Marion was old for a guerrilla.*

There are many stories that are told about happenings in Hill Grove during the Civil War. Most of them have to do with the guerrillas and later the "nightriders".

The Partisan Ranger Act in Practice

In 1862, an act by the Confederacy entitled "The Partisan Ranger Act", allowed troops to fight behind Union lines to disrupt supply lines and communications. There were many of these loosely organized bands of men operating in Kentucky Counties.

Before the war actually broke out, Kentucky formed militia units; these later became Union Home Guards that were stationed in cities and towns and became the chief defenders against the Partisan Rangers. Thus, each county in Kentucky found itself not only inconvenienced by the national Civil War, but were more directly affected by intra- county war that brought terror to their doors.

There were a number of differences in the Confederate Army and that of the Union. One such difference was that Confederate soldiers had to supply their own horses in order to be in the cavalry; Union cavalrymen were issued horses. To supply the northern forces, horses were often procured from farmers unwilling to sell them. The government procurers often paid less than the horse was worth, in effect stealing at least a part of the horses' value. Most of the horses so procured by the Union came from farmers favoring the Confederacy, or those willing to sell to the Union voluntarily. On the other hand, Confederate guerrillas that needed a horse would prefer to steal it from a Union favoring farmer. The end result was equal, no matter if you were a Rebel or a Unionist your horse was at risk.

Chapter 5

1863 Morgan's Raid and the Partisan Connection

John Hunt Morgan's "Great Raid" is a story that has been told and retold again and again, and yet it is one of those evergreen tales worth telling and hearing one more time. I will refrain from the temptation to restate the details, but will discuss how the raid and the scouting activities that preceded the raid fertilized the garden of guerrilla warfare and tactics.

The story begins with the entrance of approximately 2,100 Confederate Cavalry into Meade County and the taking of Brandenburg, the fight with the Indiana Militia, a cannon duel with gunboats dispatched from Louisville, the crossing of the Ohio, and the raid through Indiana to Buffington Island, Ohio, where the great Morgan and most of his "terrible men" were captured.

Not only were Morgan and his men a fighting force much feared, but they also provided the training for three of the most notable guerrilla raiders: Henry Clay Magruder, Jerome Clarke, aka Sue Mundy, and Thomas Dupoyster. These men were with Morgan at some time in their careers and it was in their service with Morgan that these men learned the craft of guerrilla warfare.

Thomas Henry Hines and Morgan

Thomas Henry Hines was a remarkable man, who was born May 15, 1838, in Butler County, Kentucky. He was destined to become one of the Confederacy's most daring soldier, spy, and secret agent. He was largely unschooled, but was self-taught to the point where he became a teacher at the Masonic University in LaGrange. In 1860 Hines was 20 years old, and a member of the 9th Kentucky Union Cavalry where he rose to the rank of lieutenant. Because of his love for Kentucky and the belief in the southern cause, he resigned, traveled to Virginia and enlisted in the Confederate Army. Hines was 5-feet-9 inches tall, and weighed 140 pounds. He was of slender frame, making him ideal for the cavalry, he loved music and horses, and was something of a ladies' man. Hines was sworn in by, and attached to, John Castleman's Cavalry. Castleman was another cavalry soldier, scout and spy, and both men became part of Morgan's Raiders. Early in the war Morgan entered Kentucky, and led a raid to disrupt Union communications, divert Union troops, and re-establish Confederate control of the State. On July 19, 1861, he assembled his command and marched from Georgetown, Kentucky toward Winchester, Kentucky, where they had multiple routes back to Tennessee.

Castleman's force, Co. D, with Tom Hines was to march to the outskirts of Lexington in a diversionary move to provide cover for Morgan's main force. He was, whenever possible, to cut telegraph wires and destroy railroad bridges, and sometime on July 19th-the following day-he was to bring his company into Winchester and rejoin the regiment.

This was quite an assignment for a 21-year-old captain who had been soldiering for only two months, but both John Morgan and Basil Duke were confident that Castleman, and the 81 men in his company, "each one capable of commanding," could pull it off successfully.[33] Castleman's scouts met Union Pickets and fired on them, driving them back to Lexington, but he knew the Federals would be after his small force as soon as they could form them up. Castleman, with Hines, flanked the first small force to attack them. Hines laid out a plan for Castleman that was readily adopted and was used again three years later in a West Point, Kentucky, guerrilla-action led by Hines.

Hines suggested that he take five men and lay an ambush along the road the Federals would travel. He volunteered to handle the ambush and selected five sharpshooters; they left their horses behind the church, walked across the road concealing themselves in underbrush, where they could deliver a blast of fire into the flank of an approaching column...they waited. The dust rolled closer. They could see the first horsemen now.... Across the road Hines and his sharpshooters lay on their bellies in the green sunlit brush.... A moment before Castleman was certain they would see his men, Castleman shouted: "Charge!" and they came out in a sweeping line, firing by squads. At the first sound of fire, Hines' sharpshooters blasted the Federal flank. "The accurate fire of the sharpshooters", said Castleman, "was of great service", and although the enemy gave the mounted men the credit, no one can fire rifles accurately in a cavalry charge.[34]

That early battle was a prime example of a small force, employing guerrilla tactics, in this case an ambuscade and a cavalry charge from a hidden position. Morgan's Raiders used such tactics anytime they were deemed to be effective. Prior to his "Great Raid" Morgan sent now Captain Thomas Hines and Sam Taylor to gather intelligence he would need to make a successful raid. Crossing points, lines of communications, the available roads, Home Guards, and citizens willing to give the raiders aid were all matters that concerned Morgan. To this end he ordered two of his best men to bring him what he needed to know.

Captains Thomas Hines and Sam Taylor were sent north on separate missions. Taylor was a nephew of "Old Rough and Ready" Zachary Taylor. Hines took a number of men into Indiana, scouting for practicable river crossings west of Louisville and raiding routes around Cincinnati. According to Duke, Hines was supposed to "stir up Copperheads" and locate southern sympathizers who might be useful while a raid was in progress. Captain Taylor's mission was to scout fords and other escape routes along the Ohio River east of Cincinnati.[35] By July 2 the rains had stopped and Morgan held a final conference with his regimental commanders, informing them definitely that they were going across the Ohio. He traced the route on a map, indicating four main danger points, the crossing of the flooded Cumberland just ahead of them, the crossing of the Ohio west of Louisville, the long march around Cincinnati, and the re-crossing of the Ohio east of Cincinnati. Later he told Duke privately that they might not have to re-cross the Ohio River: he had learned that General Lee was invading Pennsylvania, and if all went well Morgan's men might keep marching eastward and join Lee.[36]

Hines and his men crossed into Indiana near Stephensport in Breckenridge County, with more than two dozen men. I described his spy mission in a 2010 article I authored about Thomas Hines, for the Meade County *News Standard*. In part it reads:

> *"Hines was a scout and he and his men were dressed in Union clothing and carried fake orders to search for AWOL's and deserters. While engaged in their cover orders they were actually scouting for crossing points into Indiana. His secondary mission was to search out "Copperheads" (southern sympathizers) living*

in Indiana to see if they could give help to Morgan's Raiders after the invasion was made.... Hines made contact with a copperhead named William A. Bowles in French Lick, and soon after they met he was told he could expect no help from the citizens of Indiana. Hines and his men were discovered and fired upon in Valeena, Indiana. A hot firefight near Leavenworth, Indiana caused Hines scouting party to disband with every man caring for himself; and, Hines, to make his escape had to swim the Ohio River at Blue Island, under fire with bullets splashing all about him. When Hines was safely across the river he contacted Morgan making his recommendation for a crossing, and was found leaning against a building waiting as Morgan rode into the river town of Brandenburg, Kentucky, to start his 'Great Raid.'

"Morgan fought a short battle at Brandenburg between his forces, Union gunboats, and some Indiana militia, before crossing the river. Twelve days after commencing his raid it ended at Buffington Island, in Ohio, where Morgan and a number of other raiders were captured."

"Jerome Clarke was captured with Morgan. Henry Clay Magruder, 'Billy', who also rode with Morgan describes escaping from Union forces according to his confession, 'Three Years In The Saddle', stating that he and three other men, Hopkins, Morris, Cushingbery, and himself went in a squad.... 'We four traveled, I judge about eight miles, and laid over in daylight. The next night we traveled on, and so for four nights, with nothing to eat but onions which we could find in Dutch gardens.'

"'We had no guide but the North Star, and with our backs to that we trudged the long miles away. While we lay in the woods on the fourth day, we heard the whistle of a boat, and on the fifth night we came to the river at Mauckport.

"'Going below the town, we were in despair of finding a skiff, when in the dim light of daybreak we saw a fisherman come from a cabin, and with a net on his shoulder, and start toward the river. As stealthily as a cat I followed him, and while he was losing his boat, I put a pistol to his ear and told him to keep still. We then took the skiff and almost in the shadow of a gunboat lying out at anchor, we pulled from those "inhospitable" banks over to fair and friendly Kentucky.

"'When we reached the good old State, we sat down and "were glad." We remained ten days near Richardson's, in Meade County, and succeeded in getting horses.'"[37]

Why was this particular area of Kentucky, specifically Meade, Hardin, Spencer, Nelson, and Breckenridge Counties, so favorable for guerrilla operations? No guerrilla war can be successful without support from the local population. Food, munitions, horses, information about where the enemy is located, and safe houses, that provide a place to rest and hide, owned by those sympathetic to the guerrillas were necessary for their success. This area of the heartland was such a place. The question once again is why? And to answer that, one must look at the composition of the community and what was going on to create a prejudice favoring the South.

William Boling wrote on January 27, 1938, that Meade County supplied an even amount of men to the United States and the Confederacy.[38] The county was evenly divided, and approximately one in three families owned slaves. I suspect one half of the two thirds of the families that didn't own slaves, wanted to. If so, it would reinforce the fact that Meade County was about evenly split between Union and Confederate. Many areas of the heartland of Kentucky were more strongly Confederate. According to Watson, Bloomfield flew the Confederate flag throughout the war, from a pole in the middle of the town. All it would take to tip the scale away from being loyal to the Union would be mistreatment or perceived mistreatment of the citizens, who in the beginning of the war were about evenly divided in their loyalty. Such detrimental treatment occurred, even to people with excellent reputations. Those actions after Lincoln's election, including suspending Habeas Corpus served to reinforce the loss of freedom by all citizens. Even before that, it was reported by W.M. Boling, that in 1860 Lincoln received only four votes from Meade County, showing the distrust if not disdain the area had for a Lincoln administration. Circumstances worked to harm the Union favor.

In a letter written on October 31, 1862 by Col. Robert Buckner to his daughter, who was attending college in Louisville, reads in part:

"...Our little town is still in an uproar. No man or family feels safe in life or property...The Lincolnites have run of several

families viz Taylor and many others the 2 Wathens, Miss Abbey Thompson, some 3 or 5 other families besides many gentlemen that has been dragged to prisons in Ohio and other places. I was yestiday arrested by orders of a tyrant captain with pistols and other weapons drawn and pointed at me and was compelled to take the oath or be sent to Camp Chase, and there I would have died, being so old and feeble as I am. I had just got my horse to gow down town. They arrested Jackson Alexander and many others yestiday and today. They have got three cannon planted on the hill where the courthouse is. They have all those intrenchments around the hill. Now of all tom foolery I ever saw it beats all. There is no enemy in armes here, nor will I venture to say, non within 50 or 100 miles of this place. I say there never has come to this place a Body of Southern soldiers, not eaven one, that seem to belonged to the Southern army, and this a doo and all our troubles are brout on us by wicked & malicious neighbors claiming to be Union men, and I am sad to say nearly all are members of the Mehodis Church. The last people under the sun that should take sides against the south when they know it was the abolishion of the North that split and divided the Methodis Church. I have not been to Church or class since last July. I have no fault to find with our preacher. It is a dozen or moore of the members that have offices, that is lionizing over their Bretherand neighbors, non-escapes their malice. But for such wicked and malicious men of our Church & town we would be living in a parradice compaired to many other places in Kentucky, where rechednous and woe is...One thing I must tell you my daughter, you know my life Policys is near six thousands dollars and if I had not taken the oath, and had died in prison, the office would set up a plee not to pay you on account of my violating the law or policy. So I had to take the oath not willingly but to save my life & your money insured.

Dear Daughter you know and all my relations that I am not capable of doing a mean act nor would I persecute my neighbor or do him any rong no matter how much I may or mite dislike him I have done my neighbors no harme. It is true we have and do differ in opinion about the Right and Rong concerning this unholy War for which difference I have been basely persecuted and don't hardly hope for anything better during the few days months or years that the good Lorde may permit me to suffer here at the hands of my enemys.

Your ever devoted Father

R. Buckner"[39]

Buckner was a relative of Confederate General, and future Governor of Kentucky, Simon Bolivar Buckner. His house was commandeered by John Hunt Morgan during his time in Brandenburg, and the tea set Morgan drank from continues to reside with the house. Col. Buckner complained in his letter of people in the Methodist Church holding offices. In 1863, the wife of the Pastor of the Brandenburg Methodist Church hid the Sherriff under the parsonage when Morgan's Raiders took the town. Very likely the Sherriff held one of those offices.

In the Wednesday, February 26, 1908, *Meade County Messenger*, Mrs. MRL wrote a letter to the editor that states in part:

"*...It was in the summer of 1862 and everything was topsy turvey in Brandenburg. I will tell you from the beginning we were Southern rights or rebels, as they called us. Oh in those days how I did hate anyone that wore the blue. I have said a many a time that I would never marry a Yankee, as we called them. I had a sweetheart of that town and he joined the Union. I never looked at him again. For all that wore the blue looked alike to me...Well I said, it was 1862 and my father had been for two years buying arms and ammunition for the Confederacy. In Sept. of 1862 my father was taken to prison in Columbus, Ohio. Then our hardships began. But still we braved it all. We were willing to endure hardships for the cause. At that time calico was 50 cents a yard, domestic 35 cents a yard, spool of thread cost 15 cents, coffee we did not see for better than two years. Coffee was made out of anything, rye, wheat, burnt peaches, burnt sweet potatoes, and the southern girl did not dress very fine. My song was this:*

Northern goods are out of date,
Since old Abe's blockade.
Us southern girls must be content,
With goods that southerners made,
We scorn to wear a bit of silk.

Or a bit of northern lace,
But put our homespun dress on,
And wear them with a grace."[40]

J. C. Boling writes January 8, 1908 about the guerrilla soldier:

"...A peculiar soldier was he, living as best he could generally in the saddle. He must have been a composite of the Italian brigand who is friend to no one and of the patriotic fathers like Pickins, Marion, and Lee of Revolutionary times, who would divide their wasted potatoes with the enemy. Be that as it may, the guerrilla was a Southern sympathizer, because of which many a latchstring was hung on the outside for him. He has been called a marauder, an assassin, and a coward, because he laid waste, because he did not join the ragged columns of Johnson and Lee. It is true he did all of these things principally against Unionist in extenuation of which you can only say that the war is over and that others known as Home Guards shot from ambush in Meade County and did not have the courage to charge Mission Ridge, nor the hardihood to tramp with Sherman to the Sea. Of this be sure the guerrilla and the Home Guards were not cowards. Time and again their valor was fully tested in the hills and hollows of old Meade and no braver men ever faced an enemy in war's perilous time than the sons born and reared in that community. The war was at its height and the guerrilla was at his zenith. The summer of '64 came...."[41]

The heavy-handed rounding up of southern sympathizers alienated those people who had similar leanings, even if unspoken and unknown to others, and made them feel less safe. It must also be understood that many of those who had friends and relatives that were singled out for preferential or detrimental treatment by the governmental authorities, resulted in a negative impact on the credibility of the Union. Therefore, one whose friend was treated wrongly caught a sympathetic glance from those that might lean politically the other way. If you had a good friend who was wronged by the political party you favored, would it not make you feel sorry for your friend, and question at least the motives of the offending party? Toward the war's end, there is at least one example where a guerrilla raider informed a Unionist neighbor of a guerrilla raid to be made on his place. Later during the 1870's these two men, on politically different sides of the fence, became partners in a land transaction. Interestingly, in death they are buried nearly together, and about 15 feet separates them.

Chapter 6

Guerrillas in the Midst

There were differences between the guerrilla bands. In my eyes these soldiers were either enlisted in the Confederate Army as Partisan Rangers such as those led by John Singleton Mosby, the Gray Ghost, and Hanse McNeill of McNeill's Rangers, Adam R. Johnson of the Breckenridge Guards, and John Hunt Morgan of Morgan's Raiders, or were detached soldiers separated from their units, or soldiers that escaped Federal military prisons and joined other irregulars to continue the fight. Some of these guerrillas were commissioned by other officers, and some were acting on their own judgment. These were probably the most effective, reputable, and merciful of the guerrilla soldiers. Almost in a class by himself is, William Clark Quantrill with his seconds in command William "Bloody Bill" Anderson, George Todd, and the guerrilla band known as Quantrill's Raiders. In another category parallel to Quantrill on a local level, I place Captain Bill Marion, aka Stanley Young, Jerome Clarke, aka Sue Mundy, Henry Clay Magruder, aka Billy Magruder, Isaiah Coulter, aka Big Zay Coulter, Samuel Oscar Berry, aka One Arm Berry, Captain Thomas Dupoyster, Captain John Bryant, and a myriad of other names such as Horsely, Ludwig, King White, Hedges, Hays, Dave Martin, John Nickels, Tom Henry, Flowers, Jim Davis, William Davison, and Mose Webster. All of these Confederate fighters were in the war battling against the Union and believed they were acting under the Partisan Ranger Act. Most of these men had been enlisted in the Confederate Army.

Several guerrilla hunters are notable for their success, which brought the war in Kentucky to a swifter conclusion, considering how the guerrilla activity was prolonging the war. Cyrus Wilson, Jim Bridgewater, and Edwin Terrell are three of these guerrilla hunters, sometimes called independent scouts. Edwin Terrell was more guerrilla than Union soldier. Terrell epitomized the phrase "It takes one to catch one." He rode at the head of a unit of 18 or 20 "independent scouts" charged with capturing or killing guerrillas, and his men were probably the most effective in performing this task. He fought with, shot, mortally wounded, and captured William Clark Quantrill, capturing and killing some of his men.

Terrell and his 20 scouts fought the most notorious guerrilla warriors, Sue Mundy, One Arm Berry, Big Zay Coulter, Bill Marion, Dave Martin, and Quantrill all had fights with Terrell, and Terrell was equally hated by all of the guerrillas. Coulter, Cox, Marion, a guerrilla named Ludwig, and Quantrill, were all victims of his pursuit. Terrell may have killed Coulter, Quantrill, Marion, and he shot and killed Cox. He killed the captured and unarmed Ludwig after a fight with the guerrillas. By his own admission he had killed 17 men, one of them an unarmed blacksmith named Wooten, and a young negro boy who was drawing water from a well to quench the thirst of Terrell and his men. A Shelbyville newspaper reported the incident in a 1917 article. Terrell wanted to test his accuracy with a new revolver, when he killed the boy. Edwin Terrell and his men were armed robbers, terrorists, murderers, but effective in running Confederate guerrillas to bay. A guerrilla force actually saved a town being held up by Terrell charging and firing their guns while Terrell and his men were in the process of robbing the citizens. The Confederate guerrillas routed the Federals, and the citizens cheered.

The guerrilla warrior was initially a patriot to the Confederate cause. They had the bravery and inclination to fight and face death, but not to rejoin the Confederate armies. Many of them were bored young men who yearned for a break from farm work, and desired the excitement and danger of going on a raid. Others of them were residents of the areas in which they operated who held grudges against some of their neighbors, and used the war as an excuse to get revenge. Some, such as Bloody Bill Anderson of Missouri's Quantrill's Raiders and Captain Bill Marion were outlaws before becoming guerrillas.[42]

The guerrillas were surprisingly effective in destroying communications and supply lines. These activities often meant the burning of trains and railroad stations, the cutting of telegraph lines and axing of the poles that held them. Ambushing Federal troops was a necessary tactic employed by the guerrillas. Some have criticized the guerrillas for cowardice in perpetrating the ambuscades, however they were not only necessary for success, but also would have resulted in the guerrillas own destruction had they not been used. Remember the guerrillas, especially in the heartland of Kentucky, were small bands typically of 6 to 25 men. They usually were pitted against much larger numbers, such as in the Simpsonville battle where approximately 15 guerrillas attacked a force described as about 80, and won the fight. Attacking from cover made enormous sense, and allowed them to inflict as much damage as possible reserving for them a reasonable chance for escape.

The guerrillas were able to effectively fight consistently superior numbers and to emerge victorious due to their adoption of the latest technology available, their superior skill with firearms, their proficiency with horsemanship, and the knowledge that they were fighting to defend their homeland against those that would change or destroy their way of life.

Bill Marion

There was a question in early 1865, about who exactly Bill Marion happened to be. At various times he was thought to be J.W.W. Marion, William Marion, Al Catlin, John Oliver, and Stanley Young. The first Louisville newspapers reported on his activities in January of 1865. The *Louisville Daily Journal* reported on January 19, 1865, a Thursday: "On Saturday last a scoundrel named Marion, with a small squad of desperadoes, made a raid on Samuel's Depot, Ky. and burned several cars, the railroad trestle, and about $1500.00 worth of sawed wood...."[43] The next time we hear about him is a January 24th report in the *Louisville Daily Journal*: "An official letter from Bardstown on the 19th says the guerrillas under Captains Magruder, Marion, and Davis have burned nearly all the bridges on the Louisville and Bardstown Pike. The principal bridges were across Cox's Creek, Salt River, and Floyds Fork. A gentleman who arrived here yesterday from Bloomfield states the guerrillas burned the courthouse and jail buildings in Taylorsville, last Sunday.[44] These newspaper stories were the earliest reports of Marion's actions. On March 13th, 1865, after the capture of Jerome Clarke (Sue Mundy), Marion sent a letter from Meade County, Kentucky, to General Palmer but in care of George Prentice, the editor of the Louisville Daily Journal, identifying himself as J.W.W. Marion commanding Confederate forces in Kentucky, although he signed it W.W. Marion. In April the guerrilla Marion was misidentified in a *Louisville Daily*

Democrat article as Al. Catlin: "Captain Marion the guerrilla, is said to be no less a personage than Al. Catlin of Marion County. The family of Catlin is a good and respectable one, but Al. himself always was a bad one. While quite young he attempted to kill his father and threatened to kill his mother, robbed them of money and skedaddled. He was confined in the Lebanon Jail for murder when the rebels took possession of Kentucky in 1862; and was released by them..."[45] While this is not the exact story of Stanley Young, there are some elements that seem hauntingly familiar. On April 15, the *Louisville Daily Democrat* reported the following story: "We learn that John Oliver, alias Captain Marion was shot and badly wounded last Sunday a week ago, in a fight with James H. Bridgewater and his men... There is no doubt Marion is wounded, as he has not been heard from recently."[46] Obviously this report was another misidentification. Later in December of 1865 the real Al. Catlin was caught long after the Real Bill Marion was killed in Manton, Washington County, Kentucky.

Boling and Watson both agree that Marion changed his name from Stanley Young to Bill Marion to spare his family embarrassment. Boling describes him as soldierly and gallant, proudly leading his men riding a white horse with a white pheasant feather in the band of his hat.

Other descriptions of Marion come from a variety of sources. In 2006, Richard Taylor wrote a book entitled "Sue Mundy", a novel of the Civil War, a well-researched book rich with a very descriptive section entitled "Marion." He describes Marion as: "...thickset, but modest of stature, standing about five four in his stocking feet. *Note: This is a reasonable physical description of Henry Magruder.* To compensate he wore Western boots, tooled by some nameless artisan of the Southwest, were his only concession to stylishness. Usually he wore a scruffy jeans jacket over a checked shirt much in need of washing much in need of darning.... Marion's personal habits gave little cause for boasting. He never shaved and seldom bathed. His face formed a thicket from which the eyes stared out with a blend of wonder and malice...a blunt moustache bristled above his thin upper lip. Hair thinning on the crown, he wore the scraggly remnants long and unkempt. It billowed from under his hat in dark snarls through a comb seemed never to have passed. He adopted Remington pistols as his weapon of choice because they had drop cylinders that permitted quick reloading. He never ventured out without a half-dozen or so replacement cylinders, each holding six loads...Marion had an ungovernable temper, a whiplash tongue, and weakness for peach brandy.... In fact, the man answered to every descriptor of villainy...ruffian, miscreant, wretch, monster, cutthroat, scoundrel, and blackguard."[47]

Thomas Shelby Watson in Chapter 10 of his book "Confederate Guerrilla Sue Mundy", entitled "The Guerrilla Wardrobe", gives a more revealing look at how the guerrillas including Marion dressed. Guerrillas, due to S.G. Burbridge's order No. 59, that stated they would not be taken prisoners of war, but were to be killed when captured, seemed to incite them to provocative dress. "...They wore hats decorated with ostrich or chicken feathers. Some of the jackets were red flannel and some of the guerrillas asked for red jackets and pants, an outfit that told all foes no quarter...."[48] It is interesting to note that a leader of a company of Independent Scouts, Edwin Terrell, known affectionately as "Bad Ed", also had an all red suit made for him in which to hunt guerrillas.

On April 19, 1865, after the death of Bill Marion at Manton, the *Louisville Daily Democrat* published an article that gives a different slant on Marion:

> *Marion: "We have received information which induces us to believe that we were in error in some of our representations respecting the identity and former career of the noted outlaw. His name is not William, but Stanley Young. He formerly resided in Union Co., Ky., and has been, for some years, a fugitive from justice. Some 20 years ago, Sinclair Young removed from Nelson Co., Ky., to the vicinity of Corydon, Ind. He was killed in an altercation with a neighbor, whose daughter, Young's eldest son, William had married. The perpetrator of the act was acquitted, on the plea of justifiable homicide. The Young family afterwards moved to Union County, where, we believe William still resides.... About seven years ago, Stanley Young, the second son, arranged his business, with the declared purpose of seeking out and executing private vengeance on the man who killed his father. He found his victim at a hotel in Brandenburg, and without a word of warning, shot him through the head. His plans of escape were so well laid that he easily eluded pursuit.... He had relatives named Marion, formerly living in Louisville. It is probable that this induced him to adopt the name. He was a young man of fine personal appearance. His*

address was affable and quiet, but there was a marked expression of latent firmness in his countenance...Union County has been prolific of desperadoes since the war commenced. It has been the headquarters of a large number of guerrilla chiefs, many of who have been killed. According to our informant, Maj. Walker Taylor-at present in Louisville (apparently referring to Marion) – was the best behaved Confederate officer that ever visited that section. He not only refrained from pillaging the Union inhabitants, but made war on those that did."[49]

When taken as a whole, we find that the various reports on Bill Marion's demeanor and appearance change with the describer. He is dirty, unkempt in appearance and ill-tempered according to Taylor, affable and quiet and of fine personal appearance according to the *Louisville Daily Journal* and Maj. Walker Taylor. Boling describes him as soldierly atop his white horse with a white pheasant feather in his hatband. We know from Watson and Brantley that he certainly had a bit of dash about him when he purchased his tailored guerrilla uniform and high-topped boots. But there is another side to Marion's personality that I think is even more reflective of his true values. He seems to me to be a man that demonstrated supreme loyalty on a number of occasions. John N. Edwards, biographer of Quantrill and Jesse and Frank James, referred to Marion as: "A man who never feared an enemy or forgot a friend. As none in battle were braver or more reckless, so none, in its lapse or lull were more faithful, to the hurt, or gentle with the crippled. Twenty times over he had risked his own life to save what little life yet remained to some grievously wounded yet gallant follower."[50] Edwards' words concerning Marion seem to shout loyalty, selflessness, and duty. These attributes are reinforced by Edwards, who wrote:

Marion was sent with 12 men to Bewleyville, Meade County. Thirty Federal Cavalry attacked him there and Marion charged them fiercely. Peyton Long led this charge. He was ahead of the foremost rider when shooting with the terrible effect of his old Missouri training. Four of the enemy had already fallen, shot dead from their saddles. He was close upon a fifth when an ambushed body of Federals variously estimated at from 200 to 250, rose suddenly from behind fences and trees and poured one deadly volley into Marion's little band, A heavy carbine ball caught Peyton Long's pistol belt between the U. and the S. and wounded him mortally in the bowels. Five others of the guerrillas were killed or wounded. Even under that fire, Marion halted long enough to lend a hand to Peyton Long and steady him in the saddle. For eight miles – such was his wonderful nerve and endurance – he held to his horse, riding upright as a soldier on duty. Far in the rear, Marion, with that devotion to the wounded which made him conspicuous among the guerrillas, fought back the pursuit and held it back until the sunset. Then he halted long enough for Peyton Long to die."[51] *On March 11th, 2009, I wrote in an article in The Meade County Messenger about his loyalty and bravery, it reads in part: "Marion has been described as mean, cruel, dirty, untidy, ruthless, generous, gallant, soldierly, brave and courageous. He was probably all of these things and more, but above all, he was loyal. He attempted to avenge the hanging of his leader Jerome Clarke, protected the wounded Peyton Long, and avenged his father's death."*[52]

The story of attempting to avenge the hanging of Jerome Clarke, aka "Sue Mundy", begins in Breckenridge and Meade Counties, Kentucky, in mid-March, 1865. It involves the kidnapping of Dr. Benedict Wathen and a wealthy Breckenridge County farmer named Oscar Board, in retaliation for the capture and impending execution of Jerome Clarke aka Sue Mundy, Henry Medkiff or Metcalf, and Henry Clay "Billy" Magruder. The two kidnapped men were southern sympathizers if not outright Confederates.

Note: Robert Buckner in his letter to his daughter mentions the two Wathens and other families being abused by Lincolnites in Meade County. Their kidnapping, although improbable considering their sentiments and standing in the community, was nevertheless logical and for Bill Marion was the right course of action to help save the lives of his friends and compatriots.

The Boards & Wathens

The Wathens and the Boards were related through marriage. The father of Mrs. Harrison Board was Gabriel Wathen who was born in Maryland in 1789. These were ancestors of the Wathen and Board families that immigrated to Meade and Breckenridge Counties, Kentucky before the War of 1812.

Judge Milton Board was the son of Robert and Lydia Board born in Breckenridge County, November 20, 1829. His father Robert Board was born in Bedford County, Virginia, and came to Breckenridge County in 1828. He was a wealthy farmer, and died in 1859 at the age of 59 years. Lydia, his wife, died in 1848 at the age of 49. Judge Milton Board was a Mason. The rich farmland he owned was about four or five miles south of Hardinsburg. Robert and Lydia had five children: Richard, Seany L., Oscar, Ahmed, and Walker. Three of these were still living in 1885, Ahmed, Oscar, and Walker. It is likely that Oscar and Walker were too old for military service, and were needed to run the farm. Ahmed attended Brandenburg schools until he was 17 and entered Cecelian College in Hardin County when he was aged 20 years. He attended one year before enlisting in the Confederate Army in Col. Forrest's Cavalry.[53] In Confederate service he was involved in many hot actions. The Boards were likely Protestant because of their Masonic connection.

The Wathens were also a prosperous family. Dr. Benedict Wathen was born August 15, 1801, and he died June 27, 1876 at the age of 75. He was 64-years-old at the time of the kidnapping, and Oscar Board was described in newspaper reports as an old man. Benedict Wathen and his brother George, born in 1803, were two of several doctors in the area of Webster, Kentucky, what is now Irvington. The city of Irvington was not incorporated until 1889, but the area was known as Mt. Marino. The Wathens were Catholic and purchased land between Big Spring, and Wolf Creek, called at that time, Mt. Marino. He and his brother George established the Mt. Marino Seminary, in 1838, on part of this property. Later a church and school were built. Benedict Wathen owned slaves. At the same time Benedict was practicing medicine in this area, another prominent Doctor named Jesse Pitman Lewis was also practicing. The fact that these doctors were practicing medicine in what had to be an overlapping area is important in the decision Marion made to kidnap Wathen.

Mundy, Magruder, and Medkiff

We will learn more about these men and their activities a little further on, but a brief introduction is in order to understand the circumstances of Bill Marion's actions, and to fathom why Board and Wathen were kidnapped. Marcellous Jerome Clarke was one of the most famous guerrilla fighters in Kentucky. He was famous, or infamous, largely due to his bad press in The *Louisville Daily Journal*. Magruder, Medkiff, and Clarke aka Sue Mundy, were together when they were captured, and all of these men rode with Bill Marion. On this last raid the men were traveling south toward Confederate lines to link up at Paris Tennessee. The guerrillas numbered 13 and the party consisted of Magruder, Mundy, Medklff, Porter, Turner, Jones, Bud and John Pence, White, Mercer, Grimes McMurtry, and Tucker. These men were often times on the scout, raiding together, and they were friends, as well as desperate and dangerous men could befriend anyone.

Marcellous Jerome Clarke was better known by his sobriquet "Sue Mundy". The name Sue Mundy was a creation of George Prentice the very influential editor of the *Louisville Daily Journal*, in which he would write stories about the exploits of a female guerrilla that the Union Army could not catch. He used these stories to embarrass the Union forces. How Prentice created the girl warrior is not exactly known, but it had to be at least in part by Jerome Clarke's looks. Clarke was a pretty boy. Not handsome but pretty. He had a slender waist, delicate hands with long fingers, and shoulder length black hair. He did not sport a beard or moustache. Except for his unusual height for the time, six feet, he appeared oddly effeminate. James N. Edwards describes Sue Mundy as a quiet gentle, soft spoken dandy, with his hair in love knots six inches long, a hand like a school girl, and a waist like a woman.... When he fought he fought savagely. Beneath an exterior as effeminate as a woman of fashion, he carried the muscles of an athlete and the energy of a racer. His long hair in battle blew as the mane of a horse. The dandy in a melee became a Cossack; in desperate emergencies a giant.[54] Mundy, after being separated from his company with John Hunt Morgan's cavalry, worked on a farm near Bloomfield in Nelson County, until word got out he was a detached Confederate soldier. The owner of the farm on which he was employed, suggested he join with Bill Magruder who was operating as a guerrilla in that area. Soon Sue had a band of guerrillas of her own.

Henry Clay Magruder was also a detached Confederate soldier and former Morgan's Raider who escaped being captured with Morgan. He and his companions Hopkins, Morris, and Cushingberry found refuge with the Richardsons in Meade County Kentucky who hid them for 10 days after their escape down the Ohio River. When rested and outfitted with horses, they made their way across the Cumberland River being hunted by Federal troops.[55] Later, Magruder together with Bill Marion, Sue Mundy, and One Arm Samuel Oscar Berry, formed the dangerous fearsome foursome of guerrilla elite.

Henry Medkiff, sometimes spelled Metcalf was a guerrilla who was sent to Kentucky by General Lyons to round up detached Confederates and guerrilla fighters and have them rendezvous in Paris Landing Tennessee where they would join Lyons and the rest of Breckenridge's command. He was riding with Mundy and Magruder, and unfortunately for him he bore a likeness to another guerrilla named Tom Henry. Tom Henry was at an earlier raid on the Caldwell farm where Edward Caldwell was brutally murdered by Mundy, Magruder, Bill Maraman and a fifth unidentified man. The resemblance of Metcalf to Henry served as evidence for a later court martial and death sentence for Metcalf. Magruder states he started for Lyon's command, leaving Nelson County, and traveling through Taylorsville and on to Meade County, thence to Garnettsville, on to Big Springs where he and his men camped for the night. The next day they went to Webster through Clifton Mills, and around Hardinsburg, where at daylight they camped in an old shanty, and when they stopped to get their horses shod, a man slipped away and reported them to the Federals in Owenbsboro. One hundred Federals were dispatched from Owensboro. On the way, the Union soldier turned Confederate guerrilla Bill Davison, a native of the area from Hawsville overtook the band and coming up alone, he joined them. Davison told the men where they could stay a few days, and led them toward a safe house about five miles distant from Cloverport. There they stayed another two days. Union patrols were now all around the area, and the men finally decided to break out and run. They started for Hancock County, where on a hill above the intersection of Hampton Road and Owensboro Road, two Federal scouts came up and the guerrillas began chasing them. The Federal scouts were with Captain John A. Clark's Company D, of Major John W. Swinker's Battalion of Kentucky State Troops.[56] It was raining hard on that Saturday, February 26, 1865, when the scouts dismounted and took to the trees, later retreating to a more secure position in a log house. Davison's arm was broken when he was shot chasing one of the soldiers. Suddenly a half-mile farther, they ran into the balance of Clark's 40 soldiers and their fire was delivered to the guerrillas at a distance of 20 feet. Davison was mortally wounded in the right side and again in the bowels, while Magruder was wounded in the chest.[57]

Magruder, Medkiff and Mundy retreated with the remaining guerrillas, and stayed with Magruder's cousin Mrs. Grays for two days, and then he was moved to the woods where he remained a week. From there he was taken to the Cox farm in Mt. Marino where Elizabeth Cox reportedly a distant cousin of Magruder lived, and there they stayed until they were captured. The day before Magruder left the woods he sent his men back to Nelson County under Porter's command. He then had Dr. Jesse Pitman Lewis brought to care for his wound.[58]

Medkiff, Magruder, and Mundy were captured at the Cox Farm in Meade County, where they were hiding for four days in the log tobacco barn. All three men were charged with being guerrillas and the murder of Edward Caldwell in Bullitt County, two months earlier. Edward Curtis Caldwell was a Union Soldier on leave from the 15th Kentucky Volunteers. He was given a furlough to return home and bury his father. Magruder states that he went to Caldwell's house with a squad of five men, Porter their guide, Mundy, Tom Henry, Merryman, and Magruder.[59] On the Caldwell raid, Watson states that Mundy, Magruder, Maraman, Metcalf, and a fifth guerrilla not recognized by the civilians that saw him were dressed in layers to fend off the rain.[60] That unknown guerrilla Watson speaks to may have been Tom Henry or someone else yet unidentified. It seems to me unlikely that Metcalf was at the Caldwell raid. Magruder, when he probably did the only noble thing in his life, he told the authorities that Metcalf was not at the Caldwell killing. At that moment and against advice from counsel, he admitted he was there, for that was the only way he could have known of Metcalf's absence. By doing so he put the noose around his own neck. All three men captured in the Cox barn were sentenced to hang, but Metcalf's sentence was reduced to five years in prison and he was taken to the Kentucky Penitentiary June 3, 1865, and was released later in October of the same year after a concerted letter writing campaign on his behalf.[61] It is doubtful that Metcalf was involved with the Caldwell murder. Mundy was hanged on March 15, and Magruder on October 20, 1865.

William H. Davison

William H. "Bill" Davison, according to the date on his tombstone, was born November 8, 1839. In the 1860 census he was listed as 20-years-old. He had joined the Union army and was promoted to the rank of Captain, in the 17th Ky. Infantry, which rank he held until he resigned in 1863. Davison said the reason for his resignation was because he was passed over for promotion. However, he was at the time of his resignation facing the likelihood of a court martial for conduct unbecoming an officer, being drunk and disorderly, charges of him going to bawdy houses, and for calling a sentry a son-of-a-bitch. He must have, at one time, been a good soldier to have been promoted to a captaincy, but his superiors apparently supported his resignation, because he was a young man and that perhaps his resignation would prevent his life from being ruined. He had fought in battles at Fort Donelson and Shiloh. J.B. Nation in 2007 wrote in his history of Walker Taylor, that Davison quit after the Emancipation Proclamation saying he did not fight to free slaves. For whatever reason he resigned, after his resignation, he lived quietly for a year in Hartford, Kentucky.[62] He joined or was commissioned in Col. Lee Sypert's Confederate Partisan Rangers. Sypert was associated with Adam Rankin Johnson and Walker Taylor, and curiously he, Sypert was in the last significant skirmish of the Civil War east of the Mississippi River, when his 140 Confederates drove off a Federal Force under S.M. Overby at Eddyville, on April 29, 1865. Later he surrendered on May 6th.

Davison's resignation and switching sides this late in the war was unusual, but it did occasionally happen and on both sides of the issue. Captain Edwin Terrell had been a Confederate and in 1864, switched sides to become one of Kentucky's most effective guerrilla hunters. Earlier in the war Captain William Kendall Shacklett, Captain of the Brandenburg, Kentucky Home Guard, switched sides joining the Confederate army in 1862, at Big Springs.

Davison came from a fairly well to do, if somewhat dysfunctional family, being the son of a doctor who was also involved in local politics. His mother became a pitiable figure due in part to her husband's obsession with politics, and perhaps mental illness that may have contributed to his unusual death. In March of 1859 Dr. William Davison took part in the killing of Thomas Lowe a political rival. Lowe lay wounded and locked in his jail cell in Hawsville, when he was unarmed and shot by Davison and another man. Sometime later, after the death of Lowe, Dr. Davison made an infernal machine (bomb) and hid it in a basket of eggs. He carried it into John Duncan's store where another political adversary, Mr. William Stennett was sitting next to a pot-bellied stove. Davison left the device on the counter where it was supposed to explode. When it didn't detonate on time he re-entered the store to check on it just as the bomb exploded. He was badly injured, and was suffering so badly he self-medicated and died of an overdose of Laudanum. It was a suicide because he left two letters one to his wife and another to his son. In 1893 Mrs. Jane Davison, the wife of William Davis, asked a question of a reporter who interviewed her, "Is it possible that I shall live to see all my boys come to death by violence?"[63] The interview was given on the accidental death by drowning of Lemuel Davison. Nathaniel Davison was killed by the Owensboro Police. James Davison was killed when he tried to club a dog with his musket and it accidentally fired into him, and William Davison was killed in battle by Charles Hale, Company D Green River Band when he was shot with Henry Magruder, in the same battle.[64] She had lost four sons and her husband to violent deaths. One son was alive in Wellington, Kansas engaged in the hardware business. On April 8, a newspaper article was published it stated in part: March 26th – I do hereby certify that I was present and saw my son, William H. Davidson (sic), died, on or about the 7th of March, from wounds received from someone, I know not whom. Jane E. Davidson (sic)-Attest: E. A. Faulconer, R. H. Cox.[65] How sad for Jane Davison.

The Kidnapping of Wathen and Board

Magruder and party, after his being shot, stayed two days with his cousin Mrs. Gray in Breckenridge County. On March 4th, a story appeared in the *Louisville Daily Journal*: A correspondent writing from Hardinsburg gives additional information of the late operations of Captain William H. Davison's and Henry Magruder's gang. Davison (Magruder called him Davidson as is written on his tombstone) was mortally wounded last Friday morning by a few Home Guards near Minor Pates place, in Hancock County, and carried off by his men. Thirteen of his gang went to Breckenridge County. They were met by some eight citizens late in the evening, about three miles from Hardinsburg, where a lively skirmish ensued. In this engagement one of the devils by name of Jim Jones, of Davis County, was killed, and one taken prisoner, who gave his name as Mattingly and from the same county. Five horses and saddles, and five navy pistols were also secured. Magruder commanded this force, and was wounded, and taken to the upper portion of Breckenridge County. Our correspondent heard that he had died and was buried on the same day on Mr. Oscar Board's place.[66]

On March 9th, a retraction was printed in the *Louisville Daily Journal*: We stated in our issue of Saturday that the notorious guerrilla Billy Magruder, who was wounded in an encounter with the state troops, in Breckenridge County, was taken to the house of Oscar Board, where he died. We are informed that such is not the case. If the outlaw is dead, he was not at the home of Mr. Board when he "shuffled off his mortal coil."[67] The three men were hiding in the Cox barn at this time, likely arriving there the night of March 7th or on the 8th of March. Elizabeth and John sent for Dr. Lewis to tend to Magruder. Lewis told Mundy and Metcalf that Magruder could not be moved for a month. Secure that Magruder and the others would stay put, Lewis must have quickly notified the authorities of the whereabouts of the three men, because Cyrus Wilson was given orders on March 10th to take the troops who were dispatched to Brandenburg on Saturday, March 11th, arriving there between 9:00 and 9:30 p.m.

Bill Marion and his band were roaming in Meade County at this time. Whether he was trying to locate Mundy and Magruder, or whether he was there coincidentally, no one can say for sure. On March 12th, a Sunday, Cyrus Wilson and his men surrounded the Cox barn, and after a parlay, and most say a brief gunfight, the three men surrendered. Mundy and Metcalf were placed on horseback and Magruder was loaded in a wagon, taken to Brandenburg, where they were transported to Louisville by riverboat Monday the 13th of March. News of their capture had to be spreading. On March 13, 1865, Marion sent a telegram from Meade County, to George Prentice addressed to General Palmer who had replaced the hated Stephen Burbridge as Military Commandant of the area. It stated:

> *March 13th, 1865 Meade Co., Ky.*
>
> *"to General Palmer or the Commadant of the post of Louisville, Ky., sir you have Captured two of my men Clark or Mondy you*

style him an Magruder an also lieut Medcalf Gentlemen J. W. W. Marion, Capt. Commanding Confederate forces in Kentucky do solemnly declare if you do treat them as guirillas that I will shoot or hang fifty of your men you may think got them first but you will find that I will get them I am a Confederate soldier an my men are all regular soldiers but you drive us to desperation let it be if you murder those brave men I haunt the City of Louisville until I have revenge them look how you treated one of my men when wounded and captured in Anderson County at Bacon Bush, you Brutally shot him while lying on the ground but you failed to kill him or keep him So far as I am Concerned I ask no quarters of you an if you don't treat those boys as prisoners of ware I will show none to you so if you thint there is no hell you you pitch out. W.W. Marion Capt.-CSA"-LDJ[68]

No one can accuse Marion of being an English Major, but he got his point across. This message could have been sent from Brandenburg, Garnettsville, Grayhampton and other places, but I believe it was more likely to have been sent from Meadeville, Kentucky. One theme rings throughout Marion's statement; he believes that he and his men are Confederate soldiers, partsan rangers, and are not being treated as such.

On March 17th the *Louisville Daily Journal* wrote: "Oscar P. Board an old wealthy citizen of Meade County has been arrested by a gang of guerrillas who hold him in their possession as a hostage for Mundy. We hope this is not so, as Mr. Board is a quiet, worthy inoffensive citizen that has many friends in Meade County, and is well known in the community." This was followed by a March 18th report: "On Monday last (March 13th) Dr. Ben Wathen and Oscar Board prominent citizens of Meade County were arrested by Captain Marion's band of cutthroats, dragged from their homes and sentenced to be shot to death simply because it is supposed that they had furnished U.S. authorities with information in regard to the whereabouts of Mundy, Magruder, and Medkiff (Metcalf) which led to their capture. It is almost needless to say that the supposition was entirely wrong. On a more mature reflection, a part of the band objected to shooting Mssrs. Walthen (Wathen) and Board without giving them the benefit of a trial. An order was promulgated banishing them from the county and they were released, thus escaping death. Now they are refugees from their homes. Marion says he wants no man's sympathy or friendship. His argument is the pistol. He is a desperate outlaw and compels the farmers to cook for and furnish all that his band requires."[69]

On the same day the *Louisville Daily Democrat* printed the following account: "We stated in our paper this morning that Mr. Oscar P. Board, of Meade County, who had been captured by guerrillas, who held him as a prisoner, awaiting to hear the result of the trial of Sue Mundy. We take pleasure in stating that Board and Dr. Wathen… who were captured by Capt. Marion's gang have escaped… Since writing the above we learn that Marion's intention was to shoot Messrs. Board and Wathen, he having charged them with giving information to Federal troops. It is known that in all cases where men have been captured by "Marion and his men" that he does the shooting of prisoners. On this occasion he was about to shoot Messrs. Board and Wathen when his men threatened to kill him if he harmed either of them. Marion then permitted them to go, informing them that if they give any more information he would follow them until he caught them and killed them both.[70]

William Boling wrote an article in *The Meade County Messenger*, between 1906 and 1908 that recalled the kidnapping of Wathen and Board. In it he reported: "We lose track of Marion for a while and next hear of him holding as captives, Dr. Ben Wathen and Oscar Board, whose farm adjoined that of Wathen's. The guerrilla Captain took his two prisoners up into the Hill Grove country (Meadeville) and after a military trial, he condemned them to be shot at sunrise. The morning came. Everything was in readiness for the execution of the sentence. But the night before passed which Wathen and Board thought to be their last, had hatched a plot in the mind of a young Tindall, one of Marion's best men, to save the condemned prisoners, and when the hour for execution came, Tindall together with others stepped forward with drawn revolvers and (said) quietly but sternly to Capt. Marion that if he carried out the execution he would pay the penalty with his life. Marion ordered the men released….[71] There is little doubt that Board was targeted for the kidnapping because of the report that Magruder was buried on his place. Anyone would assume from the newspaper report that Board would be aware of his whereabouts and be in a position to tell on him. Dr. Wathen was likely mistaken for Dr. Jesse Lewis the real informant. In Marion's eyes they were probably in cahoots living on adjoining property and both believed to be in a position to lead the authorities to Magruder, Medkiff and Mundy. To save face and maintain control of his band, he banished the men from Meade County and their homes. Interestingly, Magruder states in his confession that Marion killed Dr. Lewis, but Lewis lived and survived the war. Magruder was likely referring to Wathen who was supposed to have been killed by Marion, also confusing him with Lewis.

On March 25, ten days after Mundy was hanged, Prentice printed Marion's letter of March 13th, to Palmer. Another report appeared in that issue stating: "Ben Wathen and Oscar Board of Breckenridge County are now in Louisville and under arrest by Federal authorities. The Dr. is charged with being one of the Doctors attending on Magruder, previous to his capture. It is claimed that both are in sympathy with the guerrilla bands now operating in the state. They were arrested last week and are being held for trial.[72] Wathen and Board were out of the frying pan and into the fire. They were tried by Federal authorities for aiding and abetting the guerrillas had their trial on March 31, 1865. On April 1st, the *Louisville Daily Journal* reported: "Dr. Ben Wathen and Oscar Board, of Breckenridge County, Ky., who were arrested some days since, charged with aiding and abetting guerrillas, and had their trial yesterday, and were released. [73]

It is beyond comprehension to consider what these men went through, being sentenced to death by a guerrilla firing squad, only to escape and be banished from their home, traveling to Louisville only to be rearrested by the Federal Government and tried again on a hanging offense. The death of Marion came at the town of Manton in Washington County 15 days later. His death will be discussed later along with his nemesis Bad Ed Terrell.

Boling explains at the end of his article about the kidnapping of Wathen and Board. "We lose Stanley Young, alias Capt. Marion after this, but young Tindall, after the war was over, went to Dr. Wathen, who welcomed him as his deliverer in that awful moment when he was saved from a cruel death at the hands of the guerrilla chieftain. Dr. Wathen let Tindall have all the land he wished to cultivate for a number of years and charged him not a farthing. Gratitude to a savior he had not forgotten. Capt. Marion's long white feather he could still see. Peace to all. Memory is a sad, sometimes a marvelous painter. It paints best the things we have lost. The guerrilla chieftain has passed to the other side. His enemies have joined him there. The curtain has rung down, the auditorium is empty, and the theater is dark."

There are some questions I have had about Stanley Young. Why did he become a Confederate guerrilla? He was living in Indiana, a northern state, and although he was not far from Kentucky, five to seven miles from Brandenburg, most of his associates with the possible exception of some of his immediate family, would have had unionist leanings. Stanley was born in Nelson County, where his grandparents, Sinclair Young are buried "in two lonely graves on the Royalty Farm in Bloomfield, on the east corner of the intersection of U.S. 62 and 458.[74] Bloomfield, indeed Nelson County, was a hot bed of Confederate activity. The prevailing sentiments of that community certainly could have influenced Stanley. His crime of murder was perpetrated in Kentucky, but was against an Indiana man. Since Kentucky was admitted to the Confederacy, but had never officially succeeded legally from the Union, he might have felt in safer in Kentucky as a Confederate. It is evident that not all of the Young and Marsh families shared Stanley's Confederate leanings. Stanley Young's sister Amelia H. Young was married on April 18th 1858, in Harrison County, Indiana to William Henry Timberlake, a native of Maine, living in nearby Corydon, Indiana. The marriage took place 39 days before Stanley killed Uncle Marsh. William H. Timberlake resigned his commission as a lieutenant and adjutant in the 81st Indiana Infantry on April 29, 1863, before Morgan's invasion. He was a lawyer and Insurance agent in Corydon, Indiana. Interestingly, John M. Timberlake, likely a relative of William's but not likely a son or brother, resigned from the same regiment and became the Provost Marshal (Lt. Col.) of Southern Indiana. He did take part in the battle when Morgan made his crossing at Brandenburg, Kentucky and commanded Indiana forces opposing Morgan. At that fight there was a dispute between Col. John Timberlake and Lt. Col. William J. Irvin of the Indiana Legion. Irvin ordered Captain G.W. Lyons to fire their cannon at the boat that was ferrying Morgan's men, while John Timberlake wanted him to shell the Confederates at the Brandenburg landing. Timberlake was afraid there were hostages aboard the boats, and his rank being greater, he won the debate. Brazenly, Col. John Timberlake shouted across the river, "Shut down the steam on the McCombs and send over the steamer *Alice Dean* or I will blow you to hades in five minutes."[75] John was out-spoken, sometimes profane, and combative. He was killed July 10th, 1864 while attending church services in Mauckport, Indiana. His wife and another lady and some family members began arguing with some southern sympathizers, and the verbal altercation turned violent, resulting in John Timberlake's death. Even more interestingly, he married a woman named Elizabeth Young. Of course that could have been a relation of Stanley.

Chapter 7

The Capture, Trial and Execution of Sue Mundy

The capture of Sue Mundy began March 7th or 8th, when the three men found their way to the farm of John and Elizabeth Cox. They took up residence in the Cox tobacco barn that was made of logs. To the east of, and adjacent to the barn was a spring fed pond, about 100 feet east of the barn was the two story Cox farm house. A lane led from the main road past the barn and pond, and on to the house. There was a cistern on the west side of the house that was also fed by the spring. Directly east of the house approximately 80 feet away, was the Cox Family Cemetery. The house and farm was located in the area of Mt. Marino. The closest town was Webster, Kentucky, about four miles to the north and west. Between Webster and Brandenburg lay the home of Dr. Jesse Pitman Lewis. The men were in the barn about four days before their capture. A 1939 newspaper article states they were there for about two weeks.[76]

There is little doubt that there was an informant who told the Federal authorities where the three men were hiding. The most logical person to have told on the men was Dr. Lewis. He not only tended to Magruder, but he had also prescribed that Magruder stay put for at least a month. Whether this was just good medicine or whether it was for a more sinister purpose, or simply a way to protect him, Lewis, from being charged with aiding and abetting guerrillas, we may never know. By the preponderance of the evidence it seems to point to Lewis telling on the men. He also led Wilson to the barn, although Wilson states he was pressed into service. A statement I think he made to give Lewis cover from retaliation by people like Bill Marion. There are many different stories about the capture of Sue Mundy. They are not all in agreement. I will discuss four different reports that give details that call into question some of the recorded testimony. The two reports that carry the most credibility are of course the trial transcript, and in my eyes, the story John Cox related to G.A. Foote, a relative, in a letter the 78-year-old Foote wrote to a friend in 1941. Other reports however, contain details that provide information that enlighten the entire event. Still others cloud and confuse what really happened.

The capture as relayed in Watson's, Wright's, and Taylor's book is based on the trial transcript which admittedly should be correct and beyond doubt is the best information available. However, if the trial transcript is accepted as the definitive word on matters relating to Sue Mundy's capture and trial and fairness thereof, then it must, in my opinion, be accepted in its entirety including the details of the subsequent execution of his sentence. I do not think we can afford to choose what we want from the evidence, to use to bolster whatever we think actually happened, and disregard what facts support other possibilities. It must be accepted in total, warts and all.

A paraphrased summary of the transcript reveals that Mundy, on the morning of March 12, 1865, found the barn, in which he was hiding surrounded by 50 soldiers of Company B of the 30th Wisconsin Volunteer Infantry. Captain Lewis O. Marshall and the troops were under the command of Major Cyrus Wilson. The troops and officers arrived at Brandenburg, Kentucky aboard the Grey Eagle between 9:00 and 9:30 p.m. the night of March 11th. They marched about ten miles to the home of Dr. Lewis, and he was compelled to guide them to the Cox farm where they arrived about dawn surrounding the log tobacco barn where the guerrillas were hidden.

The Judge Advocate was Lt. Col. 9th Iowa Infantry, William H. Coyle. There are some inconsistencies in the testimony of Cyrus Wilson and Lewis Marshall having to do with the number of men who were wounded. While this seems to be an understandable occurrence caused by the normally expected time lag between the capture and trial of most criminals, the lag between Mundy's capture and trial was only two days. Recollections here should be fresh and clear, especially considering it was a capitol charge carrying with it a death sentence, but they weren't always. I show the questioner to be the Judge Advocate, when it fact it could be others.

There were two charges against Mundy.

Charge first: Being a guerrilla.
Specification first: In this that he, Jerome Clark, alias Sue

Mundy, being a citizen of the United States, and owing allegiance thereto, did within the lines occupied by the lawfully authorized military forces of the United States, unlawfully, and of his own wrong, take up arms as a guerrilla, and did join, belong to, and act and cooperate with guerrillas, he the said Jerome Clark, alias Sue Mundy, not then acting with or belonging to any lawfully authorized organized military force at war with the United States, and not being commanded thereto by any lawful civil or military authority.

This, at the counties of Nelson, Marion, Henry, Woodford, State of Kentucky, during the months of September, October, November, and December 1864.

Specification second: In this that he, Jerome Clark, alias Sue Mundy, a citizen of the State of Kentucky, and within the lines of the regularly organized military forces of the United States, take up arms as a guerrilla and outlaw in the county of Meade, and the State of Kentucky, and did fire upon a detachment of the 30th Regiment Wisconsin Volunteer Infantry, and belonging to the regularly authorized and organized forces of the United States, who were then present in discharge of their duty, and by reason of said shooting did wound Privates John G, White, John Robbins, and W. A. Wadsworth of said 30th Regiment Wisconsin Volunteer Infantry.

This, on or about the 11th day of March, 1865, in the county of Meade and State of Kentucky.

William H. Coyl,
Lieut. Col. & A.J.A.
Dept. of Ky.

I am including the testimony of Wilson and Marshall pertaining to the capture, and with regard to the charges. Some spelling and grammar have been corrected.

The sworn testimony of Major Cyrus J. Wilson, a witness for the prosecution, being duly sworn, deposed:

Judge Advocate: What, is your name, occupation, and place of residence?

Wilson: Cyrus J. Wilson is my name. I do not know what I will say my occupation is. I have been a soldier for the last three years.

Judge Advocate: In what capacity did you serve in the army?

Wilson: As a lieutenant, captain, colonel, last as major of the 26th Kentucky Volunteer Infantry.

Judge Advocate: State what you know of the capture of the accused, Jerome Clark, alias Sue Mundy, on or about the 11th day of March 1865, and give all the circumstances connected with it.

Wilson: I was ordered by Major General Palmer, on the evening of the 10th, to take fifty men, proceed to Brandenburg, go about ten miles from that place and catch Magruder and Mundy, if possible. I went to Brandenburg, arriving there at 9 or half past 9, o'clock Saturday evening. I held the steamboat there for a half hour, keeping passengers all on board. There were 45 men stationed at Brandenburg to picket the town. I then went out ten miles on the Brandenburg Road with fifty men I had taken from this place to Doctor Lewis. I found the Doctor, who had been tending on Magruder and having compelled him to tell of the whereabouts of Magruder, he acted as a guide. He took us to a tobacco barn in Meade County owned by a man by the name of Cox. This was about daybreak on Sunday morning the 12th. Captain Marshall, with his men surrounded the barn. They first knocked at the door and no answer was made. They then took a rock and knocked the door down. As the door fell, the men were fired upon by, I presume Mundy or Clark. There were forty shots I presume fired into them and they returned the fire upon them, occasionally as they could see them passing backwards and forwards before the door. The firing stopped at last and I sent in a flag of truce, by Dr. Lewis, asking their surrender. Mundy asked him who I was. He told them. He then asked what regiment I belonged to. He told him of the 26th Kentucky. He asked who my colonel was. He told him. How many men I had. I think I told him 150 men, but I am not certain. I think I told him I had fifty infantry and 100 cavalry. He then called for me and I met him at the door a few feet off with his pistol in his hand.

I asked him to surrender and he said, "Major, if I surrender to you, you will kill me." I told I would not then, and he said "your men will do it." I said not at that time. He said "Where will you take me?" "I answered to Louisville." He said, "You will kill me there." I told him I had no doubt of that at all, but I said "It will give you a few more days to live." We came to take you and will take you dead or alive. He invited me in. I went in and we took a smoke together. Magruder insisted upon his surrender. I spoke to Magruder. He said he had been a bad boy and was going to die. I told him I was sorry for him. He insisted upon Clark's surrendering. Clark concluded he would not surrender for a while. I then told him I would give him five minutes to surrender, and if he did not, I would open fire again. I still insisted upon his surrendering because I wished to save the lives of my men. Magruder also insisted. Finally, I told him there might be a chance of his escape that there was one chance in a thousand or in ten thousand. He said there was some grounds to escape and he believed he would surrender. I called for the Captain. He agreed to surrender, and we would treat him like a prisoner of war until he came to Louisville. He said there was enough published against him to kill him and he knew he would be killed in Louisville. I told him I had no doubt at all but that he would have a few more days to live. Upon that ground he surrendered. We talked it over there, Captain Marshall, Mundy or Clark, and myself. The men came, and he was taken from there. When I was tying them, I tied their arms behind them and then tied them together. Said I, "Mundy, this is rather hard treatment for a prisoner of war, but we are determined that you are not to get loose." The understanding was that he was only to be treated as a prisoner of war until he came to Louisville and the publication I have seen otherwise is false.

Judge Advocate: State fully what was said by the accused, Clark, or Mundy, in relation to having done enough to hang him.

Wilson: He did not say hang. I told him I had no doubt about that.

Judge Advocate: In what county did this happen?

Wilson: Meade County, Kentucky.

Judge Advocate: State what you know of certain men being wounded by the Accused and the party he was with.

Wilson: There were four of our men wounded. I do not know their names; strangers to me.

Judge Advocate: Of what regiment were they.

Wilson: 30th Wisconsin Infantry.

Judge Advocate: State, who fired first, the party you were with, or the Accused and his party.

Wilson: My impression has been that Mundy fired first. I may be mistaken. *(?)*

The sworn testimony of Captain Lewis O. Marshall, a witness for the prosecution, being called and sworn, deposed:

Judge Advocate: What is your, name, rank, Company, and regiment?

Marshall: Lewis O. Marshall Captain, Company B 30th Wisconsin Volunteer Infantry.

Judge Advocate: State what you know of the accused Jerome Clark's capture and circumstances.

Marshall: "He was captured on the morning of the 12th March. I approached the house from the front. The side door was on and the men surrounded the house and knocked at the door and told them to open it. They did not do it. I told the men to take a chunk of stone and break the door in which they did. Just as the door fell, someone inside fired. They fired in quick succession. I stepped back and told the men to go away from the front of the door and shoot any man who attempted to go out.

I also told some of the men to take some chinking out and run their pieces through and fire. I thought they could probably see them from the outside. Then, I stepped around the corner of the barn when one of the men standing by the corner said, "Captain, I am shot". I asked him where and he said, "In the foot." Just then there was a man came and called me and said two of the men were badly wounded, in the sides, one of them, the other in the breast. I asked him where they were and he pointed out the direction, 30 or 40 feet off.

I told the men to watch the building while I went to see how bad the men were wounded. I took a, half dozen men and then went up to Cox's house and caught two men in there. I asked a Negro who was in there. He said, "Cox and his brother." I told him to tell them to come out. They came out and we went in and searched the house for arms, and found two pistols, rusty, and had the appearance of not being used for a long time. One of them was loaded with two balls. We took these men down there and on getting near saw a flag of truce going up to the house, a handkerchief tied on a stick. I asked who sent up that flag of truce of a man, and he said Major Wilson. I went and saw the Major. Just as I saw him, the Dr. (Lewis) came and said they wanted to see the Major. I asked him what they had concluded on, and he said they were considering. He went out and came out again and said they wanted to see me. I went up to where the Major was, and he told Mundy who I was. I said, "Is this Sue Mundy?" and, he replied, "I am the man they call Sue Mundy." I asked him what he proposed to do, give up his arms or not? He said you will kill me if I do. I said, no, my men should not kill him. He said he was afraid they would. I said not. The Major said he might give up his arms and prolong his life a few days, and he should be treated with respect as long as he made no effort to get away, until he got to Louisville.

I did not make him any promise of that he should be treated as a prisoner of war, or anything of the kind. He replied that he was safe enough with him but he knew damned well he had got to die when he got to Louisville; that he knew there were charges enough to swing him up."

Judge Advocate: What was your reply to this?

Marshall: I do not now remember. *(?)*

Judge Advocate: State which, if any reason, you gave the accused to believe that he was to be treated as a prisoner of war after arriving in Louisville.

Marshall: I gave him no reason for thinking so at all. I told him I thought he stood a good chance of hanging or something of that kind. *(?)* There were two of my men wounded. If the flag of truce had not been sent up, I should have set the building on fire. My instructions from Colonel Dill were that this Major Wilson was going under orders of General Palmer and I should be guided by him.

Regarding specification number one, Mundy, Magruder, and Medkiff were enlisted in the Confederate Army. They became detached and operated, I believe, in their eyes, under the Partisan Ranger Act. Partisan Rangers were guerrillas and were acting as irregular soldiers under the auspices of the Confederate Army. In fact, at the time Magruder was shot, these men were in route to combine with other detached Confederate forces in Paris, Tennessee, when they were fired upon. The problem they faced was caused by the infamous Order No. 59 issued by Stephen Gano Burbridge. In that order he declared that guerrillas would not be treated as prisoners of war, but were to be executed immediately upon their capture. The order also allowed for legitimate prisoners of war, innocent of the guerrilla crimes, to be shot in retaliation for the killing of Federal soldiers or civilians, by said guerrillas. The condemned were selected by drawing lots. Four prisoners of war were executed by firing squad at or near the place the Federal soldier or civilian was killed. This exacerbated retaliation, in kind, by the Partisan Rangers. Many times the killings by the guerrillas were of Negro Union Soldiers, or other Union soldiers on leave to go home. Often enough but less frequently civilians were murdered. Most of those killings were based on the politics of the victim, which made them justifiable to their killers.

Regarding specification number two, with only two days lapse of time between the capture and trial, and with the eye witnesses fresh from the experience, there should not be such deviant testimony on events pertinent to the specifications. The specifications list three men wounded. Marshall states two men, and perhaps three men were wounded, and his testimony could even be construed to mean four men wounded. He also cannot remember exactly what he said to Mundy. Wilson states four men were wounded. Tom Watson states three men were wounded and a fourth was also hit.[77]

The Cox/ Henderson Version of the Capture of Mundy, Magruder, and Medkiff

In the spring of 1997, I visited an antique store in Irvington with my wife Fran. We were engaged in driving around Meade County and getting familiar with our new community. We had come back from Phoenix, Arizona and settled in Northwestern Meade County, just outside the town of Payneville. We stopped at a store owned by Mr. Mark Henderson, a great-great-grandson of John Cox, the owner of the farm on which Sue Mundy was captured. It just so happened that we had passed by an historic marker that commemorated the location of Sue Mundy's capture. We made a selection or two and when we were paying for the items, I mentioned the marker to Mr. Henderson. He told me that he was well familiar with the Mundy capture, but he said he was dissatisfied with the written versions of the story. Several accounts appeared in the local newspapers and Civil War magazines that did not comport with the family story. He told me that he wished someone would write the story that his Great-Great Grandfather Cox told. It was some nine years later that I revisited Mr. Henderson and told him I would like to tell his family's story. I told him I would write it in hopes that it would be published, but without guarantee. I also promised him he could review the story before I submitted it for publication. With that, Mr. Henderson took me across the street to the City Hall, where he had the clerk copy his family papers regarding the capture of Sue Mundy.

There is a letter in the file that Mr. G.A. Foote, a relative, wrote to a friend in 1941 when he was 78-years-old. It referenced a newspaper article and it read as follows:

Irvington, Ky. Aug. 6th 1941
Friend George,

Your esteemed favor to hand for which I thank you. I am sending today a newspaper account of the Sue Mundy arrest. It is not exactly like Mr. Cox related it to me. He told me when he went to his barn to feed one morning he found a full company of soldiers 100 or more had surrounded the barn and the Captain sent him in the barn to tell Mundy he demanded the surrender of him and his two companions McGruder (sic) and Metcafe (sic). McGruder (sic) was wounded and delirious was tending on him. Mundy sent Mr. Cox back to tell the Captain to come to the barn and he would discuss the terms on which he could surrender. When the Captain sent Mr. Cox in the barn he told him if you can't persuade those men to surrender I will make you burn the barn or hang you on this tree. Thereupon Mundy told Mr. Cox wrather (sic) than shoot you when you come burn the barn, I will surrender if he will take me as a prisoner of war to this the Captain readily agreed to do in the presence of Mr. Cox.

When Mundy surrendered and gave his pistols to Mr. Cox the Captain called his men and told them to bind his hands and feet and put him on a bare back horse with his hands tied behind him *and his feet tied under the horse stomach and trotted and galloped off to Louisville. One report has it there were several men killed but Mr. Cox said there was not a shot fired at the barn and Mundy surrendered only because he did not want to shoot him when he came with a tun (sic) of straw to burn the barn. This man Metcafe (sic) came to Irvington some years ago in regard to Mundy's pistols *Ruie Cox has one now which Mr. Cox gave him when he died and Bud Price the other one. These old guns are antique and I don't think you could buy one at any price.*

Repct.
G.A. Foote

Obviously, if Mr. Foote is correct, there was no shooting at the barn. The house and the barn were on about two acres of land, and shots would have been heard by anyone on the premises inside or outside the house. The threat to hang John Cox was a very real and likely prospect, because he was harboring three notorious guerrillas, a crime punishable by death. Mundy surrendered two pistols to John Cox. It may be that since Cox had heard the Captain, either Marshall or Wilson, agree to take Mundy as a prisoner of war, the surrender of his pistols to a civilian might provide a witness to the fact, and in some way cloud the military judicial proceeding. At the very least Mundy may have died as a soldier, before a firing squad. For some reason Cox was not called as a witness. It may have been that John Cox would have contradicted the testimony of Wilson and Marshall referencing count number 2, at least partially offsetting their testimony. The story Cox related to his grandson and the family story flies in the face of that evidence of a shooting. Certainly the fact that Cox was threatened with hanging is not something that would be seen as favorable press for the military, in the *Louisville Democrat* or would likely not play very well in the *Louisville Daily Journal*. Any and all of these things might have been reasons not to have Cox testify. Mundy may not have asked for Cox to be a witness, because it would have put Cox in jeopardy of a charge of harboring or abetting guerrillas, (remember Wathen and Board were arrested and charged for abetting) or he may have asked for Cox to testify and been denied. Mundy asked for certain witnesses to appear, but was denied for two reasons: firstly, it would have been impossible to get Confederate officers to come to Louisville; and secondly, that Mundy had been a soldier was not in question. Mundy's fate was sealed a day before his trial began. This story about no gunfight at the barn was also published in 1963 in the "Brandenburg Story" printed by the Methodist Men's Club, and at least in one other document.

Mundy was captured on March 12, 1865, was tried on March 14th, and effectively was not allowed witnesses. There were in fact no witnesses that testified in his defense. He was sentenced to be hanged on March 15th. He was not told of the sentence until the morning of the 15th, when Reverend Talbott informed him he was to die on the gallows at 4:00 p.m. that day. Interestingly the endorsement of his execution was dated March 13th, a full day before his trial began.[78] It has been suggested that he was not allowed to call witnesses because they would be unable to give testimony contradictory of his career as a guerrilla. The Confederacy had a different opinion of guerrilla warfare. The Partisan Rangers or guerrillas were instrumental in the disruption of Union military operations in Kentucky. They chopped down telegraph poles and cut the lines. They burned trains, train stations, bridges and trestles. They were considered a legally instituted force of the Confederate Army, as recognized by the Confederacy. There is no doubt that they robbed people and institutions as a means by which to sustain themselves. They killed Union supporters and soldiers. It is possible, if not probable, that his witnesses could have provided corroboration that he was an enlisted and trained Confederate Soldier fighting as a Partisan Ranger? And of course there is the testimony John Cox might have provided concerning Mundy being taken as a prisoner of war. The same could have been said for Magruder and Medkiff.

When word of Burbridge's order #59 was published in the *Louisville Daily Journal*, July 20, 1864, General A.R. Johnson wrote a letter of inquiry to General Burbridge, to be delivered by Major J. Walker Taylor on August 4, 1864. Taylor found himself standing in front of a Federal gunboat officer on the Ohio River, trying to secure permission to travel to Louisville to have an audience with General Burbridge. Major Taylor was allowed to travel up-river to New Albany, but to proceed no further on the order of General Ewing. In the letter Johnson asked for a clarification to define what Burbridge meant as a guerrilla, and exactly what soldiers come under that heading. Johnson specifically wanted to know if all Confederate soldiers were to be held responsible for acts of lawless men, renegades from both armies.[79] The letter was reviewed by Ewing, but was not delivered to Burbridge, unless by wire. Ewing ordered Lt. Colonel Fairleigh to draft a reply to Johnson. The letter read as follows:

Headquarters Military
Command, Louisville
August 9, 1864

A.R. Johnson
Colonel – Confederate Corps.
In Southern Kentucky
Colonel

I enclose to you herewith a copy of General Ewing's order regarding Major J. Walker Taylor of your command, and am permitted to say as reasons for the order the following:

You are in Kentucky, a state far in the rear of the Federal lines, with a small force, and in your communication addressed to General Burbridge, fail to establish any authority from the Rebel Government for your presence here. The presumption is you are here without any competent authority merely by your own will, controlled by no orders, responsible to no one and commanding an organization equally irresponsible.

The General can only regard you as a soldier, or guerrilla. You have failed to show that you are the former and until this is done, the General declines to receive any communications from you.

Since Major Taylor claims to be a Confederate soldier, the General deems it duty to place him within Confederate lines and so directed me. The order will be obeyed. The communication addressed to General Burbridge is respectfully returned.

I have the honor to be very respectfully
Your obedient servant,

M.B. Fairleigh,
Lt. Col. 26th Ky.
Military Command

General Ewing wired a message to General Hobson in Evansville, Indiana on August 17, 1864 as follows:

Louisville, Aug. 17, 1864
General Hobson.
Evansville:

If Johnson is taken he should be shot on the spot. I will be responsible for the killing of the entire command, Johnson included. This is law; I hope you will execute it.

HUGH EWING
Brigadier-General

These communications serve to prove that guerrillas or Partisan Rangers and indeed Confederate prisoners of war were to be treated as common criminals and shot where and when captured, or later in retaliation for crimes of murder by others, without trial and for which they were not responsible. Sue Mundy's execution was a dot on the exclamation point.

The Death of Sue Mundy

When the independent scouts wished to kill a guerrilla, they did so as they wished, immediately and with the impunity Order No. 59 provided. This put the guerrilla hunters in a position of being above the law, although it was legally allowable under the order. At this same time, some people were turned in by Union procurers because they would not readily sell their livestock, or neighbors who harbored a grudge against them. How were soldiers supposed to know the difference? Obviously if the person captured was fighting them in battle, then there was provocation. Short of that, unless a guerrilla was well known and easily identifiable, such as "One Arm Berry", who might have a reward offered for his capture, the scouts found themselves judge, jury, and executioner. It seems to me that the old adage, "Kill them all, and let God sort them out", seems to have been the philosophy used in dealing with captured guerrillas or Partisan Rangers, unless the captured was a high profile individual, who was afforded a trial, conducted for the public to give the perception that justice was served, or was a captured

Rebel fighter, his death was just as certain. It was just a matter of timing, and the perceived deterrent a public shooting or hanging might have on the others still fighting. The selection of prisoners of war to be shot in reprisal for acts they had no part in, added to the injustice. So it was with Sue Mundy, Henry Clay Magruder, and would have been for William Quantrill and Bill Marion, had they not died before such a trial and public execution could be arranged.

The execution of a human being is a powerful thing. I would not want to see one. The Federals made the public executions of guerrillas a somber affair with music, drum rolls, soldiers in parade dress, and of course the reading of the charges, findings, sentence and the last words of the condemned. In those days people came from all around to witness hangings because they provided a form of entertainment that was sadly lacking in that society. It was also believed to be a time when parents could show children what could happen if they were bad. There were no movie houses, radio stations, television sets, CDs, VCRs, or MP3 players. A hanging was a time where people could socialize and be entertained, albeit in a macabre way. A military execution must have been a grand spectacle of a tragedy.

Death on the gallows was not always quick. In fact death was caused by asphyxiation after the breaking of the cervical vertebrae and or lacerating or severing the trachea. Death followed immediately or as long as twenty minutes or more after the trap was sprung. There were traditions associated with hangings that may or may not always have been followed. Many times the condemned was driven to the gallows in a wagon sitting on the coffin in which they were to be buried. The rope used, was to be without stretch, or dead, because a new rope would stretch and not break the neck quickly causing additional suffering. There were by tradition thirteen steps up the gallows, and thirteen coils of rope around the noose. After the charges, specifications and sentence was read, the person to be executed was given an opportunity to make one last statement. A prayer might be read, and a hood was placed over the head, the noose was placed around his neck, the knot usually positioned behind the left ear, and the trap was sprung. The body when it came to the end of the rope would often times jerk or spasm reacting to the shock of the trauma done to the neck and trachea. The legs would pull up and push down as if trying to find the ground. Finally the body would be still and swing gently. If the neck was broken quickly, death by asphyxiation would follow after a time, with little struggle. The breaking of the neck was supposed to render the condemned unconscious and paralyzed during the choking process, resulting finally with the heart ceasing to beat. The executed person was at last lowered to the ground and placed in a coffin, usually the one on which they sat as they rode to gallows. This is not at all a pretty picture to paint.

On March the 16th, the *Louisville Daily Journal* wrote about the execution of Sue Mundy:

> *Sue Mundy was ignorant of her fate until yesterday morning. Rev. Talbott, of St. John's Episcopal Church, was his spiritual adviser. When he asked Sue if he knew what would be done with him, he said he thought he would be executed, as the court-martial refused to have him introduce witnesses. The minister then asked him if he had any idea when his execution would take place. He replied, "In a few weeks." The minister told him it would be sooner than that, "in a few days." Rev. Mr. Talbott then informed him that his execution would take place in a few hours. He was under the impression he was to be shot, but when he was told that he would be hung he manifested a little uneasiness by a sigh and uttering "Oh." After the first tidings of his fate he was cool and collected. When he fully realized his condition, he knelt with his minister in prayer, and requested him to pray with him. After instruction and confession of faith in the Church, he requested to be baptized. This ordinance was administered an hour before his execution, after he had declared that he had no malice against anyone, and loved everybody. He then requested Mr. Talbott to write letters to his sister, aunt, cousin, and a young lady of this State, having a lock of hair cut off and placed in each letter.*
>
> *He declared he was not guilty of one-tenth of the outrages that he was charged with, and that the Louisville Journal had done him great injustice. He positively declared he was not present at all when those Negro soldiers were killed near Simpsonville, but was far from the scene, and wounded at the time. He also denied being present when Kalfus and Roberts were killed, and said it was Marion and his men that did it. He stated he held a Captain's commission from Col. Jack Allen, and was a Confederate soldier.*

He requested Mr. Talbott that his body should be sent to his aunt in in Franklin, Ky., and be buried by the side of his father and mother, in his uniform, or if that would not be permitted, at least bury him in his jacket.

A Description of Sue Mundy

Marcus Jerome Clark, alias Sue Mundy, was nearly six feet high, straight and remarkably well built, and we think would weigh about one-hundred and sixty pounds. His complexion was fair, long dark hair that touched his shoulders, and a beautifully shaped mouth, and in short, was a very handsome man. His whole demeanor was firm and polite, and he bore the air of a man of culture and gentlemanly refinement. He said he "would have been twenty-one years old next August, and would have died before his manhood, and yet had been a man to *his* country." He wore a black velvet cap, a black or dark blue jacket with one row of Kentucky State buttons, a pair of dark cassimere pants, and a pair of old boots cut down in imitation of a pair of shoes.

The Gallows

Notwithstanding the result of the trial was kept secret, a large crowd gathered at the place of execution, on Broadway near Eighteenth Street. The gallows was a hastily-constructed affair. The material was the same that was used in the scaffolding on which Nathan Marks, the guerrilla, was hung some months ago, and was built precisely like the other. The platform and trap-door was supported by a prop – a rope attached to the lower end. A rough wooden coffin was brought and placed under the scaffold a half hour before the

Arrival of Sue Mundy

She was conveyed from the Military Prison in a carriage, accompanied by her spiritual adviser, under a strong guard, and arrived at the place of execution about a quarter of four o'clock, preceded by martial music. It required several minutes to form the troops in proper order, the prisoner, in the meantime, remaining in the carriage, his lips moving, as if praying, a white handkerchief up to his eyes, and his head leaning against the side of the carriage.

The Execution

Captain George Swope, of the 5th Indiana Cavalry, and Provost Marshall, had charge of the execution. The prisoner was conducted to the gallows in company with the minister. Both knelt and offered up a prayer, after which Capt. Swope read the charges and specifications to the prisoner. He seemed to pay little attention to this. His eyes were half closed, and his lips continually in motion, evidently offering up his last petition to God. "Lord have mercy on my poor soul," seemed, from the motion of his lips, to be his prayer. He was asked if he had anything to say, to make it known. He directed his remarks to his spiritual advisor in a very low voice, hardly audible.

"I am a regular Confederate soldier, and have served in the Confederate army four years. I fought under Gen. Buckner at Fort Donelson, and belonged to Gen. Morgan's command when he entered Kentucky. I have assisted and taken many prisoners, and have always treated them kindly. I was wounded at Cynthiana, and cut off from my command. I have been in Kentucky ever since. I could prove that I am a regular Confederate soldier, and I hope in and die for the Confederate cause."

A white cap was placed over his face, and at the word the prop was pulled from under the trap. The fall was not more than three feet, and did not break his neck; like the other victim he choked to death. We have seen a great many persons hung, but never before did we witness such hard struggles and convulsions. It was feared for a time that he would break the lashings. His sufferings, however, were of short duration. Thus ended the career of the notorious Sue Mundy.

He was left hanging some twenty minutes before he was cut down. Immediately a crowd gathered around the body, some trying to cut off a button, others snatching at the cord to secure a piece as a memento. A rumor was started that his jacket contained a lot of greenbacks, carefully sewed into the lining. Accordingly, before he was placed in the coffin, a general search was instituted, but nothing was found.

As an evidence he did have a heart and a fellow feeling in his bosom, we append a letter to a young lady of this State, written in the Military Prison a few moments before he was taken to the place of execution:

*My Dear: I have to inform you of the sad fate which awaits your true friend. I am to suffer death this afternoon at 4 o'clock. ***I send* *you, from my chains, a message of true love; and, as I stand on the brink of the grave, I tell you I do truly, and fondly, and forever love you. I am, ever truly yours. M. Jerome Clark.*[80]

I have questions about the execution of Mundy. It appears to have been botched, or at least poorly conducted as was the previous execution on this same gallows. It is also possible that the rope could have been new, or the length of the drop had been miscalculated. It would seem that Mundy's neck was not broken; however, Richard Taylor states that in 1914 when Mundy's coffin was relocated to the Confederate section of Green Lawn Cemetery in Franklin, Kentucky, the coffin was found to contain a skeleton that bore the remnants of a Confederate Uniform. The skull was nestled in long black hair, and the neck vertebrae were broken. On a more personal note, I question how the very private letter to his sweetheart found its way into the newspaper. It seems out of character for Reverend Talbott to have leaked its contents, but however it happened it is wrong, and very sad all around.

Chapter 8

Dupoyster and Bryant

The David Henry Raid

Thomas Carlin Dupoyster became an item of news reports beginning in July of 1864. His name has been spelled many different ways. It has more or less commonly been spelled Depoister, Deporster, Deposter, and I even found one reference to a Dr. Roister. There are at least 10 different spellings of the name.[81] He was born in 1843 in Johnson County, Illinois. His father was Thomas Dupoyster and his mother Elizabeth Echols Dupoyster. Thomas Senior, his grandfather, was a Methodist Minister. Thomas C. Dupoyster Jr. moved from Illinois thence to Tennessee, and finally settled in Ballard County, Kentucky near Wickliff at Fort Jefferson. Their descendants still reside in that area today.

Thomas Dupoyster joined the Confederate States Army July 5, 1861, at Camp Boone, Tennessee. He enlisted as a private in Company A, Woodward's 2nd Cavalry, under Colonel Hanson. Dupoyster was captured in Fort Donelson, February 16, 1862, and sent to the military prison, Camp Douglas, in Chicago. Efforts were made to get him paroled from the camp but to no avail. By December 9, 1862, Thomas Dupoyster escaped from the camp and rejoined Woodward's Regiment renamed the 15th Regimental Cavalry. At some point and for some reason Dupoyster became a deserter, and gathered together a band of guerrillas that operated mainly in Meade, Hardin, and Breckenridge counties. His first act as a guerrilla fighter on his own may have been an ambush on Captain James Ashcraft's 20 man force about eight miles south of Brandenburg, near Big Spring, Kentucky. On July 16, 1864, the *Louisville Daily Journal* wrote:

Capt. James H. Ashcraft, Co. G, 26th Ky. Inf., with a small detachment of his men numbering 20, was bushwhacked by a party of guerrillas in Meade County, about 8 miles south of Brandenburg. The guerrillas were concealed in the woods, fifty yards from the road. They permitted the advance guard to pass them unmolested, but when the main body came up, they fired a murderous volley into the exposed ranks with telling effect. Lt. Samuel Jones, 12th Ky. Inf., who accompanied the expedition, was instantly killed, and Capt. Ashcraft and two privates were severely wounded... the body of Lt. Jones and the wounded men were removed by their friends to Brandenburg.[82] *James Head in his book, "The Atonement of John Brooks", states that Dupoyster perpetrated the ambush.*[83]

Dupoyster in his short guerrilla career of about 90 days in the area of Meade, County, seems to have been forceful enough or politician enough to hold together various guerrilla factions that may have been competing with each other for publicity, prestige, or villainy. In his band of 20 to 40 men, he had a second in command named John Bryant. Bryant was a young man from Hopkinsville. Some also say he was from Arkansas, and barely 20 years old. Dupoyster was about 21 when he was killed in September of 1864 in the town of Taylorsville, Kentucky. Bryant first shows up in the newspaper in the August 12th *Louisville Daily Journal*, when Dupoyster and Bryant with about 20 men attempted to take the town of Brandenburg. The paper wrote:

> *...20 guerrillas under command of the renegade Frenchman Capt. Duposter, made a dash into the town and demanded the surrender of the place. They were met in the street by five of the valiant Union citizens of the town, armed with double-barreled shot-guns, who refused to accede to their demands. A brief skirmish ensued, in which the 20 cowardly cutthroats were completely routed.... After the decided repulse, Dupoyster rallied his panic-stricken gang on the outskirts of town, and a short time after, sent a flag of truce, with a demand for immediate and unconditional surrender:*
>
> *Headquarters, 7th Ky. Cav. [CSA]*
> *Home Guards:*
> *We demand an immediate surrender of the town. We expect to come in at 10 o'clock, and if there is a shot fired at us from any person in the town we will burn the place, and shoot every citizen that is caught bearing arms. Capt. Dupoyster; Capt. Bryant Commanding Confederate Forces in Meade Co., Ky.*[84]

This choice piece of literature and model manifesto was written in pencil mark, on a stray leaf torn from a pocket memoranda book. The note was returned to Dupoyster with the message that if he or any of his men came into the town they would be shot down as if "they were a pack of ravenous wolves." The guerrillas were confused and dumbfounded by this determination. The guerrillas departed; however, later that evening a mail-steamer reported shooting coming from the direction of town.

Dupoyster and Bryant became infamous when they murdered a prominent Meade County farmer a little more than two weeks after their Brandenburg defeat. David Henry was a farmer who lived a few miles southwest of the town of Ekron, in Meade County. Anecdotal information has it that Henry was a Union man, and sometimes sold or procured horses for the Federals. Living in the counties of the heartland was difficult and dangerous during the Civil War. If you openly favored one side or the other you became a potential target of the Confederate guerrillas, or the Home Guard units.

David Henry became a target of Capt. Bryant and his band of six or eight guerrillas. One afternoon about suppertime on or about the 16th of August, Bryant and his men rode into the farm lot of David Henry. Bryant demanded that Mrs. Henry cook for his men, and that David Henry feed and water their horses. The Henrys had little choice but to comply. After the horses and Bryant and his men were fed, they went into the lot and mounted their horses. As they trotted off, one account states Henry grabbed a gun of some sort and fired it into the air yelling, "There they go Captain. Get them." Hearing this, Bryant's men thought a cavalry patrol was chasing them, and they put spurs to their horses and quickly fled up the road. David Henry was highly amused by his joke, and word of it got around in the county. Captain Bryant didn't think much of the joke and vowed he would return to deal with Henry. A week later, on the 23rd of August, Bryant returned with Captain Dupoyster and perhaps as many as 30 guerrilla raiders. David Henry hid upstairs, but the guerrillas told him to show himself. The Louisville Daily Journal wrote the following stories which were printed and picked up by newspapers in Evansville, Indiana and Nashville, Tennessee: On August 31st, the first of two articles appeared in the Louisville

Daily Journal, stating: *The citizens of Brandenburg have made ample preparations to protect themselves against guerrilla incursions, but still Capt. Dupoyster's cutthroats are doing a great deal of mischief throughout Meade County. On Tuesday afternoon, they killed David Henry, Esq., at his own house, 8 miles south from the town. Of course, he was unarmed and their prisoner at the time, for we have never yet known such cowardly thieves to lift a hand against an armed man, who had the opportunity to use his weapons. It is recklessly dangerous for any Federal officer, civil or military, to go within Dupoyster's "department" to collect taxes or procure recruits, for he has declared his intention to kill four unarmed, defenseless citizens for every cutthroat guerrilla who may be executed under the orders of the military authorities.*[85]

In another section of that paper, the *Louisville Daily Journal* printed a letter, dated Aug. 29, 1865, that was sent to them by a private citizen who happened to arrive on the scene of the Henry Murder about an hour after the incident. It reads:

One of the most cruel, bloodthirsty, and fiendish-hearted scoundrels brought to light by that damnable policy, guerrilla warfare, is the unprincipled devil who commands a gang of villainous cutthroats, and signs his name Dupoyster. On Tuesday evening, the 23, Capt. Deposter, with twenty two of his guerrilla band, went to the house of David Henry, and, after cursing and abusing him and his family, demanded all the arms and money in the house; took the guns, two rifles and a shotgun, and broke them to pieces over the trees standing in the yard; broke his clock, looking glasses, table ware, and some of his furniture to pieces.; took from him his best suit of clothes, all the jewellery his daughter's possessed, all the shirts he had, his daughter's shawls, and then shot him down while standing in his door, witnessing the destruction of his property. One of Deposter's men, by the name of Bryant shot him through the left breast, the ball coming out under the shoulder blade. He gave one shout for mercy and fell back dead, his daughter catching and easing him down on the floor. While placing a pillow under her father's head, mourning bitterly over his dying form, Deposter approaches, cuffing or slapping her on the side of her head, telling her that if she did not stop her noise, "God d__her" he would kill her. He then went to her mother who was screaming and wringing her hands in great distress, and told her if she did not stop her wailing he would blow her d__ed brains out. He then returned to where Henry lay on the floor, examined the wound, felt his pulse, and said the "d__ed old abolitionist has had about enough." He arrested Henry's youngest son, and left, saying there were three other men in the neighborhood he intended to kill before nightfall. A short distance from Henry's house, he arrested Mr. Wm. Brown, and sent some of his men to Neal Neafus and arrested him. He threatened to kill them both. Other men were sent to John B. Shacklett to know if these men (Brown and Neafus) were the men he wanted. Shacklett replied that they were innocent men, and he must let them go. Deposter obeyed the order, and they were released. I was at the house in less than an hour after the murder was committed and a more distressing scene, I have never witnessed.[86]

The three men that Dupoyster wanted to add to Henry's death were likely to match the Burbridge quota of four men to be killed for the death of a Union Soldier. The killing of four men by Dupoyster mentioned in the first report refers to a reprisal by him for Burbridge's Order No. 59. Anecdotal stories state that Henry was trying to hide from the guerrillas in an upstairs room, but they persuaded him to come down the stairs because of threats to his family. When he stepped out on the porch, and was in the doorway, Capt. Bryant stepped up and shot him in the chest, the ball passing through him, and lodging in the doorframe. The Henry house has been remodeled and added onto over the years, but still stands in its new configuration where the raid occurred. Some say the lead ball is still in the woodwork, others state it was removed years ago. As additional accounts of this story have come to light, I have written about them. Thanks to the courtesy afforded me by the current owner Mr. Clark I was allowed to go into the upstairs room where David Henry hid from the guerrillas. While there, I noticed there was a different level to the floor. The old upstairs floor is slightly lower than floor of the new addition. The well that was outside in the yard, is now located inside the house near the kitchen, and the house has been enlarged. When I was there, in the room where he hid, I wondered how David Henry felt hearing the threats of the raiders abusing his family, and what courage it must have taken for him to come down the stairs to their aid. It is strange how fate takes a hand in things and seems to make people account for their actions. After

Henry's murder Dupoyster had three weeks to live, and John Bryant only one.

The Coome's Cabin Raid

In 2007, I was speaking with Herb Pollock, a friend of mine who lived on New State Road about three miles from my house. I bought firewood from him. He had read one of my stories in the *Meade County Messenger*, and told me that I should write about the Confederate raid and battle that occurred on the property now owned by the Kurtz family, and is located a half mile west of, and in the direction of my house. I asked Herb about the story, and he told me that he was not familiar with the details, but that there was a gunfight between Confederate guerrillas and the Coomes family. He suggested I speak with Peggy Greenwell, and since she lived on my way home, on the road my street turned from, he telephoned her and I stopped by to hear about the raid. There, I met Peggy and her husband Larry. Peggy is an artist, genealogist and historian, and Peggy and I wrote several stories together for the newspaper, and "The Coomes' Cabin Raid" was the first. Peggy, Larry, Fran and I became fast friends, and Peggy along with Steve Straney, Donna Brown, James Mitchell, Myself, and a few others formed the Meade County Archaeological Society, later to become the Meade County Historical and Archaeological Preservation Society, or MCHAPS.

Peggy showed me a picture of the Coomes Cabin as it looked in 1913. The photo was of the Pollock family, outside the cabin, when celebrating the birthday of Uncle Milt Pollock. The Coomes family built the log house, and it was completed in 1861 when Lincoln was sworn in as President. It was a two-story building of hand hewn logs, carefully dovetailed, with a massive stone chimney at the rear of the house. Just outside the front door was a free flowing spring of excellent water. The Coomes family, were gunsmiths, and were Union men. A quarter mile or so west of their cabin was the home of Tom Hall, also made of logs. The Halls and the Coomes were friends and neighbors, although, during the Civil War they were on opposite sides of the political fence. Bob Coomes and Tom Hall attended Bunker Hill School also, located off the road on which they both were raised. These men were born a few months apart, and being the closest neighbors, no doubt hunted, fished, and played together. Their friendship transcended the Civil War. In life they became partners after the war, and in death they are buried some fifteen feet apart, having died as they were born, just months apart.

As I wrote several articles about the story, over time more and more facts came to light that gave a somewhat more complete account. Bryan Bush and James Head both have written accounts of this story, and both seemed to have relied on a newspaper account for certain facts. The name of Joseph Coomes, in the Head book "The Atonement of John Brooks", and in Busch's book "Butcher Burbridge", is identified as Uncle Joe Coonas. This is apparently a typo, or mistake in a *Louisville Daily Journal* article dated September 5, 1865. The raid, as described, is also incorrect in several instances, as is another story that was written in the 1913 *Meade County Messenger*. In the *Louisville Daily Journal* and in the *Messenger* article, both stories state that the raid was an all-day battle and Joseph Coomes was killed along with Captain John Bryant. Bryant was supposed to have lain dead in Joe Coomes' yard. Neither of these accounts is correct if we rely on the information supplied by 97-year-old Hobart Coomes in July of 2007.

Peggy told me that there were some Coomes family members in Meade County, and that Hobart Coomes was in the Medco Nursing facility after suffering a stroke. By coincident, when making inquiries about the Coomes family, I found out that a man with whom I did business was married to a Coomes. I had met her before, and called to ask if the family would allow me to speak with Hobart. She arranged a meeting about two weeks later for me, with her brothers, and Hobart at the Medco facility. The nursing facility provided a meeting room for the interview. I was surprised when I heard that Hobart's children knew nothing of his story. I was told in the interview that Hobart's wife would not allow talk of violence in her house, and this was a violent page in the history of the family. There we sat, and Hobart seemed pleased to recount the story, as he was the only living person who had knowledge of the incident directly from the participants.

I was most interested in how long the battle raged and how many people were involved. Hobart said that Captain Bryant rode up with six or seven men and found the three Coomes men hiding behind the large stone chimney. They had been told of the raid by one of Bryant's men, their neighbor Tom Hall. Hobart said the Coomes were gunsmiths repairing or building a multi-shot repeating gun. It may have been a Henry Rifle. Captain Bryant wanted the gun. Bryant wore a small Confederate Flag on his hat, and was clearly identifiable. I asked Hobart if it was a long battle, and he answered "no, there were only two shots fired." Captain Bryant's men fired, and hit Bob Coomes in the right forearm. Hobart said he used to play with the ball taken from Bob Coomes' arm. "I rolled it across the cabin floor like a marble, he said. Our men fired back hitting Captain Bryant in the stomach." A stomach wound in those days was almost always a mortal wound. Bryant's men became demoralized and rode off with their wounded Captain and about a half mile up Arnold School Road, he slipped from his horse and fell against a tree. For years it was called Captain Bryant's Tree. For a long time after the tree fell, the stump remained until in the 1960's, it rotted away. Bryant's men picked up their leader, and carried him down a bluff and hid him in a shallow cave, called forever after, Captain Bryant's Cave. Later that night they returned with a wagon and took Bryant from the cave to the house of a Mr. Kerrick where in the early morning he died. His betrothed was sent for, but she did not arrive in time to see him before his death. A week after the death of Henry at the hands of Bryant, the 20-year-old Captain of guerrillas was dead. Dupoyster would follow him two weeks or so later when he was shot dead in the streets of Taylorsville, Kentucky. By the 12th of September both men involved with the Henry murder were dead. Dupoyster had gone alone to Taylorsville to secure the release of one of his men from jail, and was killed by either Pratt or Hedge. He was shot in the arm and fell from his horse and was then killed by follow-up shots.

This did not deter Burbridge from sending four prisoners of war to Meade County, and having them shot by a firing squad just south of the Henry farm. The four victims were John Brooks, Robert Brooks, Julias Bradas, and Francis Marion "Frank" Holmes. They arrived in Brandenburg and were transported by wagon, sitting on their coffins, to the front yard of the Henry house, their place of execution. Mrs. Henry declined to have them shot on her place. She reportedly said, "There has been enough blood shed here as it is." The men were taken 300 yards down the road, and were allowed to sit stand or kneel when they were shot. All but Bradas knelt, and all but Bradas accepted a blindfold. Anecdotal evidence states that the ground was somewhat wet, and Bradas dipped his hand into the wet ground and marked an X with mud upon his chest, and said, "Be sure to take good aim."[87] He was reading his prayer book. And their aim was good. Four innocent men were killed that had absolutely no connection with Henry's murder.

I recently met a man named Ronnie Hall who resides on part of the original land owned by Tom Hall. He has the muzzle loading doubled-barrel shotgun that Tom Hall carried in the Civil War. Ronnie let me hold the old gun, and it was quite a thrill. Interestingly, the old Tom Hall log cabin is still there, but it is sided over, and looks like any other farmhouse. The current owner is Tom Hall, the great-great grandson of the original Tom Hall who Hobart said, tipped off the Coomes about the raid. Hall knew that the war was winding down, and that a good friend and neighbor was worth more than allegiance to the murderous renegades Bryant or Dupoyster. In the 1870's, Robert "Bob" Coomes and Tom Hall partnered on a farm they bought together in Meade County.

The current owner, Tom Hall, allowed me to search for Captain Bryant's Cave on his property. His son searched with me, and following the old description of about a half-mile up Arnold School Road to the tree, and down a bluff, we found the cave. It is interesting in several respects His men likely chose it because there is a large natural rock formation that sits in the middle of the opening that would hide the body from view. I took an eighth grade class to the cave to explore, and a Native American Petroglyph was found pecked into the interior side of the rock formation. It was in the shape of a turkey track, and was later authenticated by archaeologist Dr. Fred E. Coy. When the Meade County Archaeological Society visited the site, a large "lap stone," a type of stone mortar was found atop the formation. To the rear of the cave opening, and around the outside edge, a spring of water constantly drips. This may have been a reason the Native Americans and the Confederate Raiders found it a good place to hide.

Chapter 9

A.R. Johnson, Newburgh, and the Breckenridge Guards

One of the most colorful Partisan Rangers, and certainly one of the most resourceful, was Adam Rankin Johnson. Johnson was one of the earliest Partisan Rangers, and formed a Confederate company called the Breckenridge Guards. Johnson was associated with General Forrest's cavalry, but was loaned to General Breckenridge along with Bob Martin. They were to serve as spies and couriers for Breckenridge and were stationed with him at his headquarters. Later, Martin and Johnson were joined by Frank Owen, and entered Kentucky at the direction of Breckenridge to raise recruits for a Partisan Ranger force. Johnson, who had removed to Texas, was born in Henderson, Kentucky, and it was here (along the Ohio, River towns that the men concluded to use as their center of operations). They called themselves the Breckenridge Guards.

The idea was for them to organize a behind-the-lines unit to fight the Federal forces. Johnson and his little band of three men armed themselves with double-barreled shotguns, and attacked the Provost Guard in Henderson. His three men fired six quick shots from their guns, before reloading. The wounded were quickly taken inside, except for a hog that had been accidentally wounded and roamed around the area lying first one place and then another. Every place the hog lay left a blood spot. The next day the local newspaper estimated the Confederates at 300, and from the blood spots, it seemed the Provost Guard managed to wound a great many rebels. One thing this escapade did for Johnson was to spur recruitment and soon he had over 20 men. Two men that came to his group had just escaped May 11th and 12th, 1862, from Camp Morton, Illinois named Marcellous Jerome Clarke (later to become Sue Mundy) and John L. Patterson.[88] Both of these men were captured at Fort Donelson, and had artillery training. Johnson welcomed them into the "guards". Now he needed something to do that would be spectacular, and make his band a force with which to be reckoned.

Just across the river from Henderson was the sleepy little Indiana river town of Newburgh. It was a collection of warehouses connected by docks and wharfs that stored goods to be shipped up and down the Ohio River by the steamboats. Johnson was encamped on the Soaper farm when he was told that there were hundreds of stands of guns in the arsenal of this town of Newburgh. He immediately decided to get them. As soon as they finished their supper, he ordered his 27 men to saddle up, and they were en route.[89] They crossed the Green River near its mouth and soon stood opposite the river from Newburgh. The guns were in a two-story brick building that was a storehouse belonging to Colonel Bethel, of the Indiana Militia. The plan was to row over two skiffs. The first boat with two men would take possession of the storehouse serving as an armory, and a second boat would transport the arms back to Kentucky. Other boats were on the far shore should they be needed. The remainder of Johnson's men would cross on the ferry several squares above, and should they meet with opposition they would fight their way to Johnson and secure the arms.

Johnson determined that they had to move swiftly because Newburgh was connected by telegraph to Evansville, Indiana, where a company of Home Guards were stationed. He made a speech to his men, saying that the plan was a dangerous enterprise to be undertaking. He stated he desired no man whose hand and heart did not feel equal to the occasion. He said, "Soldiers, as soon as you reach the other side of the Ohio, you will be standing upon a powder magazine, and cowardice would be the match to ignite it. All who are willing and confident take a step to the front." All of his men stepped forward.

Johnson had his men search for materials with which he could fashion two cannons. From a blacksmith shop they found two pair of axels and wheels. They took some stove pipe and a log which they painted black, and thus constructed two fine pieces of fake artillery. Taylor in his book states that Mundy and Patterson manned the two pieces of artillery. This makes sense because they knew the correct procedures and drill for artillery men. Johnson had them man the cannons while his men debarked for Indiana. Johnson directed his boat with Frank Owen, and Felix Aiken and Holms in the other, rowed toward Newburgh. Martin and 21 men boarded the ferry to make the crossing.

Johnson reported that a few minutes after they landed they reached the storehouse and found the doors wide opened, and the guns in plain sight. Holms and Johnson began blocking up the windows and closed the door until Martin came up. While completing this task, Johnson noticed armed men moving into the hotel situated close by. He decided to go to the hotel and allay the fears any of the people had. On the way to the hotel he saw a man lean out of an upstairs window holding a cartridge box. This made him feel uneasy, and he realized that if he had to make a fight with a large number of citizens, his chances of securing the arms for the Confederacy would be diminished. When he got to the hotel he saw through the double doors about 80 men with their rifles cocked, all ready to fire. Johnson, with rifles pointed toward his face knew that hesitation meant failure and death. He did not halt, but stepped forward, and commanded them in an authoritative voice, not to fire a gun. He pushed aside the rifles of the first rank with his shotgun, and walked into the midst of them. He told them if they put down their guns before his men came in they would not be hurt. The citizens complied, and Johnson conducted them upstairs to the dining room. Just then he heard footsteps on the rear stairs, and a Union officer burst through the door, his face red with excitement. "Where are our guns?" he asked as he came closer. When the Union officer was within 20 feet of Johnson, he (Johnson) covered him with his shotgun, and said, "If you come, a step closer, I will fill you with buck shot." The officer froze to the spot. The Union officer was a fine specimen of a man, in full uniform, and soldierly looking. Someone called out, "They, Johnson's men, have all the streets guarded and are coming this way." Only then did the Union officer consent to surrender.

Johnson told him to get his muster rolls and that he would parole his men. Martin rushed to the hotel to relieve Johnson. The Confederates pressed into service two wagons, and soon two wagon loads of arms were on their way to Dixie. It was at this time that Johnson was informed that the Home Guards were ready to attack, and their officer Colonel Bethel, was in sight standing on the bank of the river near his store. There were 250 Home Guards, prepared to join fight. Johnson walked toward Colonel Bethel where he was talking with several citizens. Johnson addressed them, "Gentlemen, I hear there is a Home Guard near town that is about to attack me, and I must say that I came here to get these guns, I have them, and I propose to keep them; I want nothing more and do not intend to disturb any of the citizens or their property, but if I am hindered or fired on, I'll shell this town to the ground."

Addressing Colonel Bethel, Johnson said, "I see sir that you have a field-glass and by looking across the river you can see that I am prepared to carry out my threat." The Colonel, after observing Johnson's cannon, glanced at his house, the tallest and grandest in town reflecting that it would likely be the first knocked down, and turning pale, he quickly sent men to call off the impending attack on Johnson. Martin at this time had his last stand of guns to be loaded, and Johnson and his little guard went down to his boat and pushed off to the Kentucky shore. They were unmolested.[90]

This most audacious ruse earned Adam Johnson the sobriquet "Stove Pipe Johnson". It was a term used throughout the war, proudly by the southerners, and derisively by the Yankees. This excursion was the first invasion of the north, and it was completely successful. Johnson was in fact a Partisan Ranger, and General Ewing later in the war ordered Hobson to shoot him on the spot. He was a Confederate soldier. He was blinded in battle, and after the war returned to Texas where he became a millionaire. It was after the war that he was given a new sobriquet more in keeping with his talent for war, "The Swamp Fox of Kentucky."

Chapter 10

Quantrill Comes to Kentucky

William Clarke Quantrill's name has been confused at times. Carl Briehan, his biographer, spells it William Clarke Quantrill. John Newton Edwards spells it Charles William Quantrell,[91] while Tom Shelby Watson spells it William Clarke Quantrill. In Shelby Foote's first book in his trilogy "The Civil War", he has his name Charles Quantrill.[92] I spelled his name Quantrell, but finally settled on William Clarke Quantrill, which I believe to be the correct spelling of his name. William Clarke Quantrill, to say the very least, was a complicated man. It is likely that he would be considered eccentric and at times perhaps psychotic. If he was nothing else, he was a brave and courageous fighter for the Confederacy. His rank and standing in the Confederate army is somewhat clouded; however, he fought in battle with other Confederate soldiers, and held the confidence, at least for a while, of others such as General Jo Shelby, Sterling Price, and Kirby Smith. He served gallantly in the battle at Independence Missouri, and was given a commission of Captain for his efforts.[93]

Quantrill had a checkered past. When he was a boy in Canal Dover, Ohio (now Dover, Ohio), he was cruel with his boyhood pranks. He tied cats' tails together and hung them over a wire fence or clothesline and watched them claw and fight frantically until both of them were dead.[94] He played other pranks such as locking a young girl in a church belfry where she was found, hours later, suffering from shock and exposure. He was reputed to nail the heads of snakes to trees and leave them to die. Once, when he was a young man courting, he took a young lady out for a carriage ride. Beside the road on which they were traveling, he spied a tree with a limb jutting out long and straight. He commented to her that he could hang seven men from that limb. She was shocked, and I suspect the lady just didn't appreciate the physics of the thing.

His mother sent him away to live with the Clapp family in Illinois. She said she hoped that a change of scene might improve him. He wrote home that he needed money and asked his mother to send his books and a few other belongings so that he could sell them and buy things he needed. She sent them, but he was unable to do so. He was discouraged, and feeling that he had been cast off by his family, he stopped writing home.[95] The next time she heard from him was in February of 1856 when he was teaching school in Fort Wayne, Indiana. Later she found that there had been a murder in Illinois and that her son had been arrested. He was arrested on suspicion, and when confronted he said he was working in a lumber yard when he was attacked, and shot the man in self-defense. Since there were no witnesses to the contrary, he was released and advised to leave town.[96]

Quantrill fought in the 1850's border war between Kansas and Missouri, and when the Civil War broke out he naturally became a Confederate Partisan Ranger. In the Missouri state militia he was a private, and a sergeant, and was promoted to Captain in the Confederacy. He sometimes referred to his rank as Colonel.

He controlled a band of guerrilla fighters that numbered as many as 400 and in the beginning, as few as three. His band was known as Quantrill's Raiders, and they were reputed to fight under a "black flag". Over a period of four years of fighting, he had been hard pressed by the Federals, and there was little room, within the borders of Missouri, for him to operate or even hide. His second in command William "Bloody Bill" Anderson had been slain, his head impaled on a telegraph pole, and his headless body dragged through the streets of Richmond, Missouri, and Todd, a lieutenant, who had taken control of Quantrill's Raiders after Quantrill became ill and seemed to lose his nerve, was killed near Independence. According to Edwards, Quantrill became ill, and was nursed and closely guarded by 20 loyal men, including James Younger and Frank James. These men later, along with Cole Younger and Jesse James, formed, after the war, the nucleus of the famous James Younger Gang. It became clear in the fall of 1864 that the war was winding down, and badly, for the Confederacy. Missouri was too hot for the guerrillas, whose numbers had dwindled as they became ineffectual with fewer and fewer places of refuge. Quantrill believed, after Price had retreated southward from Westport, baffled and broken up, that the end of the regular war was at hand.[97] Quantrill believed he must move his theatre of operation from the west to the east. Edwards writes that his wish was to continue guerrilla warfare in Maryland, and the mountains of Pennsylvania. He considered assassinating Lincoln. There is little doubt that he had read of the successful exploits of John Mosby, and perhaps of those of the guerrilla forces in Kentucky. He wanted to take as large a band as possible across the Mississippi River, moving northward through Tennessee into Kentucky and thence further east. He would be out of his familiar territory with no support from the population. There would be no safe houses or havens for him and his men.

On November 20, 1864, Quantrill sent John Barker and James Little to notify the command to meet at Mrs. Wiggenton's on the 4th of the following month. Mrs. Wiggenton lived five miles west of Waverly, Lafayette County, and was a refugee from Jackson, whose husband had been killed, whose property been destroyed, and whose sons had been fighting the long merciless fight of the four year war.

The word of the rendezvous spread swiftly. Frank James gathered up Donnie and Bud Pence, Oll Shepherd, and George Robinson, and made haste to cross into Jackson. On the 4th of December, 47 men were at the Wiggenton's. Quantrill made a speech to the assembly, saying:

> *"I have called you together that I might say to you what I have not yet said to myself, and ask of you to my proposition the simple answer, yes or no. This side of the Mississippi River the war ended with the abandonment of Missouri by General Price. The west is overrun with Federal Soldiers. No food, no horses, no hiding places, no traffic any more with the posts – if we operate longer along the Kansas border we operate at a disadvantage altogether disproportionate to our means. My intention is to cross east of the Mississippi River, pass through Illinois and Ohio as a Federal Scout, gain Maryland, and carry into the heart of Pennsylvania the torch and the black flag. If I live, I mean that they should feel in the east what we have felt in the west. How many will follow me to the end?" As one man those stern, scarred guerrillas, shouted "All!"*

Some of the men present were Payton Long, Will and Henry Noland, John Barker, Chat Renick, Ben Morrow, Rufus and Babe Hudspeth, John Coger, Oll Shepherd, Frank James, William Hulse and many others.[98]

On January 1, 1865, the guerrillas crossed the Mississippi River at a place 15 miles north of Memphis called Devil's Elbow, and marched northeast of the river and reached Brownsville, Tennessee. They were wearing the Union uniforms of the 2nd Colorado Cavalry with which Quantrill carried orders and a commission of their officer, Captain W. C. Clark.[99] Quantrill and his raiders, about 45 in number (three of his men returned to Missouri after he was safely across the river), shot and hanged their way through Tennessee and into Kentucky, and because of their Union soldier disguises they took occasional fire from General Forrest's Cavalry in Tennessee. He learned of the guerrilla Captain Sue Mundy, probably from the *Louisville Daily Journal* articles and editorials written and published by George Prentice. Quantrill needed the support group and network of southern sympathizers that had been aiding the fearsome four-man guerrilla team of Oscar, "One Arm" Sam Berry, Henry Clay "Billy" Magruder, Stanley Young aka "Captain Bill Marion," and Marcellous Jerome Clarke aka "Sue Mundy."

William Clarke Quantrill and his men entered Kentucky and headed in the direction of Leitchfield, in Grayson County. They moved on to Upton's Station, in Hart County, Kentucky, he and his men still wearing the blue Yankee uniforms. They moved north and east into Marion County and onto the Lebanon Campbellsville Turnpike, at Rolling Fork, and traveled north to New Market and east from Bradford towards Hustonville where 30 Federal soldiers were garrisoned. Here the next day Allen Parmer killed a Federal Major when the Major objected to losing his horse. The rest of the Federals were disarmed, and the guerrillas acquired new fresh, fine horses, but at the price of losing their heretofore protecting disguises. The word was now out, and Quantrill became once again Quantrill. At Danville, the next day a lady recognized Quantrill, and addressed him by name. A Federal Lieutenant overheard the remark and got the drop on Quantrill a while later. John Barker jumped on the soldier and shoved a pistol in his face and ended the matter without bloodshed. After dinner, Quantrill marched toward Washington and halted his men at a place eight miles from Harrodsburg, Kentucky. According to John N. Edwards, by this time Little had been killed, and Quantrill ordered John Barker to go to a house nearby and secure rations and feed for the horses, while he continued on for a mile or so. Quantrill and Lieutenant Renick took the balance of the men to a mansion a mile or so further up the road. Just as the guerrillas had finished their evening meal, gunfire was heard toward the house where Sergeant John Barker had taken his men. Quantrill ordered Frank James, William Hulse, Allen Parmer, and Payne Jones to go to the sound of the firing and ascertain the good or bad of the situation. While engaged with this task, they found the body of Lieutenant Renick dead in the road, from a rifle ball to the head. Sergeant Barker had 11 men with his group, ten plus himself. With him, were Ves Acres, Richard Burnes, Richard Glasscock, George Roberson, James Evans, James Williams, Andy Maguire, William Gaugh, and William, and Henry Noland. They had unsaddled and fed their horses, and were about to eat supper, when the Union guerrilla fighter Major Bridgewater and 180 Federal Cavalry surrounded the house and began a fierce firefight. The guerrillas gathered the family to whom the house belonged and shepherded them into interior rooms where they would be safer. Ves Acres picked up a baby and placed it in the arms of its mother, saying, "Don't expose yourself; for the sake of this little thing, not much bigger than a rabbit." He returned to the fight, and fought well until he was shot down. Eleven men against 180 was a fight typical of guerrilla warfare. Bridgewater suffered the most in this fight with 30 men killed and eighteen wounded. Sergeant Barker was killed, and Henry Noland fell next. Then, William Noland was killed, joining his brother in death. Ves Acres was shot in the right side and the left shoulder, and was down. The ammunition of the guerrillas was almost given out. Bridgewater rushed the house, and Glasscock, Williams, and Maguire were down. Roberson, Evans, and Gaugh were surrounded and out of ammunition and thus surrendered to Major Jim Bridgewater.[100]

The four men that Quantrill sent back to determine the situation, came up and fired point blank into the Federal mass gathered around the guerrillas. Frank James, Hulse, Parmer, and Jones rode back and informed Quantrill that the 11 men were killed, wounded or captured. The next day Quantrill knew that Bridgewater would be after him, and so he laid a trap. He arranged an ambuscade across a creek and along a road that led up from the stream. He positioned six men on either side of the road in an area that was rocky and wooded. Quantrill took nine others and held them massed in a reserve command to attack when the time seemed appropriate. Four men were sent back up the road to skirmish with Bridgewater, and to lead him chasing them into the trap ready to be sprung. The four riders, John Barnhill, John Mc-Corkle, John Ross, and John Graham were the bait. These four were young men unafraid of any danger. Barnhill took charge of the group, and posted two on one side of the road and two on the other. Bridge-water and his men came on at a trot, following the tracks of Quantrill's Raiders. Barnhill took a position in the middle of the road, and fired at the foremost ranks. The rest of the guerrillas fired in a volley, and then rode toward the creek road ambush. Bridgewater's men gave a yell, and were off on the gallop. When they crossed the creek, and up the road that hid the 12 men, what seemed like an explosion filled the air as the Union Cavalry were fired upon at close range. The four Johns were behind them now and delivered a deadly fire, while it seemed to the Federals that the very trees were shooting at them. The Feder-als bunched up as Quantrill and his nine guerrillas charged, and in that wild moment of fear and agony they realized they were trapped. Bridgewater in less than 20 minutes, lost killed 52 men, with seven wounded. Quantrill had eight men with minor wounds. Bridgewater withdrew from the fight.[101] Note: Edward's numbers are highly ques-tionable, as we will find.

Bridgewater, a determined guerrilla hunter, never left the chase entirely and after attending to his men he followed the trail from a distance. A beautiful winter moonlit the sky that night, and the next day a blanket of snow four inches deep lay upon the ground and for the next 52 hours. Some place in Washington County, Quantrill and his men eluded Bridgewater, and made for Chaplin Town in Nelson County. Chaplin was a haven for Confederates. Edwards writes that when Quantrill rode into the center of town he encountered Edward (sic) Terrell[102] (his name was Edwin), leading some 60 independent scouts hunting guerrillas. Terrell was a twenty-year-old who had been in the Confederate Army, and deserted. Later he became an indepen-dent scout in an area abuzz with guerrilla activity. He was cruel, ruth-less, tenacious, and mean, having just the right qualities to be a suc-cessful guerrilla hunter. It is doubtful he ever had more than 25 men under his command.

Terrell charged Quantrill and his men. Of the 37 men he had be-fore the fight with Bridgewater, if you subtracted the five men killed, the eight that had been captured, and the eight that were wounded but un-captured, Quantrill was not in a condition to fight, but fight he must. Those who were wounded held the rear with others unwounded, and a running five-mile fight ensued. The fight lasted two hours, and William Hulse, John Barnhill, Frank James, John Ross, John Graham, Payne Jones, Allen Parmer, Foss Ney, Clark Hockinsmith, Payton Long and James Younger were so splendid and superb in carrying the battle to Terrell, that Terrell spoke complimentarily of them, calling them devils, not men. After Quantrill turned onto the Taylorsville Road, Terrell collected his men, wounded and dead, and returned to Chaplin Town. Quantrill moved his men to the house of a well to do farmer near Taylorsville who was sympathetic to the south. A man I interviewed in 1993, James Wakefield of Shelbyville, said his great-grandfather, James Heady Wakefield, often allowed Confederate guerrillas to use his barn. It may have been his barn in which Quantrill and his men sought refuge. In fact months later it was at the Wakefield barn that Quantrill was captured.

After a day and a night's rest, Quantrill determined to find and link up with Sue Mundy. Mundy was on a scout at the time, but Quantrill met with Captain Bill Marion who was highly suspicious of him and his men, partly because of their blue uniforms. Edwards writes that Marion was naturally distrustful, and spoke with his eyes rather than with his lips. He listened with his right hand on his revolver. He had no fear of meeting and talking with Quantrill, but was in no way prepared to trust him enough to have the Missourians, who might not be Missourians, to ride side by side with him on a raid. Marion made a proposal. If Quantrill would place his men who were fit for service under Marion and his command of 40 men, and if he would agree to remain behind under control of Marion men, to insure he was who he said he would take the Missourians on a combined raid led by Marion. If the men performed as well as Quantrill had said, then he would be accepted by the Confederate guerrillas in Kentucky, and be able to use the services of their safe houses, horse procurers, hiding places and couriers, all of the things he had left behind in Missouri. Quantrill was peeved at being perceived suspiciously, but accepted the proposal because he had no other choice. If he were to continue his fight, he must join up with these hard bitten Kentucky guerrillas.

Marion began a raid toward Georgetown, and the first night he placed a secure guard around all of Quantrill's men. The next night the guard was still placed, but not so strongly manned, and by the fifth night he had become so convinced of the Quantrill men's loyalty, that he placed them to guard the camp over the Kentuckians. On the sixth day the raiders killed a party of 11 Federal Cavalry. Marion praised the Missourians for their fidelity and courage. There is no doubt in my mind that the Missourians were equally impressed with the timbre of the Kentuckians who were every bit as hard pressed and courageous as they. They both had to be glad to fight side by side with each other. The Missourians found comrades in arms and a network of support, and the Kentuckians gained reinforcements of good, well trained, and sorely needed men.

Moving on toward the Kentucky River in the direction of Georgetown, the band was attacked from the rear. Frank James led a contingent of Missourians and Kentucky boys charging up the road at the Federals who out-numbered them. Their attack was so quick and fiercely fought, that they drove the enemy back in a head long pace, about a mile, with their dead littering the road along the way. In this fight Frank James killed a Federal with the butt of his revolver. They moved on toward Georgetown, where the Union forces were in complete control of the town. Marion sent some of Quantrill's men into the garrisoned town because of their disguise as Federal Soldiers. Marion halted the band about eighteen miles from Georgetown, and encamped in a barn owned by a Union family. That night when the men were sitting around talking, one of the soldiers of Quantrill asked, "How will we fool them tomorrow, if we find them in Georgetown?"[103] This comment was overheard by a daughter of the owner of the house and transmitted it to the Federals in Georgetown.

The next day Marion placed the Missourians in the front file of men, and it was a good thing he did. Payton Long was the standard bearer, and as he moved into the center of town he stopped. Marion wanted to know why. "It does not become me Captain," James spoke up, "to either advise with you or suggest to you unless I am so requested, but I must tell you respectively that we do not like the looks of things. There are no soldiers on the streets; the picquets did not halt us; Georgetown is as quiet as a graveyard; there is treachery somewhere; if we go further without developing the situation, we shall be surrounded and savagely attacked. Ten skirmishers thrown well forward may save 30 lives further on."[104]

Indeed Marion's band estimated now at about between 60 and 70 men, were expected in the town, but not as friends. Within five minutes the skirmishers developed the enemy and a firefight had started. The Federals numbered about 182. Frank James had his horse shot out from under him. He went to a livery stable, under fire, and with a pistol in either hand he made a rush for the doors, killing two soldiers in the process. As soon as he was mounted, he rejoined his command, astride a fine cavalry horse.

From there they headed to Owen and into Woodford Counties, where they raided the stock farm of Colonel R.A. Alexander and stole 19 thoroughbred horses valued at $100,000.00. Marion was offered a $10,000.00 reward to return Ball Chief, but he refused. The men were attacked by Federals the next day as they were eating breakfast. Marion and his men fought hard, and finally extricated themselves from the fight, with eight men wounded, including a young Kentuckian named Tom Henry. (It is this man that may well have been mistaken, in March of that year, for Henry Medkiff, as they looked much alike). Lying on the ground, shot through the chest, Henry was shot in the face two more times, and left for dead, but yet he lived. Marion reunited Quantrill and his men, and told Quantrill that he would ride into any danger with such men. They parted company. The February weather was cold, and Quantrill once again disbanded his men to be recalled again after they had time to rest and lick their wounds. Edward states that Quantrill did convince Marion to return the 16 remaining horses stolen from Alexander.

John N. Edwards was a prolific writer, newspaper editor, and chronicler of the guerrilla war. He was a friend of Frank and Jesse James, and many of their gang. He wrote in a flowery style, exhibiting a purple prose that today seems a quaint way of writing, but was in common usage at the time. Considering that his book "Noted Guerrillas" was written in 1877 this should be expected. Edwards who had been an adjutant to General Jo Shelby, had either a reason to exaggerate the numbers of people in a battle or raid, the killed and wounded, or simply a propensity to build up the guerrilla warriors, and give only grudging respect to their opponents. It is interesting to read some of these stories told by Edwards, compared with contemporary news reports about those same events.

In a February 2nd story in the *Louisville Daily Journal* the following article appeared:

On the 29th ult., a band of guerrillas under Capt. Clark made a raid into Danville, Kentucky. They pretended to be Federal Cavalry, but were soon discovered to the contrary. Capt. Bridgewater, whose command was stationed at Stanford, was appraised of the fact. He immediately mounted 45 men (not 180) and started in pursuit, arriving in Danville about three hours after the thieves had departed. Learning they had left in the direction of Salt River, he pressed his pursuit, driving them a distance of 20 miles. About sundown Capt. Bridgewater overtook a squad of 12 at the house of Mrs. Vernosdolls. He sent Lt. John Bridgewater with 12 men to charge the house, and cut off their retreat to the woods. The land pirates took shelter in a large log barn, a few paces from the house, where they fought desperately for 15 minutes, when they surrendered, with a loss of four killed and three wounded...[105]

On February 4th, a story appeared in the *Daily Journal* that states:

Guerrillas badly whipped....Harrodsburg, Ky., January 3oth: Our usually quiet village was aroused yesterday by the report that our neighboring town of Danville was in the possession of a band of guerrillas, numbering 38 men dressed in Federal uniform. Lt. B. F. Colwell, in command of a scouting party, was immediately dispatched. They proceeded to Danville, and found that the guerrillas had left taking the Perryville Pike, and that Capt. James H. Bridgewater, with his Kentucky Scouts had just passed on their track, and was in hot pursuit...The daring Coldwell followed on and soon joined Bridgewater. The guerrillas struck north, crossed the Harrodsburg, Perryville and Maxville Pikes, taking the roads that led them west of Harrodsburg, within 2 ½ miles of town. At 4 o'clock ten of them proceeded to the house of a widow lady named Vanarsdell, and ordered dinner. They had just placed their horses in the barn, when the brave and gallant Bridgewater appeared....The guerrillas sought refuge in the barn, with its picketed sheds, made a complete stockade; but "Waterbridge", as the darkies call him, nothing daunted, surrounded the barn and the fight began....Result in the barn – three guerrillas killed, three horses killed, when they called quar-

ter, and offered to surrender…the Captain ordered "Cease firing," and the party knocked under. The other seven surrendered. Just at this moment a lieutenant, who was with a squad at a neighboring house, hearing the firing, mounted his horse and rode up within 175 yards and inquired, "what in the hell is the matter over there?" Capt. Bridgewater espying him, leveled his unerring carbine, and fired. The guerrilla lieutenant bit the dust. (This was the lieutenant John Renick Frank James found dead on the road) These thieves say that they belong to the 4th Missouri… and are commanded by Capt. Clarke. Is it not probable that this is Quantrill's party? A wounded man told me that they crossed the Mississippi River above Memphis, Tenn., and had come this far without a fight; that they entered above Nashville, Tenn. They came from Hustonville, thence to Danville, and on near this place and have now struck for the Salt River Hills, toward Bloomfield, and Taylorsville. Let the 54th Ky. Mtd. Inf. Look out, for then they may go by way of Shelbyville and strike for Owen County. Capt. Bridgewater took eight prisoners to Frankfort, leaving one here badly wounded.

On Thursday evening, about 26 guerrillas made a raid on the Louisville & Lexington RR, striking it at Midway, and burning the depot station at that place. Stores were robbed and citizens were relieved of watches, money, etc. Quantrill and Sue Mundy were reported in command of the gang.[106]

On the same day the *Louisville Daily Democrat* wrote the following piece:

On Thursday evening, about 26 guerrillas dashed into the town of Midway…and set fire to the depot, which was totally consumed with all its contents….While the depot was burning the guerrillas robbed stores and everybody whom they met….After they had completed the job they got on their horses, and started down the Versailles Pike at full speed. It is reported that they had been to Georgetown and were run away from there by Federals, and that the gang was led by Quantrill, Sue Mundy, and Henry Magruder.[107]

On February 5, the *Louisville Daily Journal* wrote:

A squad of 25 guerrillas passed through Woodford County, on Thursday last and committed sundry depredations. At Midway, they burnt the railroad depot, robbed stores and cut down some of the telegraph posts, passed on to R. A. Alexander's place and carried off 13 fine horses. As soon as the guerrillas made their appearance in Midway, Mr. William Harper started in haste for Lexington, where he reported the state of affairs, and succeeded in getting a small force of 15 men, but on his return the robbers had fled. They had in tow Mr. Willa Vibey, of Scott County, as a guide. They left him at Mr. Frank Kinkead's, and took Mr. K. in his stead. The small guard, stationed at Versailles, 25 men are in hot pursuit, and it is to be hoped will overtake and recover the stolen horses, and punish the rascals as they deserve.[108]

The name Clark and Clarke, pronounced the same way, seems to have confused the situation in Kentucky when it was invaded by Quantrill and his raiders. Sue Mundy was a Confederate soldier named Marcellous Jerome Clarke. Quantrill was masquerading as a Colonel or Captain Clark, and his middle name was Clarke. To the press, Clarke was Clark. Prentice, the editor of the *Louisville Daily Journal*, had been for some time writing editorials and stories about the woman guerrilla that the Union (under Burbridge's command) could not catch, and in fact was embarrassing itself by its efforts. A February 10th newspaper report seems to show how the confusion was manifested, and how Sue Mundy became infamous for crimes or raids he did not make. The *Louisville Daily Journal* wrote:

Hustonville, Lincoln County, Ky., Jan. 31: Our usually quiet village was the scene of great excitement on Sunday morning last, occasioned by the sudden appearance in our midst of about 40 guerrillas, led by Clark, alias Sue Mundy. They approached the town by the Lebanon Rd., taking us by surprise. In a short time they were searching every stable in town for horses. The stable belonging to the Weatherford Hotel, being well filled with fine saddle horses, presented a fine attraction.... Our citizens were thrown entirely off their guard by being told that the party were Federal soldiers, and belonging to the 4th Mo. Cav.... They also succeeded in getting a horse from Maj. George Drye, formerly of the 1st Ky. Cav.; also the splendid horse presented by the citizens of Garrard Co. to Col, Frank Wolford....[109]

Later in the story, the murder of Lt. George F. Cunningham came to pass when the guerrillas had taken his gray mare. He went to the Weatherford stables and remonstrated with the man that had the animal.... The scoundrel ordered him to disarm himself. While in the act of doing so, the fiend in human form, shot him dead. Note: Sue Mundy was not present on this raid. There is a historic marker in Midway stating that Mundy and his guerrillas were the raiders, but in fact it was Capt. Bill Marion that led the raid with his own men combined with Quantrill's raiders.

The stories told by Edwards while pretty much chronologically consistent with the newspaper reports inflate numbers in places, but they also add rich details such as the names of the Missouri guerrillas and tell the personal stories of the individual prowess of the participants. Edward's book was published 12 years after the war had ended. Memory often times has a tendency to exaggerate things a bit, as recollections fade into the recesses of the mind. I suspect the men Edwards spoke to were old veterans who told their stories as they remembered, sitting around a barroom the exploits being enhanced by whiskey, and the odds against them seemed to grow as their deeds became more heroic, and their chivalry greater. When both versions of the reports are read together, one can get a good idea about how the fighting was prosecuted, on both sides. And after all 50, to ten, while not as lopsided as 180 to ten, are still pretty bad odds.

Chapter 11

Bad Ed Terrell, the Man who Caught Quantrill

Of all the guerrilla hunters, Edwin Terrell, pronounced Tur-al, was one of the most successful, rivaling Cyrus Wilson and James Bridgewater. Tom Watson refers to him as a decoy guerrilla.[110] Terrell was as brave and courageous as any soldier on either side during the war. He rode into the jaws of death more often than any soldier did, and like many of the guerrilla fighters, he had a checkered past, before, during, and after the war. He seemed devoid of feelings, other than those of hatred. He was a vicious fighter, and had absolutely no fear of death. He took at least one contract, and maybe two, to kill men, and he was successful in completing the work.

His most successful feats were the capture of Quantrill, the killing of the guerrillas Cox and Coulter, and in participating in the killing of Bill Marion. After the war, he was involved in a murder and a jailbreak, and was finally shot down in the streets of Shelbyville, Kentucky, by an impromptu posse hastily arranged in his honor. He survived the shooting and died a year or more later in a Louisville hospital.

In 2008, I began researching Ed Terrell, covering his youth, and his war experience up to and including his death. The material was researched in the Shelbyville Library from their collection of abstracts of Shelby County newspapers. This information was buttressed with information from Tom Shelby Watson's first book "Silent Riders", Ted Yeatman's book "Frank and Jesse James", newspaper reports from the *Elizabethtown News*, *Louisville Daily Journal*, and *Louisville Democrat*. I believe that Bad Ed Terrell is one of the most interesting Union guerrillas in Kentucky. It is also interesting that in one of my favorite movies depicting guerrillas and their type of warfare, "The Outlaw Josey Wales", the antagonist is Captain Terrell.

Since newspaper reports are frequently in error, sometimes totally, or sometimes in part where two different versions of a story are given,

I will tell both. In instances where there is only one report that covers an event, I will relate that as it appears in the original form.

Edwin Terrell was born in 1845, and he was eight-years-old when he began living with his grandfather, Robert J. Baker, who was known for abusing his slaves. Terrell's mother died of disease, and his father left and failed to return home. Even as an adult, Terrell was not a large man. His hair was light brown and he had blue eyes, as well as a slight frame. As an adult, he was less than five feet, nine inches tall, and as a child he was small for his age. His small size caused him to be teased and bullied by bigger boys, but he was imbued with the spirit of a lion, and when challenged he fought any boy regardless of his size. Terrell was a daredevil, accepting any risk, and his adventurous nature, slight stature, and being raised on a farm probably prepared him for his first real job, and later for his life in the cavalry.

Most farm boys learn early to ride a horse. The more adventuresome will begin to do tricks or stunts on horseback. Standing in the saddle, or bareback, and picking objects from the ground at a gallop were stunts often learned. Simple feats, such as carrying milk cans and other burdens on the shoulders while riding, were not considered tricks by country folk; it was just the way things were done. However, it takes on the character of a trick to those unfamiliar with equestrian skills and ignorant of such activities in a rural setting. Ed Terrell landed himself a job in Dan Costello's Circus, largely because of his riding ability. He was an athletic, bareback rider who by this time had acquired a taste for good Kentucky whiskey. It was likely his love of whiskey that was partially the cause of his first real trouble with the law.

The circus had moved to Baltimore, Maryland, where Ed Terrell visited a bar and ordered whiskey that he found not to his liking. He rudely let the bartender know what he thought of his wares, and to no one's surprise the bartender took a dim view of Ed Terrell's remarks. The insulted bartender took a double-barrel shotgun from under the counter and shot Terrell in the arm. Wounded though he was, Terrell jumped over the bar, wrestled the gun away from his opponent, knocked him to the floor and shot him in the head, killing him. Terrell found himself arrested, jailed, and tried for murder. His trial resulted in an acquittal on grounds of self-defense. With the circus having moved on, and Baltimore much too hot for him, Terrell returned to Kentucky.

During the Civil War, Kentucky was a border state that tried to remain neutral, but was unable to do so. At the onset of the war, Kentucky had the third largest number of slave owners behind Georgia and Alabama. Because of this, many people in Kentucky, more importantly in the heartland of Kentucky, were sympathetic to the Confederacy. Whether it was for this reason, or that his grandfather owned slaves, or the sentiments of his neighbors, Ed joined the Confederate army.

One of his first assignments was to go to a farmhouse where two Union soldiers were hiding and arrest them. As he and his associate were beating on the farmhouse door demanding entrance, one of the soldiers leaned out of an upstairs window and fired his gun, wounding Terrell. A 1917, *Shelby Sentinel* newspaper recap of the incident states that Terrell, although wounded, ran up the stairs and killed both of the Union soldiers. He returned to his company, where his wound was treated and he began to heal. During this time he was accosted by a superior officer, cursed and struck for some infraction of the rules. Ed Terrell drew his pistol, shot and killed the officer. Quickly taken into custody, he was placed under guard, given a drumhead courts martial, and was sentenced to be shot by a firing squad. While awaiting execution, he was placed under guard in a tent. Once again, his small size and athletic ability became an asset in his escape. He burrowed under the tent and made his way safely out of the camp and north to Louisville, Kentucky.

A different account of Terrell's activities, add details to the 1917 report. He may have begun his checkered career as a member of Company G, First Kentucky Infantry, CSA, a unit that served for a year mostly in northern Virginia. Much of his term was spent "in arrest near Centerville", and later in Chimbrazo Hospital No. 3 in Richmond. When his enlistment was up in May 1862, he went back to Kentucky and served briefly in John Hunt Morgan's cavalry, before he deserted the Confederate ranks. According to an acquaintance, "His reputation was the worst imaginable, and his fighting qualities were only developed when under the influence of whiskey." Terrell was apparently enlisted in Company D, Thirty-seventh Kentucky Mounted Infantry, on October 7, 1863, but put under arrest seven weeks afterward and was kept in the guard house at Bowling Green, Kentucky until he and other members of the unit were mustered out at Louisville, Kentucky, on December 29, 1864. Terrell and several of his companions were hired by the Louisville commandant, Col. Fairleigh, on January 2, 1865 as civilian "guerrilla hunters." On January 6th, he and some of his men were captured by a Captain John Smith, who commanded an independent Unionist unit nicknamed Company Q. Thought to be guerrillas, Terrell and his comrades were lodged in the Springfield, Kentucky, jail until their real identities were established. Terrell when he was released became a terror to the population of Washington, Marion, Shelby, and Anderson Counties.[111] While this last statement is true, Nelson and Spencer Counties were also blighted by Terrell and his men.

On January 28, the day before Marion and Quantrill's men encountered Bridgewater, Terrell and his self-styled Home Guards moved through northern Nelson County, "robbing citizens as they went." In Chaplin, they lined up citizens and robbed them of money, watches, and other articles. Moving on to Bloomfield, they robbed the post office, lined up more citizens and robbed them.[112] Heroically, a band of Confederate guerrillas rode into town and attacked Terrell and his men, and drove them back to Mt. Eden, Terrell's home, to the cheers of the local citizenry.

January 24th is the first mention of Ed Terrell in the *Louisville Daily Journal*. In a short article it read: Capt. Edwin Terrell, with 13 men, encountered about 20 guerrillas near New Haven on Wednesday the 18th. In the desperate fight, which immediately ensued, this gallant party succeeded in killing three of the thieves. The remainder owing to their superiority, in number, was able to affect their escape. No casualties on the Federal side, except the killing of one horse.[113]

April, 1865, found "Capt." Ed Terrell on the payroll of the U.S. Quartermaster's Department for "Secret Service" work and commanding about 30 scouts. General Palmer recalled that "Terrell was an exceedingly dangerous man, and "I never let him enter my quarters without keeping a revolver at hand."[114]

Terrell knew the neighborhoods in which the Confederate guerrillas operated, and was familiar with the safe houses and people that supplied the guerrillas. Many of the rural southern sympathizers, who at one time trusted Terrell, were now wary of him, and people of the Union persuasion were also in doubt because of his previous allegiance.

He was considered a conquering hero, especially when he met Captain Henry Cox, a daring guerrilla fighter in a face-to-face gunfight on horseback along the Bloomfield Pike. Cox was killed in the fight and Terrell was badly wounded. Shelbyville was still smarting over an 1864 raid by the guerrilla "Black Dave Martin". Black Dave was Caucasian, but of dark complexion. He wanted guns that were stored in the courthouse for home defense. When he began his raid, two citizens, Mr. Thomas A. McGrath and Mr. J.H. Moosenheimer, opened fire and a terrific battle ensued that killed three guerrillas, and a blacksmith. Because of this raid, the people of Shelbyville welcomed Terrell and his men into their town, and treated them royally. They considered Terrell their protector in these times of peril. Whenever Ed and his men were around, it was "Hail fellow well met." They showered his men with food, drink, and lodging as an enticement for Terrell and his men to frequent Shelbyville, and the town picked up the tab. Terrell normally stayed at Mrs. Burnett's boardinghouse owned by his great aunt Mrs. Lucy Burnett, but his men often stayed at the Merritt, Redding, or Armstrong Hotels, where the accommodations were first class.

The most active time for the guerrillas was the period between the fall of 1864 and June of 1865. Part of the reason for this was because of the migration of the Missouri guerrillas into Kentucky. Partly it was because the war was going badly for the Confederates, and the disruption of infrastructure behind the Federal lines was more important than ever, if the Confederacy was to endure.

Captain Bill Marion and Edwin Terrell hated each other. Both men boasted about what they would do to each other if they ever met. On January 23, 1865 that almost happened. There was a combined guerrilla raid on Federal troops herding a thousand head of Cattle through Simpsonville, Kentucky. There were approximately 80 Negro Federals, under the command of white officers, driving the cattle to Louisville. They were part of the 5th Regiment Cavalry, United States Colored Troop.[115] Later the battle was called the Simpsonville massacre, Terrell missed his chance at Marion, and conversely, Marion missed his chance at Terrell.

On the 28th of January, Terrell and 20 of his men were not far away from Bloomfield, Kentucky. Captain Marion, Captain Mundy, Captain Magruder, and Captain Isaiah "Big Zay" Coulter, were in close proximity. The guerrillas were opening a farm gate to pass through, when Terrell and his scouts spied them and charged. Terrell was firing his pistols, maneuvering to out flank the guerrillas. The guerrillas, five in total, were badly outnumbered four to one. The guerrillas turned and opened fire on Terrell's men forcing them to withdraw to a field 100 yards away. Terrell circled toward the Bloomfield Pike, while Magruder and company kept a respectful distance, expecting Terrell to spring one of his tricks, when Big Zay Coulter arrived with 10 men who were cheered by the five guerrillas, and changed the tide of battle. Coulter, Magruder and company charged Terrell, who made a run for a barn on the May place. When he began losing men and horses, he withdrew to a barn belonging to Hedge, where his men and horses could get cover. As Terrell's men were dismounting, Coulter and several of his men charged Terrell, firing as they came, and Terrell shot Coulter in the side with a rifle. A 1904, Elizabethtown News report that originally appeared in the Bardstown Standard, said Coulter had picked up a little girl, and carried her on his horse in front of him to shield himself from Terrell. That seems out of character for Coulter, but if it happened, Bad Ed took no notice of the child, and fired anyway. That would be expected from Ed Terrell. The Friday May 19, 1904 issue of *The Elizabethtown News* recounted the story:

> *Terrell and Zay Coulter's Death*
>
> *"Big Zay" Coulter met his death in Spencer County. At the Heady farm house some Federal soldiers were entrenched and the guerrillas coming up not being strong enough in numbers to storm the place a regular exchange of shots was kept up for several hours. Finally, Coulter said he would fire the house, catching up a little girl and placing her in front of him rode up to the building thinking he would not be fired at while holding the child. He rode to within fifty yards of the house when a sharpshooter fired at him from an upstairs window. The bullet went just over the head of the little girl, and entered Coulter's body. He rode back, and placed the girl on the ground. The shot he received was a fatal one, and he died the following morning.*[116] *– Bardstown Standard*

It is likely that Terrell killed Coulter. He was certainly firing at him. The guerrillas no longer had the advantage, and withdrew soon after Coulter was shot. Other reports said that Coulter died two days later from complications associated with his wound. Marion escaped Ed Terrell once again, and vice versa.

Terrell and his men on a scout in Shelby County, stopped at a farm house to get a drink of water, and he ordered a young Negro boy to draw a bucket of water from the well so his men could cool themselves. Bad Ed had just acquired a new revolver, and decided to test his aim. As the boy went to the well, Terrell shot him and he fell, dead, head first into the water. Ed and his men had to go to the next house to quench their thirst, because the well at the first house was spoiled.

On April 27, 1865, Terrell rode into Jefferson County, Kentucky, and thence north on the Preston Street (plank) Road, to the house of Hercules "Herc" Walker's father-in-law, Col. Montgomery, who lived on Flatlick Road. Walker was an outlaw, who was accused of killing the Hill family in 1860. He was successful in having his trial delayed until most of the witnesses against him mysteriously disappeared. He was also suspected of supplying arms and ammunition to the Rebels. Rumor had it that Jefferson County officials had contracted Terrell to assassinate Walker. Terrell rode up, and Walker was plowing in a field when Terrell asked him to sell him and his men some of the ammunition he was known to traffic-in. As he unhitched his mule from the plow and went back to the barn, he was shot dead.

The report of his death appeared in an April 29, 1865, *Louisville Daily Journal* article, which stated:

> *Hercules Walker whose name is familiar to everybody, was killed day before yesterday at Col. Montgomery's place about ten miles from Louisville, on Flatlick Road. We learn that about 20 of Captain Ed Terrell's scouts surrounded the house of Col. Montgomery's (Walker's father-in-law), who was absent at the time. They then went to a field where Herc Walker was engaged in Ploughing. After parlaying a few moments, the soldiers compelled him to take his mules from the plough and go with him to the house. Here they demanded Walker's pistol, which his wife at first refused to deliver, but finally procured it at Mr. Walker's own request. Walker was then requested to step outside toward the barn. While on the way he was shot in the back of the head by someone of the company who was behind him, and instantly killed. Our informant said the scouts afterwards asked for the watch belonging to the deceased, and then carried off all the clothing belonging to Walker and Mont-*

gomery; also the two mules and a horse. This appears to be strange conduct. The Coroner's jury will elicit the facts in the case today.[117]

The *Louisville Daily Democrat* had the following report on the same day:

> *The killing of Hercules Walker...The person who fired the shot is said to have made the following remarks: "You have strutted through the streets of Louisville after killing several persons, including the Hill family, but you will not kill another." It will be remembered that Herc Walker and others were arrested in Louisville on the 21st of January, 1860, charged with the murder of the three brothers named Hill, who resided near the L&N R.R. a few miles from the city...The case was postponed from time to time until the parties were acquitted. It is not positively known who fired the shot, but he is supposed to be a relative of the Hill family.*[118]

Watson states a slightly different version of the events, and includes some details not in the news reports. The scouts rode up the Preston Street Road (now Preston Highway) and when Terrell called Walker outside, he said he was a leader of a guerrilla band and understood Walker had been supplying rebel guerrillas. Walker acknowledged that he had been supplying ammunition to guerrillas and agreed to sell some to Terrell. As walker was heading to the barn, one of Terrell's men rode up and killed Walker.[119]

Walker was reported in an April 29th newspaper report to be killed on April 27th. In an April 30th report, it seems the *Louisville Daily Journal* might have been giving some cover to Terrell, "Our report of the killing of Hercules Walker in yesterday's Journal [April 29th] was in the main correct. It is not quite certain who did the killing, but it is supposed to be one of the members of the Hill family. Captain Terry's (sic) object in visiting the neighborhood was to clear it of guerrillas."[120]

The next day, however, the paper took a different view of Terrell, and perhaps tried to backtrack a bit. On May 1, 1865 it wrote, "...Terrell's company of scouts may very properly be termed guerrillas, for it is self-constituted by the call of a single individual, not according to the general law of levy, conscription or volunteering; it is disconnected from the army as to its pay, provision, and movements, and it is irregular as to the permanency of its company, which may be called together and dismissed at any time. On Saturday, April 29, Coroner J.C. Gill, being under the impression that Capt. Terrell was or ought to be responsible for the killing of Walker, had him put under arrest. He was however, immediately released, and is now on a guerrilla hunting expedition."[121]

Terrell's lawless reputation coupled with his effectiveness in killing guerrillas caused the Federal authorities the same consternation that these back to back newspaper reports seems to have caused the Journal.

Terrell and the Death of Bill Marion

There are two accounts of Bill Marion's death, one of which I believe resulted only in the wounding of Marion, and the other in his demise. Marion had a bit of a dash about him. He sported at one time a white pheasant feather in his hat, and the only known photograph of him he is wearing a cavalry styled hat pinned up on one side. He was known to wear Polk leaves and other things in his hat, from time to time. He had special guerrilla clothes made for himself, and a pair of exceptionally well made, high-top riding boots, custom made by a shoemaker in Bloomfield named John Broderik. Terrell had learned of these boots, and bragged that he would soon be wearing Marion's boots. A 1917 article in the *Shelby County Sentinel*, states that Marion and Terrell who were bitter enemies, met on the Bloomfield Pike near the fairgrounds, and a gunfight ensued resulting in Marion's death. Terrell supposedly rode through Bloomfield to show off his new boots. There may have been a running gunfight between the men, and it is entirely possible that Terrell took Marion's boots after he (Marion) was killed. On April 16th, *The Louisville Daily Journal* wrote:

We learn that Captain Terrell, with only 16 men, met Capt. Marion and his gang, numbering about 30 men, on the road between Bloomfield and Taylorsville, last Thursday. Terrell retreated to a house and barn near the road and for some time a lively fight was kept up. Marion sent a flag of truce to Terrell, with a demand to surrender, informing him that he would be reinforced by Quantrill's command numbering about 40 men. Terrell replied, "Come and take me," and immediately dispatched to Bardstown for assistance. The courier met Capt. Robert H. Young, 54th Ky. Mtd. Inf., at Bloomfield with 35 men, who arrived at the scene of action a few minutes after the arrival of Quantrill. After a lively skirmish the guerrillas were routed and closely pursued. Marion was wounded in the thigh by Capt. Terrell, who was only 20 steps behind the guerrillas. We heard also that a heavy bunch of hair was cut from the side of Marion's head. Several others of the gang were severely wounded. One man by the name of Booth was killed on the Federal side, and another, Lt. Thompson, shot in the foot….About 7 o'clock on the same evening Maj. Cyrus Wilson's men fell into an ambuscade. One, of the party, was killed, and one wounded. The guerrillas were attacked and routed.[122] I suspect that the thigh and head wound Marion received, coupled with his death a day or so later, gave rise to the notion that he died from a shoot-out with Terrell near Bloomfield.

The death of Marion occurred in Washington County, at a town called Manton. Marion and Washington Counties abut, and Manton lies approximately 200 yards inside Washington County, causing some confusion in Captain Penn's initial report. Springfield is the Washington County seat, and three different groups of men were there hunting for Marion. Cyrus Wilson and Captain Penn had troops that converged in Springfield. Ed Terrell and several of his men were also in Springfield trying to locate Marion. Two roads lead from Manton to Springfield. Manton itself was a distillery town, having two distilleries making Kentucky Whiskey, and had at least one "still house" where spirits could be imbibed. Between Penn, Wilson, and Terrell there were about 100 soldiers. A plan was devised where the forces would be about equally split and would move on both roads, from Springfield, toward Manton. Penn's men had been driving him in the direction of New Haven, and Manton might be where Marion would stop and rest. The *Louisville Daily Journal* wrote on April 17, 1865, the following report:

> *Major Cyrus J. Wilson telegraphed us yesterday from New Haven that the notorious guerrilla leader, Capt. Bill Marion was shot and killed at a still house, near Manton, on Saturday evening, by one of Capt. Terrell's Union Guards. The body of the dead guerrilla will be forwarded to Louisville today. Marion was one of the most bloodthirsty and desperate outlaw leaders operating in the State, and news of his death will create intense delight. But a few days ago he threatened to avenge the death of Sue Mundy a hundred-fold.*

Thanks to a Union guard, he will not be able to put boasted threat into execution.[123]

On April 18, another lengthy account of the killing of Marion was printed in the *Louisville Daily Democrat*:

Marion killed...We will here relate an incident in connection with the above affair. A short time ago Capt. Edwin Terrell was in the presence of Major General John M. Palmer at his headquarters...General Palmer knew the young man with whom he was engaged in conversation. He stood before him his slouched hat in his hand, while his face presented a cool, disinterested look. "Terrell" said the general. "There is a certain man (naming him) that I want to have caught, and I want you to catch him." "Will you make me the present of a good horse if I do?" said Terrell. "Yes," replied the general, and Terrell pulled his hat over his eyes and stated, "Does it make any difference to you, general, whether I bring him dead or alive?" The general gave a look for a reply, and Terrell closed the door after him. Yesterday morning Terrell reported to Gen. Palmer with the man he wanted – Bill Marion[124]

Mean: When Bill Marion was killed by Capt. Terrell, on last Saturday, near Mantoon, they were two hundred yards apart. His body had scarcely fell out of the saddle and struck the earth, and before Terrell could reach the corpse, some of Marion's guerrillas robbed their leader in the jaws of death, of all the money and valuables about his person. It is said that Marion had a large amount of money and valuables.[125] *Other reports of Marion's death circulated, Maj. J. Walker Taylor in self-defense was reported to have killed Marion with a pistol shot. The fact is that it was likely one of Penn's men that killed Marion. Marion was killed by a rifle bullet, and Terrell and his men were armed only with pistols.*

On May 2nd, a report appeared in the Journal that was headed, who killed the guerrilla, Marion – Lebanon, Ky., April 28th. It reads:

Since there have been various written reports through the country as to who was entitled to the credit of killing Capt. Bill Marion, the notorious outlaw, I will give the following facts connected with the killing of Marion, and then submit the matter to the people to say whether the parties heretofore claiming the honor are justly entitled or not.

I was on the 15th of April, ordered by Hobson to take my company and scout the country in the direction of Bloomfield. I accordingly proceeded to Springfield. There I joined Maj. Wilson and Capt. Terrell, and after consulting with Maj. Wilson, we agreed to send out several scouting parties, who were to meet in Manton, Washington County, Kentucky, on the same evening. And having arrived at Manton first, with my company, I sent Sgt. Hughes in charge of twelve men to a still-house on the road leading to Loretta Station. While there on pickett, Capt. Marion and four of his men rode up to within one hundred and fifty yards of, inquiring of the sergeant whose men they were, at the same time firing at the squad. Sgt. Hughes ordered his squad to fire, which they deliberately did, resulting in the killing of Capt. Marion on the ground. The other four fled through the woods in different directions. In a few minutes, Capt. Terrell and myself, came up, and found my men still at their post. They had not yet been to the body of Marion. We then pursued them a short distance, when Capt. Terrell and his command turned back, and as I afterwards understood, took the body of Capt. Marion to Louisville. I still pursued the four for some four miles, after Capt. Terrell left me, and finding my pursuit was hopeless, I returned. I cannot say positively which one of my men did it, but I am satisfied one of my men did it, from the fact that the ball that he was struck with was a carbine ball, and there were only two of Capt. Terrell's men present at the time and they were armed with pistols only, while my men were armed with Ballard carbines. Very respectfully, your humble servant, George W. Penn, commanding Casey County State Guards.[126]

Terrell did take a heavy gold ring from Marion, and perhaps he did wear Marion's boots, no one can say now for sure. We do know that Terrell claimed the killing, and brought the body to Louisville where he likely claimed his reward, a good horse from General Palmer.

Chapter 12

The End of Quantrill and His Raiders

April and May of 1865, were climactic months for the guerrillas and especially for Quantrill and his men. The weather was warming and more clashes with Bridgewater, Terrell, and Wilson were being encountered. Quantrill and One Arm Sam Berry were apparently looking with an eye to the future, when they talked Marion out of killing Spencer County Judge Jim Davis for not burning the Spencer County Courthouse as Marion wanted. By this time Lee had surrendered, Lincoln had been assassinated, and everyone could see the war was near ending. General Burbridge had been replaced by General Palmer, who tried (it seams) to deal more honestly with the guerrillas and sort out the outlaws from the Confederate fighters. The guerrillas were looking for ways to be able to survive the war, and neither Palmer nor the Guerrillas found that an easy task.

At the same time Quantrill's nerves seemed to be fraying, and he appeared to be coming apart at the seams. He rode into a farmyard just north of Taylorsville with 13 men, overpowered Lucinda and Joseph K. Hughes, the owners of the farm, and threatened to hang Joseph. He told the man's wife, Lucinda Taylor Hughes, to bring out the "cookie jar". Not understanding that was his way of asking for their money, Lucinda said they didn't have one. With that Quantrill hoisted Hughes up from the limb of a tree in their yard, and had him dangling by the neck, choking to death. Suddenly she understood, and went back into the house and got all the money they had and gave it to Quantrill. Then, the 13 raiders rode off, after exchanging their spent horses for fresh ones, and she cut her husband down, just barely alive. But live he did, thanks to quick thinking Lucinda.[127] In 1875, Joseph was murdered in an unsolved case. Joseph was in a late card game, and family lore states it was with the Spencer County sheriff and his deputy. The sheriffs were big losers. The next day Joseph was found shot to death at a spring where he stopped in the early morning hours to get a drink. When his body was found, he had no money on his person.

Interestingly, Bud Pence and Doniphan Pence, two of Quantrill's raiders, stayed in Kentucky after the war. Doniphan was so popular that he was elected sheriff of Nelson County, while Bud Pence was elected town marshal of Taylorsville. Bud Pence could well have been, and likely was, in the group of 13 men that raided the Hughes farm and hanged Mr. Hughes. He was in the group of 13 when Quantrill was mortally wounded.

Another example of Quantrill seeming to lose control occurred at the small hamlet of Smiley, Kentucky. Smiley lies between Wakefield Station and Taylorsville, about four miles or so south of Taylorsville on State Road No. 155. The only thing that marks the place is an intersection of a two lane county road and Hwy. 155. On the west side of the road, is a one-room schoolhouse, the Smiley School. The school is freshly painted, and is well kept, even today. It was at this school that the Wakefield children attended classes. Joseph William Wakefield was one of the students that attended class at Smiley. I had read in the *Courier Journal* Newspaper about the sword of Quantrill, and in 1993, called the paper and got as much information as I could about who had the sword. I wanted to swing that sword once around my head before I died. All the paper could tell me was it was owned by a Wakefield in Shelby County. In 1993, I spent the better part of a day with James Wakefield of Shelbyville. James was a gunner on a battleship in the U.S. Navy during WWII. The large 16" guns he fired had taken a toll on his hearing. I found him by calling every Wakefield in Shelby County. I would call, and ask if they knew anything about Quantrill's sword? Most who answered said no, one or two hung up, but after some five or six calls, a young lady said, "We don't know nothin' 'bout swords," when a voice far back from the telephone said, "I'd better talk to 'em." He told me he was a nephew of Jo Morry Wakefield, the son of Joseph Wilson William Wakefield, who was given the sword by Quantrill, and who was the grandson of the man in whose barn Quantrill was captured. We then made a date to pack a picnic lunch, pick him up at his home, where he agreed to show my wife Fran, my mother Virginia, and me the places where his family history and the last battle of Quantrill took place. We picked up Mr. Wakefield and he showed us many sites and cemeteries, and told us of Quantrill and the Wakefield family lore. We had a great day together. He was 74-years-old.

When we got to Smiley Town, he pointed out the small asphalt road that intersected the state road. He told us how on this steep-sided road, how Joseph William, a boy, got the sword of Quantrill. In 1971, Tom Shelby Watson wrote a magazine article about this incident, and James Wakefield's story is nearly the same, saving only the weather. Coming down the road, which was steep sided and deep, was a log wagon on its way to Fairfield, a short way down the road, and between the steep banks on either side of the road, the wagon got stuck in the mud. This was likely because of the heavy load, and because of rain, and the horses could not advance. Meanwhile Quantrill and his raiders, coming up from behind and, in a hurry, were held up by the mired, log wagon. The wagon had seven horses. Quantrill could not pass, and frustrated, he drew his sword and killed all seven horses. He may have thrust the sword into them, or slashed at their heads and necks, but whichever way, the horses were slain in the road. Joseph William was walking home from school, and Quantrill saw him, and threw down the sword, sticking it blade first into the ground at his feet, and said, "This is for you." Joseph took the sword home. Unfortunately for me some two years before, in 1991, someone broke into Jo Morry's home in Oldham County, and stole his sword and arrowhead collection. There remains a mystery about why there were seven horses. Six would pull the wagon and logs, and perhaps the seventh was trailing behind to be ridden somewhere else, sold or whatever. No one knows. James told us the Wakefield family had always puzzled over that question.

May 10th, 1865, in the morning, Quantrill was in the Spencer and Nelson, Counties area. Watson states he was visiting with the McClasky families. It rained that day. Quantrill had some 13 to 21 men with him. At the hanging of Joseph Hughes, several days before he was captured, he had a company of 13. Watson states that, counting Quantrill, that is the most likely number of his party,[128] and that is consistent with the number of his party at the Hughes farm. Yeatman gives the number a variance between 11 and 21. Various others have estimated the number between 15 and 20 men.

Terrell likely had between 15 and 20 men with him on his scout in Spencer County, on May the 10th, a Wednesday. There was a county road that ran west off of what is now Hwy. 155, just across from the newer of the J.H. Wakefield houses, the old house was up this road, and a barn sat on the northwest corner of the intersection. Near this place a Negro blacksmith operated a shop on Wakefield's property.[129] The shop may have been in or adjacent to that barn. Terrell was on the scout searching for guerrillas, and noticed hoof prints of a sizable party in the mud leading up the county road to Wakefield's. There was a Wakefield barn and silo to the south of this farm lane, where Quantrill and his men took refuge from the rain. A stock pond was adjacent to the barn. To the north across the road from the barn sat the Wakefield house.[130] Wakefield had supplied the raiders with whiskey, presumably to ward off a chill from the rain. The raiders were sopping wet. There were sheds projecting out on three sides of the barn where the raiders sheltered their horses.[131] Quantrill climbed into the loft to nap, while his men had a sham fight with corncobs. The raiders needed time to talk, and consider their options. Lee had surrendered and Lincoln was dead. Quantrill was 27 years old, and most of his men were younger; and, they were all tired of the war. Terrell and his men rode up the steep road toward the Wakefield house, and when he crested the hill, looking down on the barn, he spied the horses tied, and charged ahead. Dick Glasscock who was outside the barn at that time, near where the horses were tied, called out "Here, they come!" With that the fight was joined.

John N. Edwards lists the men in Quantrill's company as John Ross, William Hulse, Payne Jones, Clark Hockensmith, Isaac Hall, Richard "Dick" Glasscock, Robert Hall, Bud Pence, Allen Parmer, Dave Helton, and Lee McMurtry,[132] and of course Quantrill. There could have been and probably was another of the Kentucky guerrillas riding with Quantrill. I will describe the battle at Wakefield's as Edwards says it happened. Even though Edwards, once again, seems to overstate the odds against the guerrillas. He says that Terrell had fifty men with him, when it was likely the number was not more than 20, and perhaps was even less.

The Battle at Wakefield's Barn According to John N. Edwards

On the morning of May 10th, Quantrill and his men took shelter in the barn of James Heady Wakefield. His men and he were given whiskey to drink by Mr. Wakefield. The guerrillas, who were full of youthfulness, were having a corncob fight while their leader was trying to nap in the loft. Quantrill was as ignorant of Captain Edwin Terrell's scouts being nearby as Terrell was of Quantrill's whereabouts.

As Terrell passed by the road where Quantrill's raiders had ridden to the Wakefield barn, if he had not seen the hoof prints of a sizable force in the muddy road, he would never have discovered the guerrillas, and a fight would not have occurred. This trail Terrell had followed to within sight of the barn, and understood in a moment the character of the men sheltered there, and closed upon it rapidly, firing as he came on. Before a guerrilla could put a single bridle on a horse, Terrell was at the main gate of the lot, distant some fifty feet from the barn, and pouring such a storm of carbine bullets among them that their horses ran furiously about the lot, difficult to approach and impossible to restrain. Fighting desperately and deliberately, and driving away from the main gate a dozen or more Federals stationed there, John Ross, William Hulse, Allen Parmer, Lee McMurtry, and Bud Pence cut their way through mounted and defiant. The entire combat did not last ten minutes. It was a fight where every man had to do for himself and do what needed to be done speedily.

Once, above the rattling of musketry, the neighing of horses and the shouting of the combatants Quantrill's voice rang out loud and high: "Cut through boys; cut through, somehow. Don't surrender while there is a chance to get out!" The fire upon the guerrillas was furious. Quantrill's horse, a thoroughbred animal of great, spirit and speed, could not be caught. His master, anxious to secure him, followed him composedly about the lot, for several minutes, trying under a shower of balls to get hands upon his favorite. At this moment Clark Hockensmith, who was mounted and free to go away at a run, saw the peril of his chief and galloped to his rescue.

Quantrill, touched by this act of devotion, recognized it by a smile, and held out his hand to his comrade without speaking. Hockensmith dismounted until Quantrill could take his place in the saddle, and then sprang up behind him. Another furious volley from Terrell's men lining the fence about the great gate killed Hockensmith and killed the horse Quantrill and Hockensmith were upon. The second hero now gave his life for Quantrill. Richard Glasscock had also secured his own horse as Hockensmith had done, and was free to ride away in safety as he had been.

Opposite to the main entrance of the barn lot there was an exit uncovered by the enemy, and beyond this exit a stretch of heavy timber. Those who gained the timber were safe. Hockensmith knew it when he faced about and deliberately laid down his life for his chief, and Glasscock knew it when he also turned about and hurried up to the two men struggling there, Quantrill to drag himself cut from under the body of the horse, and Hockensmith in the agonies of death. The second volley from the gate mortally wounded Quantrill and killed Glasscock's horse. Then a charge of 50 shouting and shooting men swept over the barn lot. Robert Hall. Payne Jones, David Helton, and Isaac Hall had gone out sometime before on foot.

J.B. Tooley, A.B. Southworth, and C.H. Southworth, wounded badly, escaped fighting. Only the dead man lying by his wounded chief, and the dauntless Glasscock, erect, splendid, and fighting to the last, remained as trophies of the desperate combat. Glasscock stood over his wounded chief and emptied the remaining barrels of his last loaded revolver, killing two of Terrell's men almost upon him, and wounding three. The Federals fired full upon Glasscock, and beat him with pistol butts; he was later killed trying to escape. Two balls had hit Quantrill. The first, the heavy ball of a Spencer carbine, entered close to the right collarbone, ranged down along the spine, injuring it severely, and hid itself somewhere in the body. The second ball cut off the finger next to the little finger of the left hand, tearing it from its socket and lacerating the hand itself painfully. The shoulder wound did its work, however, for it was the mortal wound. All the lower body of Quantrill was paralyzed, and as he was lifted and carried to Wakefield's house his legs were limp and his extremities were cold and totally without sensation. At no time did he either complain or make moan. His wonderful fortitude and endurance remained unimpaired to the end. His mind always clearest in danger seemed to recognize that his last battle had been fought and his encounter finished. He talked very little. Terrell came to him and asked if there were any good service he might do that would be acceptable. "Yes," said Quantrill. "Have Clark Hockensmith buried like a soldier." After he had been carried to the house of Wakefield and deposited on a pallet, he spoke once more to Terrell: "While I live, let me stay here. It is useless to haul a dying man about in a wagon, jolting out what little life is left in him." Terrell pledged his word that he should not be removed, and rode away in pursuit of those who had escaped.

Isaac Hall and Payne Jones took refuge in a pond a number of yards from Wakefield's house. Gathering together sticks and bunches of grass they made of them a sort of screen for their heads, which from the nose up was all that remained above water. Hunted everywhere, they remained in the pond for an hour, chilled to the marrow but undiscovered. Thus, the battle ended.[133] A newspaper report of the battle on May 13th, which stated:

> *On Wednesday evening Quantrill of Kansas notoriety, with some ten or twelve guerrillas were in Taylorsville. They had not gone more than 20 minutes when Capt. Edwin Terrell, with his scouts entered the town. Hearing that Quantrill had just left, Terrell started in pursuit and came up with Quantrill and his band in a barn a few miles from town, where they were feeding their horses. A fight took place at once and the result was that Terrell shot Quantrill through the breast, lodging the ball against the backbone. One of Quantrill's men was killed on the spot, four or five badly wounded, and the balance took to the woods and made their escape. Terrell captured a number of their horses and equipment's... From the description of the man it must be Quantrill...but be that as it may, the man who has thus met his fate is said to have been a most desperate individual.*[134]

It seems to me at least that Quantrill did not get the press coverage that Sue Mundy, Bill Marion, and Billy Magruder did.

According to the Shelby County newspaper, Quantrill paid Terrell $500.00 and his watch to allow him to stay at Wakefield's. He promised more money for a worthless parole Terrell wrote him. Terrell was under the impression that Quantrill was Captain Clark. Wakefield gave Terrell and his men whiskey, and Terrell $20.00 and Harry Thompson, his Lieutenant, $10.00, to stop the ransacking of his house. Terrell took his men in search of the remaining guerrillas. With the capture of Medkiff, Magruder, and Quantrill, along with the hanging of Mundy, and the killings of Cox, Marion, Coulter, and Walker, Terrell was running out of business, and on Thursday May 11th, the city fathers of Shelbyville voted to stop paying for Terrell and his men's room and board. Twenty-year-old Baby Faced Ed Terrell would not be happy at the news.

This is a photo of the grave of William Kendal "Billy" Shacklett, who died April 29, 1863. He was a former captain of the Brandenburg Home Guard. He deserted the guard and joined the Confederate Army in 1862, at the town of Big Spring, Kentucky. He, along with his cousin John Wimp, gun runner, James Gorsuch, Dan Morgan Shacklett, a man named Jarrett or Garrett, Duke, about four others were attacked and killed at some over-hanging rocks known as the Sheep Shed, by Captain Hare and his 100-man force. At least four of the men were murdered after being captured or after they surrendered. Note: The United Daughters of the Confederacy placed a new stone on Shacklett's grave engraved with the emblem of the Southern Cross of Honor awarded for heroic action in the Civil War. Photo by author.

The photograph of John Wimp's grave shows his date of death to be April 29, 1863. He died along with Billy Shacklett. After emptying his pistols, he surrendered and with his hands raised was reportedly shot in the back of the head by Hare's orderly, Amos Griffin. Both men were buried the next day in the Meadeville Cemetery. Photo by author.

The Shumate Schoolhouse as it appears today. The battle of the Sheep Shed occurred near the school, and Jarrett was captured about 60 feet from the front door of the school. The children witnessed some of the fighting, and assisted in the death hunt for the bodies of the slain Confederates. Author's collection.

The Meadeville, Kentucky Baptist Cemetery as it appears today. Photo by author.

The improved spring at Meadeville, Kentucky that served to water the horses on the Hardinsburg–West Point stagecoach route. The Shumate School sits atop the hill in the woods overlooking the spring. The school children and the Confederates obtained their water from the spring. Meadeville is now a ghost town. Author's collection.

Historic marker commemorating the Robert Buckner House used by Morgan as his headquarters in July of 1863. Robert Buckner, an aged man, was forced to take the oath of allegiance to the Union at gunpoint. Photo by author.

Brandenburg's Main Street looking north toward the Ohio River, as it appeared in the late 1890's. On the right side of the street, the second building is the bank building where Frank James committed his first crime after taking the oath to rejoin the Union. On the left, hidden by trees, is the Ashcraft Hotel, where Stanley Young killed his Uncle Marsh for the murder of his father, St. Claire Young, when Stanley was 9-years-old. Stanley Young came back during the Civil War as guerrilla captain Bill Marion. Photo courtesy of Jess Scott.

The tombstone of Dr. Benedict Wathen, who was kidnapped, tried and given a death sentence by Captain Bill Marion, who confused him with Dr. Jessie Pitman Lewis, the doctor treating Billy Magruder for a bullet wound and who guided Cyrus Wilson to the Cox farm where Magruder, Mundy and Medkiff were captured. Photo by author.

Close up of wording on Benedict Wathen's tombstone. Photo by author.

Jack and Pete's tombstone. Jack and Pete were Benedict Wathen's slaves. They were well treated and buried in Mt. Marino Catholic Cemetery beside Benedict Wathan.

Artist's rendering of Sue Mundy, adapted from a tintype in the Filson Club collection. Author's collection.

The author is studying the sandy floor inside Captain Bryant's Cave. The Confederate guerrilla captain was hidden in the cave until early the next morning, when his men removed him to the home of a Mr. Kerrick where he later died. A spring of water was near the cave, and the large boulder in the foreground hid his body from view. Photo courtesy of Peggy Greenwell.

The Coomes cabin as it appeared in 1913 when Uncle Milt Pollock celebrated his birthday. From left to right, Octavia Chism Pollock, Cornelia Pollock Morris, Uncle Milt Pollock, Gertha Pollock Phipps, Mary Jane "Mollie" Pollock Chism, and Carrie Pollock Basham. The final raid of Captain John Bryant began and ended on or about August 30, 1865, when the Coomes', who hid behind the large stone chimney, engaged Captain Bryant and his six man guerrilla force in a gun battle, resulting in Bob Coomes being shot in the right forearm and Captain Bryant being mortally wounded in the stomach. Captain Bryant was carried a half mile up the road and was hidden in a shallow cave. The cave forever after became known as "Captain Bryant's Cave." Bryant was about 20-years-old when he died. Photo courtesy of Meade County Fiscal Court Judge Executive Harry Craycraft, and Peggy Greenwell.

The David Henry House as it appears today. It was on the front porch of this house where Captains Dupoyster and Bryant raided the Henry farm with an estimated 35 guerrillas, and murdered David Henry. Dupoyster slapped Mrs. Henry, who was trying to comfort her dying husband and told her to shut her wailing or he would kill her as well. The murder turned many people against the guerrillas. Photo by author, courtesy of Mr. Clark.

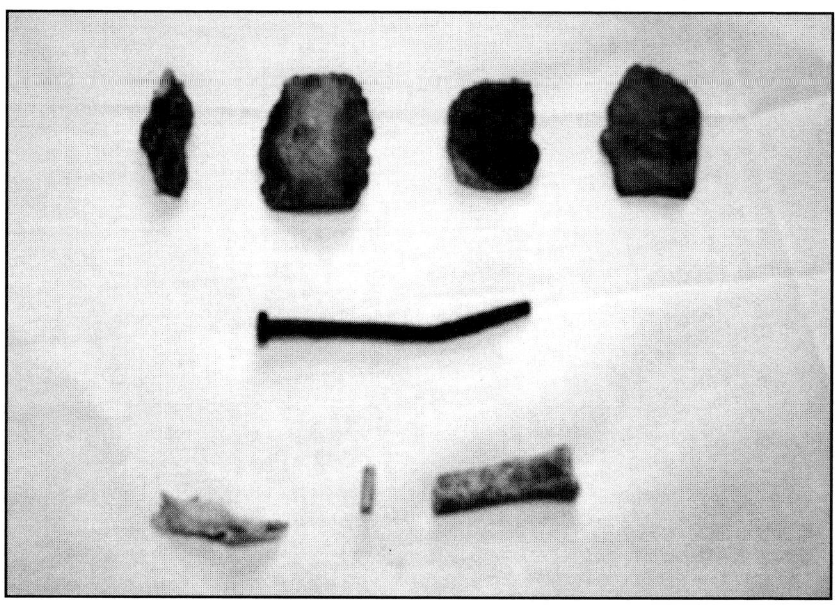

Artifacts found in the Midwife's Cave. The iron nail could have been made by James Irvin Newton. Photo by the author.

This is the top view of the gravestone of James Irvin Newton, who was killed in a guerrilla raid on his property across the road from the Meadeville Cemetery. Newton, although Catholic, was hurriedly buried the night he was killed in the Baptist Cemetery. A large slab of natural limestone disguised the grave. Fear that his burial would be desecrated, a permanent marker was not placed on the grave until 1998. Photo by author.

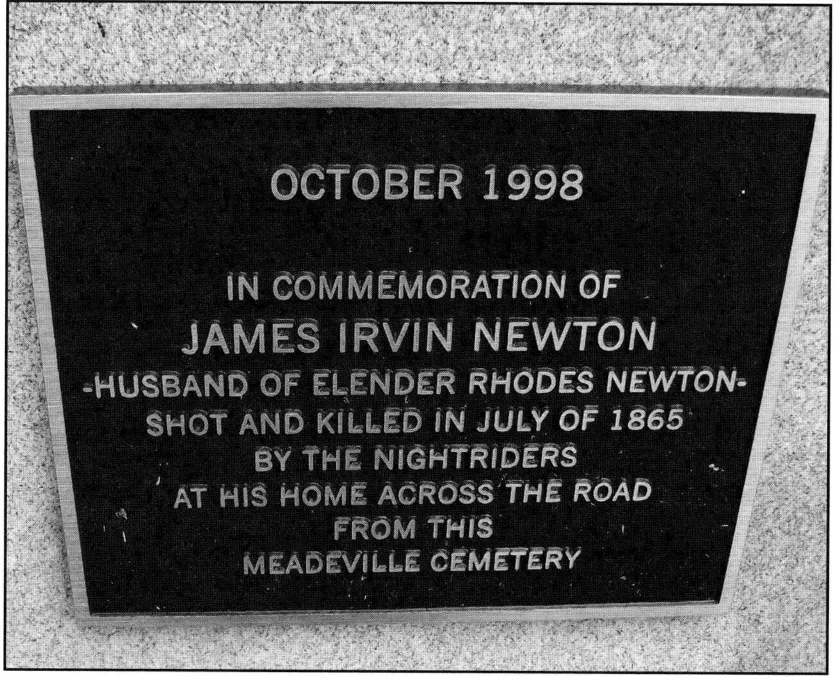

The side (front) view of the marker tells the story of the "Nightriders" that assassinated Newton at his home. An 1865 newspaper story states that Henry Clay Magruder's brother did the murder. Two men were arrested on suspicion, but the case has gone unsolved. Photo by author.

Overview of the heavy granite headstone of James Irvin Newton. Photo by author.

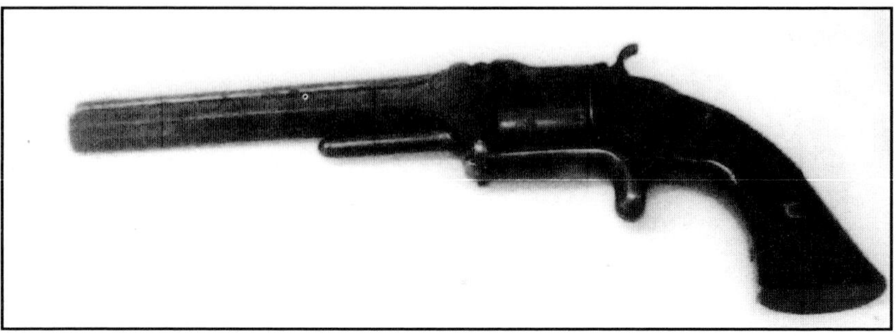

This photograph is of one of the two pistols Sue Mundy surrendered to John Cox, the owner of the farm on which Sue Mundy, Billy Magruder, and Henry Medkiff/Metcalf were captured by Major Cyrus Wilson, March 12, 1865. Mundy asked for treatment as a prisoner of war, and by surrendering his pistols to Cox he may have tried to cloud his trial proceedings. Photo by author, courtesy M. Henderson.

The grave of Marcellus Jerome Clarke, aka "Sue Mundy", lies in the Confederate section of Green Lawn Cemetery, in Franklin, Kentucky. He was captured in Meade County, March 12, 1865, tried on March 14, 1865, in Louisville, Kentucky, and hanged on March 15, 1865. The endorsement for his execution was entered on March 13, 1865, a full day before his trial was held. He was approximately 20 years and seven months of age. His execution may have been botched as he struggled at the end of the rope. Photo by author.

Historic marker commemorating the capture of Sue Mundy. Photo by author.

William Davison's historic marker in Hawesville, Kentucky. Davison, a Confederate guerilla in Lee Sypert's partisan rangers, was mortally wounded in the same engagement with Henry Magruder, dying on March 7th, 1865. Magruder's wounding led to the capture of Sue Mundy, Henry Magruder and Henry Medkiff, March 12, 1865. Photo courtesy of Debra Masterson.

Davison's new tombstone; note the Southern Cross of Honor. Photo courtesy of Debra Masterson.

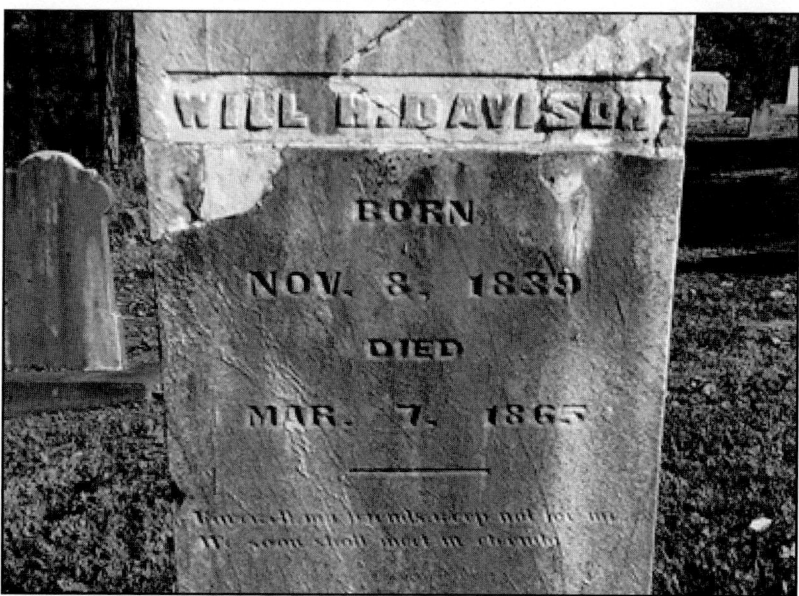

Davison's original tombstone in Hawesville, Kentucky. Photo courtesy of Debra Masterson.

Samuels Depot, where Quantrill's men were allowed to take the oath of office after Frank James killed the rapist brothers and One Arm Berry turned in the rapist Texas for trial. Photo by author.

The Smiley Schoolhouse from where Stillwell Heady was walking when William Clarke Quantrill threw down his sword and told Heady, "This sword is yours." Photo by author.

The road leading to the Smiley School where the wagonload of logs got stuck and Quantrill killed seven horses with his sword because his men could not pass. Photo by author.

The dirt road through this farm gate was a Spencer County Road in 1865. The road winds up a hill to the James Heady Wakefield barn, where Quantrill was captured. Terrell noticed the tracks of a large body of horsemen in the muddy road leading to the crest of the hill. From there the barn could be seen. Today only the silo remains. Photo by author.

The grave of William Clarke Quantrill, in St. John's Cemetery in Louisville. The stone of William Clarke Quantrill is flush with the ground and is engraved with the Southern Cross of Honor. He may have written the verse engraved in the stone. The priest had him buried and disguised the grave fearful it would be desecrated; although Quantrill paid for the grave and a marker, a marker was not originally placed on the interment. Some of Quantrill's skeleton is still in the Louisville grave. Other portions are in Missouri, and the bulk of his remains are buried in the family plot in Dover, Ohio. Photo by Frances Fischer.

Historic marker noting the capture of Quantrill just feet away from the gate and road that leads to the Wakefield barn. Photo by author.

April 1993, panoramic view of 74-year-old James Wakefield standing beside the Quantrill Historic Marker, with the two James Heady Wakefield barns to the left, facing the old county road that Terrell rode up to attack Quantrill and his raiders. The barn farthest left is the one in which the blacksmith shop was located in May of 1865. The barn with the silo is the one in which James Heady Wakefield boarded Jesse James horse, after the war. Jesse was flat broke, and gave Wakefield a silver watch to settle the $8.00 bill for feed and board. Both barns are now gone, lost to age and the elements. Photo from the author's collection. Photo by author

The bank building in Brandenburg, as it appears today, where Frank James had a gunfight with four Union soldiers in the late summer or fall of 1865. He killed two, mortally wounded a third, and was shot through the hips by the fourth soldier who fired and fled the contest. Frank and Jessie returned to Brandenburg in 1869. Photo by the author.

Jessie Woodson James made a number of trips to Kentucky. Sometimes he traveled with his brother Frank, with Jim, Bob, and Coleman Younger, the famous James Younger gang. Photo from a postcard in author's collection.

Henry Clay Magruder's grave; the stone was placed in 2000 by the Sons of Confederate Veterans in the Ezekiel Magruder Cemetery. To reach the lonely, wooded cemetery that lies atop a small Bullitt County, Kentucky knoll, a walk of about 60 yards must be made through tangled brush and trees. The cemetery quietly looms into view, a scattering of graves mingled amidst a grove of ancient Cedars. Many of the tombstones are toppled or broken. Somehow it seems a fitting place for the grave. Anecdotal evidence states that Magruder's first two headstones were destroyed by friends and relatives of the men he murdered. Photo from the author's collection.

Thomas McCormick tombstone. McCormick owned a store in which he hid John Hunt Morgan and Thomas Henry Hines in Larue County, Kentucky after their escape from the Federal Penitentiary in Columbus, Ohio in 1863. Photo from the author's collection.

Thomas Franklin Crady's grave. Crady, a Union Soldier on leave home, was shot November 18, 1864 by the guerrilla Sol Thompson, and while he was alive on the ground clinging to life, he was shot again and killed by Thompson's companion, Henry Clay Magruder. Photo from the author's collection.

Captain Bill Marion, aka Stanley Young, was shot and killed at a still house at this location in Manton, Ky. He was shot with a Ballard rifle ball; while Ed Terrell claimed the kill, he was armed only with revolvers. Photo by author

This photo covers the pathway between two large hills near West Point, Kentucky, where Captain Thomas Henry Hines and six hand-picked men attacked a group of 50 drovers who were herding 500 horses through this pass to be loaded on boats and sent down river to remount Union soldiers. The attack was made on a moonlit night and many of the drovers were killed and wounded. The horses were scattered. The six men that Hines selected made their way home and were safely in bed before sunrise. Hines revisited a safe house in Vine Grove, Kentucky before rejoining his regiment. Photo by author, at the Bridges to the Past West Point, Kentucky City Park.

Catty Rhodes, standing in the front yard of Edward Rhodes. Edward Rhodes was the Payneville, Kentucky Postmaster. Photo courtesy of Peggy Greenwell and Dennis Staples.

Cattie Rhodes, standing in the doorway of the smokehouse owned by Edward Rhodes, in Payneville, Kentucky. Cattie was born into slavery, and spent her entire life taking care of others. Photo courtesy of Peggy Greenwell and Dennis Staples.

Chapter 13

Bad Ed's Exploits and Death

On May 18, 1865, a number of Negro soldiers were stationed at the courthouse in Shelbyville, and requisitioned a "market house" leased by Mr. Thomas McGrath, where he kept stocks of goods. The soldiers were supervised by white officers who were impudent and overbearing. The soldiers, imitating their officers, broke in the door of the market house, and began chopping up merchandise to use as kindling for their cook fires. Mr. McGrath promised the soldiers he would have a load of firewood brought up if they would stop destroying his property, when one of the Negro soldiers shot and killed McGrath. The citizens, aghast at the dastardly deed, demanded the officer turn over to them the Negro soldier, but he refused. Shortly later, Ed Terrell and his men rode into Shelbyville, were told about the killing of Mr. McGrath, and the lieutenant's refusal to turn over the man.

Ed Terrell, no stranger to climbing stairs and fighting the men at the top of them, marched to the top of the stairs, and demanded the Lieutenant turn over the soldier. He refused. Upon hearing his refusal, Terrell took the lieutenant by the ear and proceeded to kick the officer down three flights of stairs. He then ascended the stairs, tied a rope around the Negro's neck with the other end tied to the balcony railing, and was proceeding to throw the soldier over the railing, when Colonel Buckley's regiment of soldiers, who were stationed at the fairgrounds, arrived in time to prevent the hanging. The town's people cheered Ed and his scouts, and supplied them with the room and board taken away a week earlier.

The *Louisville Daily Journal* reported on the event:

We regret to learn that Mr. McGrath, a well-known merchant of Shelbyville, Ky., was killed by a soldier of the 13th U.S. Colored Heavy Art. About 6 o'clock Friday morning. Mr. McGrath has been using the market house to store agricultural implements in, and Friday morn-

> *ing he found it had been broken open by some of the Colored soldiers. He went to Capt. Kent to make a complaint, and on leaving was followed by one of the Negros and shot. Mr. McGrath was a thoroughgoing Union man, and the pretext cannot be given as a palliation of the act that he was a secession sympathizer.*[135]

On the 21st of May the following story appeared:

> *We are called upon to record another outrage committed by Negro soldiers. The affair…happened in Shelbyville…Mr. Thomas C. McGrath a well-known merchant was shot and instantly killed by a soldier from the 13th U.S. Colored H.A.…Mr. McGrath lived in the house adjoining the courthouse and was a dealer in hardware and agent for various patent agricultural machines. Back of the courthouse there is an old market house, which he used in storing some of his machines. Yesterday morning a citizen of the place by the name of Hastings observed that the back door of the market house had been broken open, and that several Negro soldiers were inside. He immediately informed Mr. McGrath, who hastened back, and found them hammering a lock on the front door, and told the Negroes not to break the lock, that he would get a key and open it. After a few insulting remarks by the negroes he got the key, and while in the act of opening the door he was shot in the back with a musket, the ball coming out of his abdomen, killing him instantly.*
>
> *The murder of McGrath: In a few minutes after the occurrence there was a scene of the wildest excitement. Citizens were going hastily along the streets men were carrying guns and pistols hurrying to the courthouse and groups standing about everywhere. Everyone wanted to visit immediate punishment on the murderer, and Capt. Edwin Terrell and his men armed themselves for the purpose of taking him out…When the officer commanding said he would deliver the Negro to Col. Harvey M. Buckley, 54th Ky. Mtd. Inf.*[136]

Meanwhile, a Dr. Wooten living in Fairfield and sympathetic to the southern cause, aghast at the disregard for the law that Ed Terrell exhibited, complained to Union authorities about his abuses, and on May 21, 1865, Terrell decided to kill the doctor. On his way to Dr. Wooton's, he stopped at Bloomfield and told a relative, Mr. John A. Terrell, of his intention. John Terrell begged him not to kill the doctor, because he was one of the few remaining in the area. Terrell promised not to kill the doctor, but when he arrived in Fairfield, he procured a rope, tied Wooton with the rope, and with the other end tied to his saddle, he proceeded to drag the doctor up and down the main street. On May 22, 1865, Asst. Adjutant, General E.B. Harlan, by orders of General Palmer, rescinded the commission of Terrell.

A May 26th article appeared stating: *We announced yesterday that by order of Maj. General John M. Palmer, the bands of scouts – Capt. Edwin Terrell's and others – have been disbanded and dismissed. These bands have been employed in breaking up and capturing guerrilla squads that have been roving around and plundering the country. As they are disbanded, we suppose it is because all the guerrilla bands in this State are broken up and there is no more need of independent scouts....*[137]

Three days later on May 25, 1865, whether by chance or design, Terrell and his men were in Taylorsville, and stopped by the blacksmith shop of Innis Wooton, the brother of Dr. Wooton. Innis was busy shoeing a horse, when one of Terrell's men named Weathers demanded that Wooton shoe his horse. Weathers apprenticed as a blacksmith with Wooton, and Wooton told him that he was busy, but that he was free to shoe the horse himself. A fight between Wooton and Weathers ensued, when Terrell rode up and shot Wooton dead. Soon after Terrell got word that General Palmer wanted to hang him for his outrageous acts, Terrell left Kentucky.

A report appeared in the newspaper, June 1, 1865 stating: Innis Wooton Killed: *We learn that on Saturday Capt. Edwin Terrell and his men were at Taylorsville. Terrell went to Mr. Wooton's to have his horse or horses shod. Mr. Wooton referred him to another blacksmith shop. Warm words followed between one of Terrell's men and Wooton, whereupon a fight occurred during which Terrell rode up and shot Wooton dead.*[138] *On the same day the Louisville Daily Democrat reported on Henry Metcalf (Medkiff) Having his sentence reduced to five years imprisonment, down from the death sentence. Magruder was still to hang at some future date.*

Sometime in August 1865, Terrell returned to Shelbyville. He and his lieutenant, Harry Thompson, were staying at the Lucy Burnett's boarding house. On August 24, 1865, William R. Johnson of Sangamon

County, Illinois, a stock buyer, arrived by stagecoach from Louisville. He had sixteen hundred dollars in gold on his person, and a substantial sum in cash, and he also took a room at Lucy Burnett's boarding house. It was at the boarding house that Thompson and Terrell teamed up to murder William Johnson. After dinner they convinced him to accompany them for a walk. The walk took them out of town down by Clear Creek, where Johnson was shot and relieved of his gold, and much of his cash. Johnson's body was weighted with stones and sunk in a deep hole in Clear Creek.

The next Sunday, "Irish Tommie Fox" went down to the creek fishing and as he threw in his line, his hook snagged on Johnson's clothes. Tugging on it, trying to get it loose, Johnson's body was pulled into view, and Tommie Fox was almost "skeered to death." He quickly gave the alarm, and it was determined that Terrell and Thompson were guilty of the murder. A warrant for arrest was sworn out by the Coroner, and the sheriff was to make the arrest. Sheriff Harbison, a big man, knew who he was dealing with, a desperate killer. And, with Terrell being slight in stature, he grabbed him firmly from behind in a bear hug, which prevented Terrell from reaching his revolvers. Thompson was caught later and both men were housed in the Shelby County Jail.

Two weeks later at the regular September meeting of the Circuit Court, an indictment for murder was rendered in the case of Edwin Terrell and Harry Thompson. The trial was set for March 12, 1866, and three defense attorneys represented Terrell and Thompson, W.C. Bullock, M.C. Taylor, and W.C. Taylor. Since there was no evidence other than the three men took a walk together, for the jury to make a ruling was impossible, and the jury was dismissed. The accused were remanded to the jail, and within 48 hours of the dismissal of the jury, on March 26, 1866, Terrell and Thompson escaped from the new cells that were steel lined. They pried up a steel plate and made a hole large enough for them to wiggle through.

Thompson left Kentucky for Texas, and Terrell made his way to the south part of the county, and went into hiding. Terrell was caught and arrested for the killing of Innis Wooton, and was housed in the Spencer County Jail in Taylorsville. On April 13, 1866 four days after his capture, Terrell was broken out of jail by some of his old gang. By April 24, Governor Bramlett placed a $500.00 reward for the capture of the murderers of Wooton, Johnson, and Herc Walker, and their incarceration in the Jefferson County, Kentucky Jail. Terrell once again in hiding, and drinking heavily, began to blame the people of Shelbyville for all of his woes. Sometime later he would begin sending messages to Shelbyville telling various people that he would make the town pay.

On May 26, 1866, Terrell had been drinking heavily at Jack Eade's Barroom in Clayvillage, with his uncle John Baker, and Love Head. The Shelby County jailer, David J. Thompson, was in the barroom when Terrell talked himself into making a raid on Shelbyville, to "bluff" the town. Thompson unsuccessfully tried to talk Terrell out of his plan and Baker, Head, and Terrell began riding north to Shelbyville. They entered the town from the east, however, and Head, riding behind Terrell and Baker slipped off. The two men arrived at the Armstrong Hotel bar where they kept drinking, signed the guest register, and began calling for sheriff Harbison, his deputy, or the town marshal to come arrest him. It was near twilight and the town was quiet except for Terrell's loud talk. Baker and Terrell remained at the bar for a half hour, while a posse of five or six men armed themselves and with guns loaded, started walking toward the men. As Baker and Terrell started up the street, after speaking to Merritt Redding, someone called "Halt!" at which Terrell drew his revolver and fired into a building, both men spurring their horses. The report of his weapon caused 20 shots or more to be discharged by the posse and Terrell fell wounded from his horse, before it advanced 50 feet. Baker continued up the street for four squares before he fell dead in the street. Several Shelbyville citizens were wounded in the fight, and Merritt Redding was killed, the last man to die at the hands of Bad Ed Terrell.

Mr. Moosenheimer was credited with the shot that brought down Terrell, and though badly wounded and partially paralyzed, Terrell kept firing his pistol until Mr. J.Q. Johnson grabbed the gun placing his thumb under the hammer preventing it from firing. Johnson's thumb badly injured, was later amputated. Terrell was taken to the nearest hotel and given emergency treatment, and moved to Jefferson County, where he underwent surgery in the city hospital and was incarcerated in the jail. Partially paralyzed and no longer considered a threat, he was released later under a $5,000.00 bond, and placed under the custody of his grandfather. While home at Mr. Baker's, Terrell got hold of his revolver and tried to shoot his brother-in-law at which time John Baker notified the court that he could no longer be responsible for his grandson.

Continuing to suffer pain and paralysis, Terrell entered the City of Louisville Hospital, in December of 1868, unpublished and without fanfare. He hoped that another operation would remove a piece of lead shot Ed thought remained in his body. The surgery did not locate any additional foreign matter, and when he took a turn for the worse, Ed Terrell's doctors told him to prepare to meet his maker. He asked one doctor, "What makes you think I am not prepared?" He asked for whiskey, and while drinking, regaled his nurse with stories of his exploits, as his condition worsened. He died December 13, 1868, survived by a brother, a brother-in-law, and his grandfather. He bequeathed to his brother the only things he truly valued, his revolvers and Bill Marion's gold ring. Bad Ed Terrell, the terror of Shelby County and of many guerrilla fighters, was dead at 23 years of age.

Chapter 14

Quantrill's Death and His Burials

The night of May 10th, there was a knock on the door of the Wakefield house, and Frank James was there to take Quantrill to another safe house where he could not easily be found, and hopefully heal. Quantrill refused to make the trip because he knew he was mortally wounded and had but a short while to live. He bade his men to take the oath of allegiance should the war end, and they were allowed. He knew he had a parole, not realizing it was worthless, and should he be wrong about his prognosis, and get better he might be able to return to his home. James left. Quantrill was on a low bed, covered with his army blanket. According to James Wakefield, Frank James came to the Wakefield's after the Civil War, and traded a blanket of his for the one of Quantrill's. Frank and Jesse were pretty famous at that time and the trade was easily made. The blanket of Frank James and a silver watch of Jesse James in 1993 were in possession of a family member some place in southeastern Kentucky. Quantrill's blanket now resides in a Missouri Museum.[139] Unfortunately, James Wakefield could not remember which museum. The watch was given as payment to the Wakefield family for boarding Jesse's horse on one of his several trips to Kentucky after the war. Jesse had run up an $8.00 bill and did not have any cash about him. He offered his watch and James Heady settled the bill.

Watson writes that it was two days later that Quantrill was readied for his trip to Louisville. He further states that Quantrill was covered by a blanket of Frank James that was provided for Quantrill.[140] This could conceivably be the same blanket in the story James Wakefield told to me. Ed Terrell reported to his superiors that he had wounded a Captain Clark, killed two guerrillas, wounded and dispersed the rest. He was ordered to bring Quantrill into Louisville.

Edwards states that three days after the battle, Terrell, against his word to let Quantrill peacefully die at Wakefield house, returned for

Quantrill. Time would have been needed for Terrell to call off his chase of the other men, and time would have been required to send his report, receive his orders, as well as arrange transportation of Quantrill to Louisville. Two or three days to begin his transportation to Louisville, is not unreasonable. Quantrill was placed in a wagon on a bed of straw and transported to Jeffersontown, where he passed the night, and made the remaining 9- or 10-mile trip to Louisville, Kentucky, where he was treated in the military prison hospital. While at the military hospital, Quantrill was treated by the prison doctors. Until it was definitely established that he had no possible chance to recover, he was not allowed visitors.[141]

After a while, and with pleas made on his behalf by a Priest (possibly Hugh J. Brady), he was transferred to the Catholic Hospital and was tended on by the Sisters of Charity. John Ross's mother visited with Quantrill; her son was one of the guerrillas in that last fight. Edwards states she left at 1:00 p.m. on the 4th of June. Quantrill lingered for nearly a month after he was shot. The priest and nuns must have had a significant influence on him, because he converted to Catholicism, after making a long confession of his sins. Before he died at 4:00 p.m. on June 6, 1865, according to Edwards, he awoke and called for water. A Sister of Charity provided him a glass, and touched it to his lips, but he did not drink. According to Edwards she heard him murmur, "Boys, get ready." And then there was a long pause, and one word more, "Steady," and Quantrill was no more. Because of his conversion, Quantrill was allowed burial in the Catholic Cemetery and had paid for a burial plot and marker, in St. Mary's Catholic Cemetery. He was buried in a simple wooden coffin. The priest fearing vandals and perhaps desecration of Quantrill's corpse did not mark the grave, and the ground was returned to its natural condition in order to further obscure the interment. Quantrill's lot in that cemetery is No. 224. Twenty years later, a childhood friend, W.W. Scott, accompanied Quantrill's mother, Mrs. Caroline Clarke Quantrill, to the gravesite. While a request to take Quantrill's remains back to Ohio was denied, permission was given to dig up the body and view the remains. Scott hired a man to exhume the body of Quantrill. Mrs. Caroline Quantrill identified the skull by a chipped tooth as that of her son.[142] Some of the bones were in very fragile condition and disintegrated into the dirt of the grave, where they remain even until today as part of the soil. Having excavated nine Native American burials as an archaeologist, I can attest that often osseous material can turn almost to a paste until exposure to the air can harden it so the bone can be lifted. The bones that could be lifted were placed in a box and under cover of darkness the entire box was stolen.

Upon return to Dover, Ohio, the bones were interred in the family plot in the Dover 4th Street Cemetery minus the skull, and various long bones that were removed and kept by the friend Scott. Some bones ended up at the Kansas Historical Society, and the skull went to the Dover museum until buried in a separate container in the family plot. The skull had been displayed as a relic, and used by Scott's son in a fraternity initiation ceremony before it was returned for burial in Dover. Therefore, there are three resting places for William Clarke Quantrill: parts of his skeleton are in Louisville, some few bones are buried in Higginsville, Mo., with the majority of his skeleton buried in Dover, Ohio.

Reflections on Quantrill

William Clarke Quantrill, like all men, possessed a flawed personality. He could be cruel and desperate, but he loved the south, and he had the ability to instill loyalty and devotion in some of the sternest most desperate and determined of men. He was also a visionary and a sort of a geek when it came to adapting the latest technology to military uses. He improvised tactics that could be likened to the German Blitxkrieg of WWII.

He required that his men be able to shoot proficiently, with either hand from horseback. He armed his men with as many as six revolvers, and one or two double barrel shotguns. This way a small company could win over ten times their number by exceeding the larger force in firepower. He had his men carry extra pre-loaded cylinders in their saddlebags in order to extend their force of fire even more. While the Union and Confederate armies were using single-shot rifles, muzzle-loaders at that, ten men armed with six shots in each of six revolvers and with one two barrel shotgun, would command at least a 380 to 100 shot advantage, over a force of 100. Taking into account that all of those shots fired by Union forces would require as much as a minute to reload, on the ground, and which was practically impossible to do on horseback, the guerrillas, small in number, would prevail far more often than not.

Quantrill and his associates in Kentucky were out in front of the armies in terms of their adoption of technology.

While like his mother in not attending church services, he seemed to find religion at the last and to win the confidence and approval of the priests and nuns. Interestingly, Carl Briehan, a biographer, reflects that many intelligent people in the Southland who persist in depicting Quantrill as a brave and misunderstood commander, must be ignorant of the facts, for there is nothing in the documents to warrant their admiration. As a matter of fact and record, Quantrill never rode with all his men except once – for the pillage of Lawrence, Kansas he was accompanied by three hundred men, but between 150 and 180 were Confederate regulars. At all other times he sent out a small detachment of from twenty to thirty (occasionally as many as 50) under the command of his lieutenants who owed him no actual allegiance.

These petty leaders, who by no means considered themselves Quantrill's subordinates, include Bloody Bill Anderson, George Todd, Bill Gregg, Fletch Taylor, John Thrailkill, John Jarrett, George Shepherd, Cole Younger, Kit Dalton, John Hildebrand, Arch Clements, and occasionally Frank James....It was Quantrill's custom to pillage then put to the torch small undefended towns or villages, deliberately murdering any who dared protest.[143] Even with this scathing indictment, Quantrill had the confidence and loyalty of some 47 men who crossed the Mississippi River with him in January of 1865, and who traveled, fought, and raided with him to the last. It was said that if you were captured by Quantrill, you had a chance for life. If so captured by Bloody Bill, death was certain.

The fact is that the name Quantrill still conjures up images of a heroic guerrilla fighter, or a devil on horseback murdering and pillaging, depending on the politics and proclivities of the individual. He was a complex man.

Chapter 15

The Rape of Mrs. Clark

I got my copy of John N. Edwards book "Noted Guerrillas" in the summer of 1993, on the same trip from Phoenix, Arizona to Louisville, where I had the honor to meet James Wakefield. There was a rare book dealer on Bardstown Road in Louisville, Kentucky, that had a copy of the 1877 book. I confess that I really didn't want the book, because I was searching for a copy of a book by a Bob (later I found was named Thomas Shelby) Watson, entitled "Silent Riders." I am glad I bought the book; however, James Wakefield convinced me "Silent Riders" was a must read to understand the guerrilla war and Quantrill. I bought the book "Noted Guerrillas" and could not find "Silent Riders". It was not until 2008 or 2009 that I learned in a telephone conversation with Tom Watson that he had been "Bob Watson" the News Director for a radio station in Louisville, WAKY in about 1969 or 1970, when he wrote "Silent Riders." It is out of print now, but I highly recommend it to anyone.

I grew up listening to that station and the morning radio Jock, Bill Baily, and his sidekick Reed Yadon, with whom I attended the same school, and although I didn't know him, shared part of my high school years at Dupont Manual High School. In 2009 I was working on a presentation about Ed Terrell, when I called a lady editor of the Taylor County newspaper, named Robin Bass, to see if she could direct me to some people who knew the old stories. I loved her name because it was a combination of my favorite bird and fish. She was very nice and told me I had to speak to Thomas Shelby Watson. It was in this first of two or three calls I made to him when I learned he not only wrote the book "Silent Riders" I was searching for, but also had written the newly released "Confederate Guerrilla Sue Mundy." I later ran across a copy of "Silent Riders", and through it and some telephone conversations, Tom Watson filled gaps in my research as well as corroborating some of my information. I appreciate the work he and author Steve Wright have done, because I too have wandered the fields, farms, and cemeteries in order to research my stories. This leads me to tell of a story I found in "Noted Guerrillas" that I freely admit I did not fully understand until I began doing more research on the old newspaper reports of the *Louisville Daily Journal* and the *Louisville Daily Democrat* for 1865. It is the story of a rape and sexual assault on a Nelson County woman that almost precluded the remaining guerrillas of Quantrill from surrendering and taking the oath of allegiance, allowing them to return home.

There seems to be some confusion about the date when the rape of Mrs. Mary Clark occurred. Yeatman states it was in late April or early May[144], and Watson gives the date of April 25th 1865.[145] Edwards does not give a date. Mrs. Clark lived in Nelson County. Some say she lived in Bardstown and others in the town of New Haven, but wherever she lived, she was riding alone to get medicine or medical attention. While riding outside of town in a rural setting she was approached by two horsemen, John Brothers, and a man named Haskins or Hoskins, who attacked Mrs. Clark and sexually assaulted her. This was Victorian America, and crimes of this nature were not only uncommon, but also looked upon as a particularly atrocious crime against non-combatants. The attack and rape of Mrs. Clark when it came to the attention of General Palmer caused the general to suspend any of the guerrillas operating in that area from surrendering and taking the oath of allegiance. Palmer seemed much more just than General Burbridge, but, when he made war, he made a mean war, and when he made peace he made a mean peace.[146] This outrageous act perpetrated upon Mrs. Clark was rumored by some to be committed by the Missouri guerrillas. This was especially hard for Quantrill's men, who were told by their leader to quit the war. They had been operating in an environment, foreign to them, since mid-January and most of those with whom they were aligned, had been killed or imprisoned. More importantly they were innocent of the assault. One Arm Sam Berry and William Clarke Quantrill seemed to me to be trying to gain some credibility when they talked Bill Marion out of killing the Spencer County judge. To gain an ally like a judge might just be enough to be allowed to take the oath and go free, and now this outrage was laid at their door. The only choice was to bring in the guilty parties, or be tried as an outlaw, and have a fine chance to be hanged. At this time Berry, extended through a third party, a man named Kirk, an overture to Palmer to come in and surrender; however, Palmer issued order No. 64 that placed a $500.00 reward, dead or alive, on the two men who committed the act, and then stated that no paroles would be issued until these men were killed or turned in for prosecution. This was extremely important to Quantrill's men as well as a few Kentucky guerrillas like Berry.

There is little specific to note in the Louisville newspapers about the assault on Mrs. Clark, but reports on Texas and Brothers are later mentioned in connection with the incident. The real story lies not with the crime, but with how the criminals were brought to justice at the hands of the guerrillas, and Major Cyrus Wilson. Wilson entered into an agreement with One Arm Berry and Dick Mitchell that if they would turn over Texas, he would write for them a parole, providing they had murdered no person for money, or Union sentiments, and that, if he should find they were accused of any murder, he would retake them if possible.[147] Brothers and Texas had ridden with Berry, but were not Quantrill's men. According to Edwards, Frank James and William Hulse went on the scout for Texas and Brothers. Edwards states that Texas was likely named Jonathan Billingboy, but Hoskins or Haskins was probably his name. Hulse and James came upon the two men in the company of a third man in no way connected to the outrage at a farm house just as they were sitting down to dinner. In the version of the story related by Edwards in 1877, James and Hulse realized that the three men would likely be in the fight against their two. James said, "Yes, there are three. If there were six it would not matter." With that, the two men dismounted and tied their horses in the timber. The men they sought were at dinner, indifferent and unaware. Throwing back the door of the dining room, the two guerrillas strode in, wrathful and unceremoniously. Frank James called out in a placid, penetrating voice: "Keep your seats, all of you; keep your hands up; keep your eyes to the front." Brothers, desperately grabbed for his revolver, and Frank James blew his brains out across the table. The other two did not move.[148] According to Edwards, Texas, who had been with Brothers at the assault on Mrs. Clark, was later killed by Allen Parmer.

Newspaper reports tell a different story, although it is probable that James did kill Brothers. James and Hulse wanted to go to Sayers house in Deatsville, to ascertain if Texas was with Brothers when Mrs. Clark was outraged. Edwards further relates that One Arm Berry was well acquainted with Texas, and went to Sayers to find him, but, the fact remained that until he was surrendered, Berry, nor any of the other guerrillas could take the oath and go home free men. A June 6th newspaper report reads as follows: "Texas" the guerrilla: This notorious outlaw, who has been the terror to our loyal people for some time, has been captured at last. He fell into the clutches of Maj. Cyrus Wilson, the indefatigable guerrilla-hunter. The major had to resort to strategy to gain his point. He entered into an agreement with two guerrillas – One-armed Berry and Mitchell – that if they would surrender "Texas" they would be released from taking the oath. The two consented to the bargain and started in search of him. They found him and delivered him up to Maj. Wilson in Taylorsville on Saturday. Mitchell and Berry were released, according to the promise, and "Texas" brought to Louisville yesterday under strong guard.[149] On the same day the Louisville Daily Democrat wrote: For some time past the citizens of the southern portion of the State have been bothered by a certain set of guerrillas or robbers, under the command of one who styled himself "Texas." This notorious guerrilla was brought to Louisville last evening on the train by Maj. Wilson, and lodged in the Second Street Prison. Berry and Dick Mitchell, who surrendered to Maj. Wilson, were paroled…Texas was one of the party who, in connection with Brothers, committed the horrible outrage upon a lady near Bardstown. He should meet that punishment which his crime so richly deserves.[150] Therefore, we see that Texas neither was killed by Allen Parmer nor escaped being surrendered to the law. This can largely be credited to General Palmer for his quick determination that this man Texas had to be turned in or all the guerrillas would share his fate. I think it also points up the fact that the Missouri guerrillas of Quantrill did not want to be placed in the same category as a rapist.

On June 13th Major Cyrus Wilson wrote a letter to the *Louisville Daily Journal,* which was published on June 15th. It read:

> *To the editors of the Louisville Journal:*
>
> *Having seen an article in a newspaper published at Lebanon, Ky., censuring me for the terms upon which I released two men named Berry and Mitchell, I wish to state to the public what those terms were and the reason for making them.*
>
> *A person calling himself Texas, and well known by that name had committed a series of outrages in the neighborhood of Bard-*

stown, and had concealed himself so effectually in the thick woods of that region that he could not be arrested by any of the ordinary means within the control of the military authorities. To affect his capture I made an agreement with Berry and Mitchell, in consequence of which Texas was given into my hands by them. And this was the agreement made with Berry and Mitchell: That, if they would give Texas into my hands, I would parole them, and they should go free for any offenses they had committed, provided they had murdered no person for money or Union sentiments, and that, if I should find they were accused of any murder, I would retake them, if possible.

I have made no terms with other parties who have surrendered to me than those stated above. Cyrus J. Wilson, formerly major 26th Ky. Inf.[151]

On June 16th, another article discussed both Texas and Brothers, giving more detail:

"Texas": It will be remembered that some time ago a diabolical outrage was committed upon the person of a respectable lady in the neighborhood of Bardstown, Ky., by two fiends in human shape. Maj. John M. Palmer offered a reward for the capture of the two men, but all efforts to capture them proved fruitless until a short time ago. Lt. H. A. Porter, with a company of Confederates, most all of whom were from Missouri, was on their way to Bardstown, Kentucky with the intention of surrendering themselves to the Federal authorities. A short distance from town they encountered three guerrillas, and succeeded in killing one, capturing one, and the other escaped. The one captured proved to be the desperado calling himself "Texas." The one killed proved to be of like ilk named Brothers – both of who have been recognized as the individuals who committed the outrage. Who the other was is not known... Two of Lt. Porter's men remained with "Texas." And delivered him safely into the hands of the Federal authorities, where he is now in heavy irons, preparing to meet death at an early day. The remainder of Porter's men withdrew their intention of surrender and have been in the State ever since, in quiet and peaceable rendezvous, awaiting the action of Gen. Palmer in their cases. The deportment

of Porter and his men is spoken of as being excellent....Gen. Palmer has addressed a communication to President Johnson, asking him to allow Lt. Porter and his Confederates to come in and be fully pardoned from the past course they have pursued...it will most likely be granted.

There is no doubt that the most dangerous and effective guerrilla force in Kentucky was made up of Billy Magruder, One-armed Sam Berry, Bill Marion, and Sue Mundy. They were joined in 1865 by Quantrill's Raiders, an equally ferocious band of Confederates, and in every way just as effective. By June of 1865 most all of the guerrillas were so desperately hunted, captured, incarcerated, tried, and executed, that they just wanted to quit. Samuel One-armed Berry was the only one of the five major guerrilla leaders left free in the heartland of Kentucky. Berry, prior to the war, had been a school teacher, who as a child, was left at Pleasant Hill near Harrodsburg in the care of the Shakers. It was there he lost his arm in a hay mowing accident. There were wrongs, real and perceived, that led him to his life as a guerrilla warrior. He saw, however, his friends suffer terrible fates: Sue Mundy hanged, Bill Marion shot dead, Billy Magruder awaiting trial and execution and the mortally wounded, Quantrill imprisoned, and awaiting death. He was now riding with the dregs of the guerrilla cup, Brothers and Texas. Quantrill's men wanted out as did Berry. Allen Parmer, John Porter, Dick Mitchell, William Hulse, Frank James, Bud and Doniphan Pence, perhaps Payne Stone and two or three others of the Missouri men were not as well known in Kentucky for their bad deeds, and indeed they seemed to be well liked. Unfortunately for Berry he was fresh on many peoples' minds, because of his shootings, killings and rape of Negro women. Therefore he got bad press, as did Cyrus Wilson for writing Berry his parole. On June 26, 1865, a Louisville newspaper article appeared that was an answer to Cyrus Wilson's letter to the *Louisville Daily Journal.* It was printed in the *Lebanon Loyal Enterprise,* and carried in the Democrat, and says:

We charge Berry with having killed three Negro men, deliberately and in cold blood, in Spencer County. We charge him in the death of Weatherton and Lee, two brave and good men who were murdered in Springfield, on the first of December, 1864. We charge him with having deliberately committed rape on three colored women, in Nelson County; once in the presence of the mistress of one of the girls. We charge him with having robbed Perryville, Springfield, Texas, Pottsville, and Nevada, Kentucky. We charge him with having shot at Federal soldiers; with having murdered colored recruits, and of being the tool in the hands of the Bloomfield rebels, to prevent colored men from enlisting. If these charges are not grave enough Major, we will add to them. Now for Mitchell. We charge Mitchell with having a command of a squad of men who were with Quantrill when eight Federal soldiers were deliberately murdered near New Market, Ky. – with being with Berry when he committed his numerous murders, and with having been a robber for two years.[152]

Even with this scathing list of charges it is apparent that Mitchell's charges seem in the line of duty regarding the New Market killings and he had not been in Kentucky for more than six months. Berry's charges, however, carry more weight, largely because he had been active longer within the state. It may have been this article or condemnation from the public, or perhaps a perception that Berry continued to be a threat, but Berry's parole was later discounted by Palmer. In an August 27, 1865, newspaper article appearing in Louisville, reported:

Saturday, One Arm Berry, well-known desperate guerrilla, made his appearance in Bardstown. He was accompanied by twelve men. They remained in town long enough to get drunk, but committed no disturbances. Berry was paroled by Maj. Cyrus J. Wilson, some weeks since, but he started out with his new company from Taylorsville, and his movements are looked upon as indicative of a disposition on his part to disregard his obligations.[153]

Berry seemed to me to be drifting between quitting his guerrilla life, and starting anew, but with no war to fight. His press seems equally conflicted with their reports. On October 27th, a report states that Between Fairfield and Bloomfield, in Nelson County, on the afternoon of Monday, the 23rd, a gentleman traveler was robbed on the highway of his horse, saddle, bridle, and saddlebags, his over coat and body-coat, and pocket book containing $200.00 in paper money. The highwaymen were One Arm Berry, Owens, and a brother, it is supposed….They left the party a lame mare and an old army saddle....our informant adds, that the guerrillas on the one hand and the Federals on the other having heretofore deprived the inhabitants of their arms and best horses, outlaws assume that they can carry on their nefarious practices with impunity.[154]

Another report that same day stated: We are informed that Sam Berry, the one armed guerrilla, with several others of his like, are committing depredations in Nelson County. A gentleman was robbed of $240.00 near Bloomfield day before yesterday. They were at Deatsville yesterday. They were finely mounted and dressed superbly.

On November 4th, Berry was seen with 12 others in Meadeville, where they stayed all night at the home of James Patterson. They moved on toward Union Star, and on Wednesday morning Berry and six of his men returned going through Bewleyville, proclaiming death to all who had been in the army white and black except for drafted negroes, who had returned to their homes, and were working for their old masters. Berry and his party stated that the Yankees would not let them stay at home, and that they intended to make their way to Mexico, and designed to harm no one. A part of Marion's gang is said to be with Berry. He told Patterson he had not taken the oath, and he never would. The citizens of Kentucky have no sympathy for these proscribed gangs, and they are nowhere harbored willingly.[155]

Berry and his band were reported in Carrolton, Meade and Breckenridge Counties, Bewleyville, Stephensport, and Union Star. In Bewleyville Berry and fifteen men robbed the citizens of their valuables. In Union Star they also robbed. When at Union Star the gang made for the home of Capt. George Hammers formerly of the Union Army, for the purpose of robbing it. Mr. Hammers hearing their approach closed his house and made preparations to resist any attack that might be made. The band came for the house at full tilt, and when within some few yards of the place Hammers fired a shot, mortally wounding one of Berry's men, who fell from his horse. This unexpected resistance made the guerrillas terror-stricken and they left the town in double-quick, going in the direction of Clifton Mills.

One Arm Berry was tried by a court-martial in Louisville Sept. 13th, 1865. In it Wilson was asked if he signed Berry's parole under direct authority of General Palmer. "Well, I didn't know whether I did or not," Wilson said. "It was the first parole I had given, the first of the kind."[156] Wilson further said this was the only avenue he had open to capture "Texas." Contemporary newspaper articles differ with authors on the capture and trial of Berry. It was reported in the *Louisville Daily Democrat*, on November 7th that the raid on the home of Capt. Hammers resulted in the wounding of Tom Berry, Samuel O. Berry's brother.

It is interesting to me that Captain Hammers, who had only one leg, was successful in driving away One Arm Berry. I suspect Berry could have used a helping hand, and Hammers a leg up. Another interesting item came out of that news story. Tom Berry, who is in prison now, is really Tom F. Henderson, of Fayette County, Kentucky, and got the name of Berry by his mother, who was a widow marrying the father of One-armed Berry, Samuel O. Berry, Sr. [157] So it seems Berry and about fifteen men were still raiding and robbing in Meade and Breckenridge Counties in November of 1865.

On December 4, 1865, Berry was reported to have been in Bloomfield on Wednesday December 1st. Berry and his men entered the town, hitched their horses, and commenced an attack of a serious nature on Mr. Tinsley and his son. Several shots were fired by both parties.... The Tinsleys finally drove the villains out.... In the affray Berry was wounded. Neither Mr. Tinsley nor his son was hurt. Nothing has since been heard of them.[158]

On the 11th of December in a lengthy article it reported the capture of One Arm Berry and one of his men, King White, near Bloomfield. Berry, who was shot in the gunfight with Tinsley and his son, was seriously wounded. His men left him at the home of a Mr. Mark Thomas. Captain Cyrus Wilson and twelve men left Louisville to capture Berry and King White. White was seen alone on the road to Brunerstown, in the forenoon, and after a short chase was quickly overtaken. Wilson surrounded the home of Mr. Mark Thomas, and found Berry in bed suffering from the wound he received from Mr. Tinsley. Berry stated "he would rather surrender to Major Wilson than any other man he knew of" ...On the road to Louisville, Berry became sick and he was placed in a light covered wagon.... Arriving in Louisville, the wagon was halted in front of Maj, Gen. Palmer's headquarters at Berry's request, and he asked for the general. The general made an appearance, and looked in the face of Berry long enough to hear him plead for pitiful mercy. The general turned away silently and the procession moved to the military prison.[159]

It is interesting to me that the sweetheart of Sue Mundy (M. J. Clarke) was Mollie Thomas. In his book "Confederate Guerrilla Sue Mundy," Tom Watson states in a caption below the photographs of the twin girls, Mollie and Martha that during the war a Union officer reported to his superiors: "that the Thomas neighborhood is Rebel headquarters," and added that it was where wounded rebels were taken so they could recover in a safe place. Dr. Isaac McClaskey lived a few miles away and would attend to Rebel wounds.[160] Molly and Martha's father, Remy, or one of his relations, could have, and possibly did, provide the safe house for Berry.

On December 22, 1865, it was reported Berry, White and Henderson would be put on trial immediately after the disposal of the Well's case.[161] One Arm Berry was finally tried on February 10th, 1866 for 11 separate murders, and was condemned to be hanged March 3, 1866. As a result of the appeals for clemency by Berry's relatives and friends their came a surge of petitionary letters, including one from George Prentice, who described Berry as "the most humane and best of them all." John Palmer commuted the sentence to 10 years of hard labor at Sing Sing Penitentiary in New York. Berry died after serving seven years.[162]

Chapter 16

Billy Magruder and Sue Mundy

In the year 1865, sometime between March 12th and October 20th, Henry Magruder dictated his confession. Magruder and Sue Mundy are inextricably linked with Henry Medkiff (Metcalf) because they were captured by Cyrus Wilson at the Cox tobacco barn. Mundy and Magruder are also linked in their deaths on the scaffold, a fate Medkiff avoided. Mundy was a member of John Hunt Morgan's command, and was at the Newburg, Indiana raid of Adam Johnson, and served at Fort Donelson, where he was captured and sent to Camp Morton, Illinois. While there, he managed along with some others, to over-power their guards and escape. Both Clarke and Magruder were enlisted Confederate soldiers. Magruder escaped capture when Morgan and others were caught at Buffington Island attempting to get back into Kentucky. There have been so many books, histories, articles, newspaper reports and the like that have documented the guerrilla deeds of Magruder, Clarke or Mundy, Marion, and Berry, that events are oftentimes confused due to the fact that two or more of these bands of men came together for operations, and then were dispersed into the countryside to make individual raids on their own. It was hard to identify just whose men were whose, and who the leaders at a specific event happened to be. The guerrilla warriors and their raids bore some resemblance to a lava lamp, with images forming and reforming, only to dissolve and come back differently.

Accounts of the various raids and crimes against the Union made by Magruder and Mundy will exhibit some overlapping with regard to participants and debate about who did what and when. I plan to document some of the major incidents that led to their sentences of death, and eventual execution.

There were several occurrences that brought heat on these two guerrilla warriors. One of these incidents occurred in January of 1865. On

January 7th, a newspaper report in Louisville stated: A discharged soldier by the name of Caldwell, lately of the 15th Ky. Inf. Was murdered on the Bardstown Pike by Sue Mundy's thieves last Wednesday [Jan. 4th][163] On that same day a more in-depth article reported:

> *During Thursday night and yesterday morning two squads of guerrillas, one under the command of Henry Magruder and the other of Sue Mundy's gang, have been operating in the vicinity of Lebanon Junction, and have committed crimes which are almost too revolting to relate. Without the least cause or provocation they murdered five members of the 15th Ky. Inf., in cold blood, one at his home Thursday night, and the other four at Lebanon Junction last evening between four and five o'clock.... On Thursday night seven men under the command of Magruder went to the house of Edward Caldwell, who resides at Bullitt County, about two miles from Carpenter's Station on the L&N RR. They entered the house and remained some time, pretending to be very friendly with Caldwell. They then invited him out to look at a horse, but Caldwell refused to go, remarking at the time that they (the guerrillas) wanted to kill him. One of the men, a cousin of Caldwell, said that no one should harm him while he was present. Upon this assurance Caldwell went out, but he had not more than got out the door before they fired upon him, killing him instantly. The body of Caldwell was pierced with eight balls. He was a nephew of Mrs. David L. Ross of Louisville.... In regard to the killing of the four men at Lebanon Junction...A party of guerrillas, said to be Sue Mundy's gang, arrived in Lebanon Junction about 4 o'clock in the evening. They met there four men who belonged to the 15th Ky. Inf., and without the least provocation at once commenced firing upon them, killing three of their number and wounding the fourth. One of the gang went up to the wounded man and cut his throat from ear to ear.... The guerrillas, after committing the foul deed, turned their attention to the destruction of the rolling stock of the L&N RR. A number of boxcars, which were stationed on the side track, were set on fire and entirely consumed.*[164]

Sergeant Caldwell was home on leave to bury his father who was near death, and in fact died just before Caldwell arrived home. Mundy,

Magruder, and according to Magruder's later statement, Tom Henry, and another unidentified man were headed to the Caldwell house. When the guerrillas arrived, they robbed the house and visitors of their money. They took Edward's tobacco and pipe. Edward gave them his pistol. The name Sue Mundy was used when they referred to Clarke. The family knew Magruder and Maraman, and when Edward was asked to go out to the barn with his brother George to get a horse. Mrs. Caldwell, afraid that her son would be killed pleaded for his life, but Edward assured her that he would be all right. He was wrong and now his mother needed two coffins. This murder, for that is what it was, was totally unnecessary, and portrayed the guerrillas by shining a bright light on their worst efforts.

Metcalf (Medkiff), although tried for it, was likely not at the killing, and Tom Henry was probably the unidentified man, or was mistaken for Metcalf. Metcalf and Henry were said to closely resemble one another. Later that night, they rode down to Wilson Creek, Magruder's old home neighborhood in Bullitt County near the Nelson County line. Near the Mt. Carmel Church, they found discharged Federal Private Henry Mulligan and ended his life as well.[165] A January 11th report told of a December 29th murder by a band of guerrillas under Sue Mundy, of a Lt. Charles E. Spalding in Washington Co., Ky., He was murdered in cold blood while on a visit to the parents and friends of his young wife, to whom he was married last July.[166]

On Tuesday January 17, according to a *Louisville Daily Journal* report that appeared two days later, it read:

> *On Tuesday a concentration of guerrilla bands operating in the neighborhood took place, and at 3 o'clock in the afternoon, headed by Capt. Pratt and Henry Magruder, the outlaws numbering about 40 men, made an attack on Bardstown. The town was garrisoned by detachments of Federal soldiers, in command of Capt. G. W. Nichols Co. A, 54th, Mtd. Inf. The guerrillas succeeded in reaching the railroad depot, which they set on fire, hoping that the conflagration would attract the attention of the soldiers, and that they would be able to reach the jail and rescue Robinson with but little effort. The building burned rapidly, but the fire was kept from spreading. Pratt and Magruder dashed wildly up and down the streets, shouting to their men and urging them on toward the jail. Our soldiers*

fired on them from the courthouse, and kept them at bay. Captains Nichols and Robert H. Young, of the Ky. Mtd. Inf., superintended operations, and the outlaws were greeted with showers of musket balls. Lt. Robert A. Hancock, with a handful of men, charged the desperadoes in the street. After a brisk fight, the guerrillas were driven from town. Capt. Pratt was shot and mortally wounded. He died at 5 o'clock yesterday morning. Sue Mundy and the scoundrel Marion were both severely wounded, and removed to places of safety by their friends.[167] From Bardstown the raiders rode east toward Simpsonville and Shelbyville. In Simpsonville, they robbed the citizens of $1000.00 in money, a dozen gold watches, and a number of silver ones. Berry was in this group of 25 men. Berry rode his horse into the post office, and robbed the mail and the postmaster. When the guerrillas were told that the Shelbyville stage coach had just left the town, the guerrillas quickly rode to overtake it. The men robbed the passengers which included a lady and her two children, who were made to get out of the stage at gunpoint, and stand in the freezing snow. After stealing all the money they could get at the stage, they proceeded to rob the toll gate keeper of $145.00 and then the Hays Spring grocery of Mr. O.C. Curry. They also burned the bridges over East Fork, Cox's Creek, Floyds Fork, and the Salt River Bridge.[168]

On January 22, 1865, a Sunday, approximately 900 to 1000 cattle were being driven from Fort Nelson in Jessamine County to Louisville, where they would be slaughtered for food supply to the Union army. Most of the troops from Fort Nelson were Negro. There were between 80 and 100 drovers bringing the cattle north to Louisville. The soldiers driving the cattle were black with white officers, and were from the 5th Regiment of Colored Troops. An article in the *Louisville Daily Journal* on January 26th, reported the incidents as follows:

A drove of cattle, about 900 head was son the way to Louisville yesterday from Camp Nelson, guarded by 80 Negro soldiers, detailed from various regiments. The day being cold and no danger being apprehended the soldiers were allowed to straggle along by themselves, while the white officers stopped to warm themselves at various houses on the road. One half of the command rode in front *of the cattle, while the other portion kept in the rear of the drove. The cattle and guards were not yet out of sight of Simpsonville, when 15 guerrillas, headed by desperate Coulter, dashed into the town. Three of the Negro officers were loafing in the tavern at the time, but succeeded in making their escape from the outlaws. The guerrillas robbed the citizens of the place of goods amounting to about $1,200.00, when they started in pursuit of the Negro troops guarding the cattle. They were not long in overtaking them, as the citizens of Simpsonville, soon after their departure from the place, heard rapid firing down the road. In about a half an hour, the guerrillas returned, loaded down with booty, and stated they had killed 25 negroes….Not more than half a mile this side of the village a terrible scene was presented to view. The ground was stained with blood, and the bodies of the Negro soldiers were stretched out along the road….The cattle stampeded and as soon as the advance guard learned of what was going on in the rear, each individual in blue, made a tall scamper for a place of safety. Coulter, One Arm Berry and Sue Mundy were the leaders of the murderous gang. In making the attack the guerrillas were only armed with navy revolvers. After the attack, they took good care to secure the arms and ammunition of the slain…The guerrillas were traveling toward Shelbyville at last accounts.*[169]

The *Shelby Record* of February 21, 1913, perhaps written by W.J. Lampton who chronicled the history of Shelby County for the *Record*, and who related stories about many of the guerrilla fighters, read:

A thousand head of cattle were being driven from Central Kentucky and through Shelbyville, stopped for the night at the farm… less than four miles west of this city. The cattle belonged to the U. S. Government and were being taken to Louisville, to be distributed among the soldiers in the Union army. The cattle had been turned into the lot and fed, the soldiers had erected their tents, and the officers were quartered in the farmhouse on the place.

Suddenly there was a loud knocking on the outer door, and a white man, who said he was employed on an adjoining farm…demanded admittance and a chance to speak with the captain…he told the captain, that the cattle were ruining a field of un-shucked corn belonging to Squire Matthews, a Union sympathizer. The captain asked what could be done. The man asked how many men he had and was told there were near one hundred, and there were one thousand cattle. The man, who was in fact a guerrilla spy, suggested the captain go out and instruct the men to each turn out ten head of cattle and in that way there would be no confusion. He said, too, that he would take the matter in charge himself, but that he had no suitable boots in which to tramp through the snow. The officer then told the man to take his boots and superintend the work. After getting the boots, the guerrilla spy…left for parts unknown, presumably towards the Spencer County line, while the Negro soldiers got the cattle out of the corn as best they could.

The next morning the soldiers and the cattle started for Louisville, about half of the men in front and the other half in the rear of the herd. As they passed through Simpsonville, the captain stopped in a store to warm his almost frozen feet and buy a pair of boots. The cattle and the soldiers, in the meantime proceeded towards Louisville. Suddenly, while the officer was looking at the boots, someone ran into the store and shouted: "Here comes Coulter and his guerrillas." The quality, price, and size of the boots had no longer any interest for the officer, and ran he out of and down under the store-room, where he remained in hiding until after his men had been massacred and the guerrillas had passed back through Simpsonville, on their way east.

The soldiers and cattle had gotten to a point on the state pike… not much more than a half-mile west of Simpsonville, when Captain Coulter and his fourteen guerrillas yelling like very devils and shooting their pistols in the air, rode rapidly towards the panic-stricken rear guard of the herd of cattle. They began shooting down the men without compunction, who on their part, made no effort to return the fire or to protect themselves in any way. Only one shot was fired by a soldier, and it went wild. In less than twenty minutes nineteen of the soldiers were dead, and more than twenty were wounded, mortally, the guerrillas believed. To get to the guard in front was impossible, on account of the excited cattle in the roadway, and the guerrillas turned back towards Simpsonville, believing they had killed every man in the rear of the herd. Every man in front of the herd made his escape, as did three in the rear guard.

One of them was found lying "flat on his face" on the ground, an hour and a half afterwards, by Capt. George and others who went to the scene of the trouble. He was unhurt as was one who hid himself under the bed of a commissary wagon that was overturned early in the action, and was not discovered by the guerrillas. The third, who was far up in the front of the rear guard, started on a run as soon as he heard the firing.

The man reached a farmers house without being seen by anybody. He immediately divested himself of his soldier's clothing and running to the woodpile, began chopping very enthusiastically. He was still at it several hours later, and when he was asked about the killing said: "Fore God, boss, I don't know nothin'.... All I know is I has to cut this white man's wood".... The white officer came out from under the store, and without waiting to buy boots, left hurriedly for Louisville. The nineteen Negroes that were killed were buried in a long trench near where they were massacred. The twenty wounded men were taken to Simpsonville by Capt. George and other citizens of that community, and attended to for several days, when Government officials sent a lot of ambulances and they were taken to Louisville.[170]

Henry Clay "Billy" Magruder was in this Simpsonville raid, and he discussed his part in his confession that was published by Cyrus Wilson, after Magruder was hanged. Magruder describes the Simpsonville raid:

The weather was bitterly cold. Here we heard of Government trains and cattle on the Shelbyville Pike. Of course we went over. We started from Thomas's, over ice and snow, at 8 A. M., reached Simpsonville at 10 o'clock A. M. I rode straight into town, and saw six or eight cavalry horses hitched. The citizens told us that a "train" of cattle had just passed. I sent Dick Mitchell toward Louisville to see what was coming from that direction. By this time the Negroes fired on him. He came back, and the Negroes thinking him alone, came on. I formed and charged them with a yell. As we came in view, thundering down on them, they fired a few shots, and throwing down their arms, ran in among the cattle. At the first fire they killed my horse. I was mounted again in a moment, and went for them with a yell. They had no officers, or at least they did not show themselves. Well to make a long story short, we just went in among the cattle and killed the Negroes wherever we could find them. I don't know how many I killed, but I got plenty of wool.

I got hold of a Government agent, and took three hundred dollars from him. My men numbered 15. They were – Whitesides, Merryfield, Froman (1), Froman (2), Johnson (1), Johnson (2), Hughes, Jimmy Jones, Marion, Clark, Colter, Magruder commanding.[171]

Clark could be Sue Mundy, although Jerome Clarke states he was not at this raid, because he was recuperating from a gunshot wound to his hand sustained in the Bardstown raid a week earlier. The Clark that Magruder mentions is probably not Quantrill. And, while Magruder does not mention Bill Davison, he was riding with Coulter and could have taken part.

The Simpsonville raid was not really a massacre. There were 15 guerrillas that were out-numbered more than five to one. The fact is that the Federal officers and their men likely felt their numbers would preclude an attack by a small party of raiders. That was a serious mistake in judgment. It seems to me to show arrogance on the part of the Federals, especially the officer that did not want to go outside and direct his soldiers, who later hid under the store, and did not emerge until after the guerrillas had left the area. It was either stupidity or naivety to give someone you did not know your footwear, and to take the word of someone you don't know that could compromise your command. The Negro soldiers were obviously poorly trained and poorly led and additionally split their force by placing one half their troops in front of the 1,000 cattle and one half behind making it even more difficult to give aid each to the other. The guerrillas on the other hand had few if any long range weapons, only their navy revolvers, and charged into the soldiers without fear, yelling and firing. If that 40-man rear guard was properly trained and willing the guerrillas would have been decimated or at least driven away. The press said it was a massacre, and although it may have been a rout, a massacre it wasn't.

The Simpsonville and Bardstown raids and the raids at Samuel's depot, including the Bullitt County murders of Edward Caldwell and Henry Mulligan, were not playing well for the guerrillas. Perception can be your best friend, or your worst enemy. And, although the guerrillas were attacking the infrastructure, bridges and railroads, robbing trains, and U. S. post offices, and army caravans and cattle trains, as they should have been, the perception of the guerrilla's actions by the public, became one of cruelty.

Henry Clay Magruder's trial, unlike the trial of Sue Mundy, seemed to be fair; Magruder even declared it so. It commenced September 14, 1865 and extended through September 28, with the result in a sentence to be hanged on October 20, 1865. The October 20th newspaper report on the day of his execution, stated:

> *October 20 – This day Henry C. Magruder will look for the last time upon his mother earth. After a tedious and impartial trial, he was condemned to die upon the scaffold. The sentence will be carried out privately in the courtyard of the Louisville Military prison, between the hours of 12 and 4 o'clock*[172]*.... The October 21st news report stated October 21 – Execution of Henry C. Magruder: This solemn event, which has been anticipated with variant feelings by the friends of the condemned and by the people of Kentucky at large, took place yesterday at the Louisville Military Prison.... The parting with his mother was said to have been deeply affecting. During the day and up to his last moments he was attended by his faithful counsel, Gen. Walter C. Whitaker and Fr. Brady (probably Fr. Hugh Joseph Brady), his spiritual advisor.... In alluding to his fate he said to Gen. Whitaker, "'Tis hard, but I reckon it is fair."... About 100 spectators exclusive of those belonging to the prison, were admitted to the court-yard. At fifteen minutes after 3 o'clock, the field band of the 125th U. S. Colored Inf. gave note of dreadful preparation. Under direction of Capt. J. P. Neal, Provost Martial, the above regiment was formed in a hollow square around the scaffold, which stood in the center of the yard, facing westward, as if to show the sun in its decline typical of the prisoner's waning life. An awful stillness pervaded the enclosure of the prison during the few moments of waiting for the approach of Magruder. About 20 minutes before 4 o'clock, the prisoner emerged from his cell, supported on either side by Gen. Whitaker and Fr. Brady. With a firm and dignified air, holding a cigar in his mouth, Magruder passed the door of his cell, through an aisle of armed guards, and ascended the gallows.... Capt. Neal, in a subdued voice, read to the prisoner*

> *the proceedings, findings, and sentence of the court.... The reading occupied about ten minutes.... He was then asked if he had anything to say, to which he replied "Not a word.".... Mr. Harris placed the prisoner on the trap, adjusted the rope around his neck, drew a white cap over his head, and at ten minutes to four o'clock Henry C. Magruder was launched into eternity.... The body gyrated and quivered for five or six minutes before life was extinct.*[173]

Interestingly, Magruder asked that the cigar butt that he was smoking be given to his mother. Billy Magruder had joined his friend Sue Mundy in death.

Henry Metcalf (Medkiff) was the third man captured in the Cox tobacco barn on March 12, 1865. He was also sentenced to be hung on the 23rd of May, 1865, but his sentence was commuted to five years in prison. An Oct. 14, 1865 newspaper article stated that by special order No. 204...the unexpired term of the sentence in the case of Metcalf, the guerrilla, has been remitted and the prisoner ordered to be released.[174] Henry Metcalf had been released the previous day, October 13, 1865. After the war, Metcalf became a farm implement salesman, and traveled doing business in many of the areas of which he was familiar from when he rode briefly with Mundy and Magruder. It was probably during the performance of these duties that he visited John Cox to inquire about Mundy's pistols.

Chapter 17

The James Irvin Newton Affair

I began researching information about Billy Shacklett in 2008, and started with locating the Meadeville Cemetery from a map that was drawn for me at the request of Mr. Board, of Breckenridge County. The cemetery was not shown on the USCGS maps of the area available to me. I had met him when I was researching the Sue Mundy Capture site. When I went to the Meadeville Cemetery, it was grown up with weeds, and deer were bedding among the toppled tombstones. Sometime in the past, cattle were allowed to graze in the cemetery, causing some of the stones to be toppled, broken, or to lean precariously. While I was in the cemetery, I took the time to see other of the graves stones and muse over them. The first sheriff of Meade County, Kentucky was buried there as well as many others notable in Meade County history.

Toward the north side of the cemetery, I noticed a newer stone that stood in stark contrast to the stones from the 1830's that appeared ancient in comparison. I was drawn to this stone, and it opened for me a mystery. It was a heavy granite stone with two bronze tablets affixed to it. One of the tablets was placed flat across the top of the monument, while a second was placed vertically on the front of the heavy rectangular monument. The bronze tablet on top of the stone read:

James Irvin Newton
Pvt Co C
12th Ky Cavalry
1819 – 1865

The vertical tablet held this mysterious message:
October 1898

IN COMMERATION OF
JAMES IRVIN NEWTON
HUSBAND OF ELANDER RHODES NEWTON
SHOT AND KILLED IN JULY OF 1865
BY THE NIGHT RIDERS
AT HIS HOME ACROSS THE ROAD
FROM THIS
MEADEVILLE CEMETERY

What else can a Civil War researcher do but raise his eyebrows and begin investigating. James Irvin Newton was a Meadeville blacksmith when the Civil War began. Meadeville was a hotbed of Rebel sentiment. It was the place where Bill Marion held court for Wathen and Board. It was some three miles or so from where Sue Mundy and Billy Magruder were captured, and it was the site of the battle of the Sheep Shed. Many raiders used the place, for safe houses there abounded, and the site lay some two miles or so from the David Henry house. Meadeville was a stagecoach stop and a vibrant town with a hotel, two blacksmith shops, two stores, a post office, and a number of houses over its two mile length.

When I first saw the stone, the thought that a Union soldier from a Rebel town could come back home and take up where he left off would likely be the ultimate challenge. As with almost all 150-year-old stories, there is usually more than one version. It is so with this case.

The story of the Newton murder was personally told to me by members of the Newton Family attending their reunion, held in the Meadeville Cemetery on October 11, 2009. I was working for the Meade County *News Standard* at the time, and writing history stories for the paper as topics presented themselves. Monday, Tuesday, and Wednesdays, I worked as a proofreader. I noticed on the bulletin board where reporters could look to see events that were to take place that they could report upon, when I noticed the Irvin Reunion. I had to go. The story I was told at the reunion was a little different from the written ones, but essentially the same.

Then, sometime later, I met a person who I consider one of the best, if not the best researcher on guerrilla activities in Kentucky's Civil War, Mr. Steven Wright. In one of the two most definitive books written concerning Sue Mundy, the historical novel by Richard Taylor entitled "Sue Mundy," he thanks Steven Wright of Elizabethtown, and Harold Edwards as "scholars who know more of the guerrilla war in Kentucky that can be found in books or fiction writers can imagine."[175] In reference to Mr. Wright, I have not met Mr. Edwards, I heartily agree with Taylor.

According to the family lore, James came home from the war, in which he suffered a wound, and he wanted to resume his place in Meadeville society as a blacksmith. The story of Newton's murder, for that's what it was, begins after he came home in May about a month after Lee surrendered, and where he resumed his blacksmithing trade. He was eating supper with his family on the night of July 9, 1865, when a voice called to him from outside the door. James went to the door and as he exited the house (here the story differs), he was met by a man on the porch, who stuck out his hand to shake hands with Newton with one hand, and with a revolver shot him with the other. This is the story told to me and believed by the family members at the reunion.

Another version probably incorrect, but written in an old church history, states the following: James heard a voice call out to him from outside the door, and when he stepped out on the porch, there were night riders gathered in the yard, and he was shot down. Whichever way it happened, the family was distraught and their father and husband was dead. The Newtons were Catholic, but they knew that they had to bury their dead quickly, because it was not uncommon for the dead to be returned for and the body to be hanged from a tree. To this end, the family took the body across the road and up the hill to the Baptist Meadeville Cemetery. The body was hastily buried and a slab of limestone was placed over the grave not only to mark it, but also to hide the excavation. They were successful, and it was not until 1998 that the family felt comfortable enough that the body would not be disturbed to have a monument placed on the grave in honor of James Irvin Newton. I was told by one of the people at the reunion, that the heavy granite monument was considered enough to continue to deter any that might want to desecrate the remains. I spoke to a member of the Meade County Historical and Archaeological Preservation Society, Mr. Rice Dugan, a local historian; he told me that sometimes the dead would later be hanged as a deterrent to others, and that the Henry family was afraid that would happen to David Henry.

The question is, why was he killed? When I first heard this story, I thought that Newton may have told on Billy Shacklett and been killed in reprisal. Even though there is no evidence of that it seemed to me to be a possible motive. Then I read there was some talk about Newton being a spy passing information to the enemy.[176] That could mean the Home Guard or the guerrillas. While that might have been possible, it would mean Newton would have had to become a sort of double agent, and that seems unlikely to me. The probability is he did not inform on the home guard or the guerrillas, and was in fact doing a balancing act on the edge of a razor, trying to reintegrate himself into a divided society where he was distrusted by many, and trusted by few. One reason for that distrust was that he served in the 12th Kentucky Cavalry, a guerrilla hunting band, that was thought to be involved with the shooting of Davison and, Davis and Magruder in Hancock County; but, that newspaper report was corrected a day later on March 6, 1865 newspaper article, with a statement that the 12th Kentucky was not involved,[177] and indeed it was Major John Swinker's battalion that shot the, guerrillas. The best thing he could have done for himself, with his history of fighting Confederate guerrillas, was to mind his own business.

I found an 1865 newspaper report, concerning Mr. Newton, with the following press release:

> *August 3rd. – Garnettsville, Meade Co. Ky., July 31st: On Wednesday, of last week (July 26th) two men, one of them calling himself Magruder, supposed to be a brother of Bill Magruder.... entered Meadeville, and after drinking a number of times, in a low groggery, Magruder inquired for Mr. James J. (sic) Newton, and being directed to his house, found him surrounded by his wife and children, and engaged him in conversation. After several ineffectual efforts to induce Newton to leave the house with him, Magruder asked him if he had not been a Federal soldier, and on Newton's answering yes, he deliberately drew his revolver and shot him dead. Magruder then quickly left the house, mounting, drove rapidly out of town, being fired upon as he left by one of the citizens.... It was thought that Magruder was wounded, as he rode from this place to Grayhampton. A peddler was also robbed last week while on the road from this place to Grayhampton. The military authorities*

at Brandenburg were informed of the fact and on Wednesday arrested two bothers named Burch, formerly in the rebel service, on suspicion of being engaged in the robbery. They are held in jail at Brandenburg.[178]

Henry Magruder, in his confession, stated that he stayed in Meade County at Richardson's for ten days after managing to elude capture when Morgan and most of his men were taken by Union forces. We know he had friends and probably relatives in the county. Elizabeth Cox was purportedly a distant cousin of his, and they lived less than five miles from the Newton home. Certainly a Magruder family member could have done the murder. The story in the paper matches pretty closely the family lore.

The Midwife's Cave

During the Civil War, midwives were sometimes the only source of medical attention in a community. Many doctors were called away to serve in the war effort, leaving the communities on their own. These midwives were women commonly summoned to assist or manage the births of babies. They were also known for their knowledge of herbal remedies, as were most farm wives up until the 1940's. I can remember my grandmother taking a paring knife and a basket and going into the yard to clip various herbs to cook with or with which to make medicine. While researching a history of various churches and ghost towns in Meade County, I found a reference to a Meadeville, midwife that had to hide her horse in a cave to prevent the home guards or the guerrillas from stealing the animal, her only mode of transportation. The only description of her hiding place was a cave that was located a mile or so behind the Meadeville Cemetery and up a hill. She supposedly tied her horse in the mouth of the cave under an overhanging rock.

One day I called Dan Redenius, the new caretaker of the Meadeville Cemetery who took over those duties after Bud Roberts, the former caretaker, had passed away, and asked him if he would like to look for the cave. He said yes, and then I telephoned Jess Scott to see if he and Frances, his wife, would like to go along. Jess and Frances are wonderful historians that have guided me to the old Shumate Schoolhouse, the old stagecoach watering hole, and around Stith Valley.

We met at the Meadeville Cemetery on a Sunday, and Jess with his son Alan and Alan's wife Ashley, and Dan and I, drove down the rough deep rutted road for approximately a mile, (four wheel drive was a necessity) and found a place to pull off and park. To the north of the road was a valley, and to the south there was a hill, and that is where we began our search. After an hour or more, we had made no progress. Dan decided to break off and search in a different direction. In a little while we heard him call out. We went directly to the sound of his voice, and he had located three small caves that interconnected with one another. The lower cave had at one time a large limestone shelf projecting out from the rock formation above the floor, which had at one time been high enough to harbor a horse. We began exploring the part of the lower cave that had a small portion of the original floor exposed. With a trowel, in the dry dust of that floor, we found several small Native American artifacts made of Wyandotte Chert, several pieces of bone, and a hand wrought square nail. I sat there holding that nail. It had very obviously been hand hammered. It occurred to me that James Irvin Newton could have made that nail. I wrote an article about that, published in the *News Standard*.

Chapter 18

Further Exploits of Thomas Hines

One of the true heroes of the Confederacy was Thomas Henry Hines. He was a soldier, spy, cavalryman, and guerrilla, as the need for his services presented themselves. Hines was born May 15, 1838, and was largely unschooled, but self-taught to the point that he became a grammar teacher at the Masonic University in LaGrange. In 1860 Hines was 22-years-old, and a member of the 9th Kentucky Union Cavalry, where he rose to the rank of lieutenant. He was 5'9" in height, and weighed about 140 pounds an ideal size for the cavalry. Because of his love for the South, he resigned his commission and traveled to Richmond, Virginia, to enlist as a private in the Confederate army. He loved music and horses and was something of a ladies' man. Captured two days earlier than Morgan, on his great raid, he was imprisoned along with Morgan and about a dozen other soldiers, in the Ohio Federal Penitentiary in Columbus, Ohio. It was here that Hines devised a plan to break his general and the other soldiers out of prison.

The ever observant Hines noticed that his cell floor was dry while the floors of the other men's cells were damp. He concluded that there must be a ventilation duct beneath the floor of his cell. He spoke to Morgan about it, and various plans were presented and rejected, until finally a plan was hatched. The men took turns chipping up the concrete floor in Hines' cell. The floor was six inches of thick concrete with a six-layered arch of brick below. The residue from the chipping was carried away in handkerchiefs, placed in Hines' mattress, or put in the coal stove used to heat their area.[179] The men did the tunneling with two Case pocket knives and a stolen spade. They tunneled from the bottom up to the floor of the cells of the men who were assigned to escape. The concrete was weakened so that a heavy heel could smash through it the night of the escape. They broke out using the 4' by 4' ventilation duct that ran through Hines' cell and the prison wall. Once on the outside, there would be two walls of stone fence to go over. The tunnel was completed on November 24, 1863.[180]

The taller of the two walls was some 25 feet high, and a rope was braided, and a hook was fashioned from a poker, and the men slipped out in the night, hoisting themselves up the outer wall and down to safety within 60 yards of the guards that were standing around a fire talking. A popular story states that Hines had been reading "Les Mise'rables" and left the book open where the escape from the French prison was detailed. I had a chance to speak to Jim Hines, a descendant who resides in Meade County and is a Meade County bank officer. He confided to me that the family history states it was "The Count of Monte Cristo" he was reading. I have to believe that the family history is more likely correct. No matter which book Hines was reading, he did leave a note for Warden Merion. A note was found written in French, that said, "La patience est amere, mais son fruit est doux." It translates "Patience is bitter, but its fruit is sweet.[181]

Hines was able to help Morgan escape once again when a Federal patrol spied the two men. Hines told Morgan to wait until he, Hines, created a diversion. Hines was captured, while Morgan made his escape, eventually reaching South Carolina. When Hines was captured, one of the Home Guards threw a rope around his neck and begged the officer to let him hang Hines. Hines had the presence of mind to ask, "Suppose that was General Morgan as you insist, and I have led you astray. Put yourself in my shoes. If you were a member of his command wouldn't you have done just what I did?"[182] The officer reflected for a moment and then decided not to hang Hines. That night, under guard, Hines told stories and regaled his guardian with tales of the wild rides and adventures with Morgan's Raiders. When the guard was suitably involved with the story, Hines over-powered the guard and once again escaped, later to reunite with Morgan.

One of my favorite stories about Hines is one that happened at the Ohio River town of West Point Kentucky. West Point lies on the southern bank of the Ohio River, and is overlooked by a large hill, known as Fort Hill. The Union Fort Duffield was situated on the hill, and was one of several forts that ringed Louisville, Kentucky. The cannon on Fort Hill commanded a stretch of the river for about five miles to the south, and protected the L&N RR, tracks and trestle from West Point to Muldraugh, Kentucky. The guerrillas in the area, Ben Wiggenton and his men as well as Dupoyster, Bryant and their gangs, Marion, Horsely, Hayes and others were often in the town, seemingly unafraid of the soldiers in the fort. General Stephen Gano Burbridge became the Military Commandant of Western Kentucky. On February 14, 1864, Burbridge was ordered to Fort Nelson in southern Jessamine County to command the district of Kentucky until relieved by General Jacob Ammen. By February 25, 1864, General Burbridge had begun to issue his first orders as commandant of the District of Kentucky.[183] The Burbridge reign in Kentucky was spanned the darkest days the State has or will ever see.

Among other things, such as his infamous Order No. 59, that allowed prisoners of war to be shot in retaliation for people killed by Partisan Rangers fighting the Federals, or the killing of Union men supporting the infrastructure of the Union army. He was also involved in something called the "Great Hog Swindle." On October 28, 1864, Burbridge issued a letter from his military headquarters in Lexington, stating that those who owned or fed hogs in Kentucky were informed by the United States Government that they wanted to buy surplus hogs in Kentucky. He stated a fair market price would be paid for all hogs that were for sale. He hoped that all hog owners would willingly sell to the government any excess hogs and not allow the excess pork to be packed in the country, which would invite raids by the Confederates to capture the excess pork.[184] Burbridge seemed to have a racket going. He told the hog farmers that the United States Government had set the-per-pound price for hogs, and that they must sell for that amount. Never mind that just across the river farmers were getting more money. Burbridge placed guards on the ferries and bridges prohibiting Kentucky farmers from taking their stock where it would command a higher price. The agents of the army paid less to the Kentucky farmers. Governor Bramlette accused Major Henry Symonds the depot commissary at Louisville, of stealing $300,000.00 from the farmers of Kentucky.[185] Hogs were not the only thing being stolen from the farmers. Horses were often purchased at less than the fair market price, and the unscrupulous middlemen then sold them to the Union procurers, and made a handsome sum. Occasionally the horse buyers would issue worthless papers to the farmers stating that they could be cashed in Louisville or other places by the army. It would be days before the seller would find he had been cheated. If that ruse didn't work, sometimes the stock buyers would insinuate that the reluctant farmer held Confederate sympathies, and could get in a lot of trouble if that were true. They would then tell the farmer that they would put in a good word for the him if he would sell.[186] There was little else he could do.

In West Point, Kentucky, one of these horse buyers was a notorious Home Guard, and Federal agent named Jarrett. Jarrett secured a commission from the Federal Army to supply horses for the Union forces. His base of operations was West Point, Kentucky. There was a port there and of course it was more or less protected by Fort Duffield. Jarrett's method of operation was to send out 50 of his men in five or six man groups. These groups would buy the horses by hook or by crook, and drive them to a prearranged point, and then they would be shipped south by whatever means were deemed appropriate. John Hunt Morgan had his ear to the ground when it came to Kentucky, and had heard of Jarrett's practices that deprived the Kentucky farmers of their livestock. He sent Thomas Henry Hines to this area to put a stop to Jarrett. Briggs states that Hines would be considered the Ollie North of today. I don't disagree with that.

Hines came to a safe house in Vine Grove. He went into the Mill Creek area of Hardin County, where he assembled a number of men. Briggs states there were seven men including Hines, but he names only six. The men were Hines, Owen Cowley, Bill Austin (a first cousin of Abraham Lincoln), Hays, Melton, and Gray. By expert intelligence, which was Hines' forte, he was able to find the date the horses were to be driven to West Point. Briggs states the date was June 20th, and there was a full moon. He stationed his men in the hills on either side of a draw called The Dripping Springs Hollow, located about two miles southeast of West Point, down which the horses were to be driven.

His men were well hidden, and Hines had armed them with the latest repeating rifles. About 3 o'clock a.m. fifty mounted drovers driving about 500 horses came down the gorge. They were to be sold at the West Point wharf the next day. When the horses and drovers were in the gorge, and between the Confederates stationed on the hillsides above them, they began the ambuscade. As shots were fired, the terrified horses bolted, running up and down the gorge trampling the drovers where they fell from the gunshots. This continued for a time, but before the dawn, all of the Confederates were home in their beds, and Hines was on his way back to the safe house. Forty drovers were killed, and buried in a mass grave at the Pleasant View Baptist Church about a mile from the ambush site.[187]

The success of this ambush was incomplete as Jarrett was not in the party. I have found other stories, which tell less dramatic accounts, but show that there were some consistent attacks by guerrillas on the horses being driven to West Point. The stories are so different, and date specific, that I do not believe they refer to the same event.

In "The Civil War in Hardin County", Mary Josephine Jones states that on August 9, 1864, about noon, an incident occurred about three miles from West Point. About sixty horses were being driven from Louisville to Gallatin, Tennessee. Nine drovers were employed, and the group was attacked by guerrillas. The first version says that a band of about 20 guerrillas rode down from the hills, and scattered the horses and yet the guerrillas gathered up 42 of them and drove them toward Meade County.[188] There was an article in the *Louisville Daily Journal*, on August 14th that stated:

> *We have learned some additional details on the attack of Mr. Leonard's drove of horses, on the Salt River Rd. It appears the guerrillas were under the command of the notorious Capt. Dupoyster and Garrett. But one of the drovers, Mr. Howard Bush, was injured by the firing. He was shot in the head, yet hopes are entertained for his recovery.... One of the drivers, a daring and resolute fellow, rode to the front of a large portion of the drove of horses, and by yelling and slashing his whip, he started them down the road on a full run. The guerrillas fired several shots at him, none of which took effect.*[189]

This story was followed five days later with the following report:

> *Mr. Howard Bush who was shot by guerrillas last week in the cowardly attack on Mr. Leonard's drove of horses on the Salt River Rd., has since died from the effects of his wound.... We are informed that the guerrilla band, guilty of the outrage...still hovers in the vicinity of West Point....*[190]

Chapter 19

Quantrill's Raiders Quit the Field

With the war quickly coming to an end, Brothers dead, Texas locked up, and Quantrill having died, the war weary Rebels were finally allowed to take the oath and leave the war behind them. On July 26, 1865, eighteen guerrillas took the oath of allegiance at Samuel's Depot. Edwards has the date the 25th of July. The oath was administered in a most reasonable manner by Captain Robert H. Young, of Co. B 54th Ky MTD Inf. assisted by Lieutenant Campbell, of the same regiment.[191] According to Edwards, these two gallant officers were especially generous and obliging.[192] These two men were soldiers themselves who saw real service, and recognized courage even in the enemy, and showed respect for the Missouri fighters. Young administered the oath, and Campbell required of the guerrillas their promise not to retain more pistols than were allowed under terms of the surrender.[193] The Rebel soldiers were allowed to retain the side arms that they needed for defense. Frank James was not allowed, by Missouri law, to return to his home, so he lingered in the river town of Brandenburg.

In January of 2008, I wrote an article for *The Meade County Messenger* entitled "Frank and Jesse James in Brandenburg". When the paper debuted, the title became the headline for that week's newspaper! Amused, I sent a copy to my Uncle Fred Fischer, with a note stating this is what happens on a slow news week in Brandenburg. Regardless of that, Frank and Jesse James did in fact have friends and relatives in Kentucky, and traveled to the state extensively. They robbed at least two banks in Kentucky, one the Bank of Columbia, Kentucky, on April 29, 1872[194], at which time they killed R.A.C. Martin, the cashier who refused to open the safe, and the Russellville, Kentucky Nimrod Long and Company Bank on March 20th, 1868.[195] They also robbed stage coaches, such as the Mammoth Cave stage coach, "Florida", on September 3, 1880[196], just after it had left the Mammoth Cave Hotel.

There were other instances when robberies occurred in Kentucky, and legends were built on Jesse and Frank hiding their treasure in various caves. It is surprising to me how many of these stories about the James boys are told, and how evergreen they stay.

I was managing the construction of a Convenient Food Mart in Columbia about the spring of 1972. Columbia is in the Central Time Zone, and my habit has always been to get to appointments early, because emergencies such as flat tires, traffic, and such can cause one to be late. Not realizing they were on Central Standard Time, and with Louisville being on Eastern Standard Time, when I got to the town square, I was an hour and a half early. The stores were not open, and so I strolled around the courthouse square, so common in Kentucky towns. At the bank building I saw a bronze plaque dedicated to Mr. Martin who was killed in the robbery, and as I walked back to the place where I parked my car, two men in bib-overalls were sitting on a bench in front of one of the stores. I nodded to one of the men, and he waved me over and asked, while pointing at the courthouse clock, high on a steeple, "Do you think it's still there?" I answered, "I don't know, what is, *it*?" He replied, "Frank James' bullet. He fired at the clock as he and his men rode out of town after killing the clerk, Martin. They stole some horses from a lady down the road, because theirs was all played out. Some folks say it's still up there." One hundred years later and people were still talking about the bank robbery of Frank James.

I took my wife and mother to a Bryant family reunion in Estill County (my mother's maiden name was Bryant). My grandfather Bryant had always been thrifty, as well as educated. At one time he loaned his brother, Mathias Marmaduke Bryant, $600 sometime before 1940, to purchase a farm in Waldo, Florida, where Uncle M.M. taught school. In Estill County there are many caves, and one or more are supposed to be where Jesse James hid loot from his holdups. One elderly man at the reunion, a cousin from Texas, got me off to the side and asked me if I knew where Uncle M.M. got his money? I told him the family story that A.C. Bryant had loaned him the money. He then asked where Papa got the money, and I told him I didn't know. That's when he told me that he was pretty sure that they had found Jesse and Frank's gold in one of the caves. Such is their fame, begun when Frank rode with Quantrill, and Jesse with Bloody Bill Anderson.

It is no different in the town of Brandenburg, where Edwards states Frank James committed his first crime after taking the oath of allegiance and being paroled. Brandenburg was a good town in which for James to stay. It was on the river, and he could get passage south into Missouri when it was safe to do so. He would also hear the latest news. At the same time that Frank James was in Brandenburg, Jesse was laid up with a bullet wound to his lung. He spent June and the first half of July in Rulo, Nebraska, where he was tended to by his mother and Aunt and Uncle Mimms, and their daughter Zerelda or Zee.[197] He left there August 26, 1865 to go south.

No one knows for sure when the shoot-out in Brandenburg between Frank James and four Union soldiers happened, but it is safe to say it couldn't have been much earlier than sometime in August of 1865 and later than January of 1866, when a group comprised of formerly Quantrill's Raiders, robbed the Liberty, Missouri, Clay County Savings Association Bank.[198] This was the first recognized peacetime robbery of a bank. Bud and Donnie Pence and Oll Shepherd, and Joab Perry were mentioned as suspects, and later Jesse and Frank would be added to the list.[199]

Whatever the date of the incident, Frank James was walking south on the east side of Main Street toward Hotel Meade, when four Federal soldiers who had heard of Frank's association with Quantrill's Raiders, were walking north on the same side. The guerrillas were looked upon as very tough men, and sometimes met with scorn by Union soldiers. As James was walking up the street, across from his hotel, he came to a place in front of the bank building. There were four soldiers dressed in blue walking abreast along the same wooden sidewalk. The soldiers decided to test Frank James's grit, and refused to let him pass by without stepping off the walk and into the street. Quantrill's men were polite and well-mannered by most accounts, but they had their own code they lived by, and Frank James was not to be bullied by these four men facing him. They decided to muscle him off of the sidewalk,[200] and perhaps rough him up a bit. That was a huge error in judgment.

Edwards writes that suddenly and without intention, or any semblance of self-control, the old passions and fire arose like the Phoenix from the ashes, and he fought like he did at Centralia, Missouri. (Note: Bloody Bill Anderson, George, and Tom Todd's men fought at Centralia, Frank James was unlikely to have been in that fight.) He literally threw caution to the wind, being out numbered four to one. As one of the soldiers' hands landed lightly on his pistol, Frank James drew his pistols, killing two of the soldiers where they stood. A third soldier was desperately wounded, and out of the fight. The fourth soldier managed to draw his weapon in the four or five seconds the gunfight lasted. His aim, although low, placed a bullet in Frank's hip, wounding him seriously. This no doubt affected his aim, and his last four or five shots were only effective in forcing the last soldier to withdraw and seek shelter elsewhere.[201] Frank James gave a derringer pistol, a pair of dice, and a letter to a citizen who helped hide him. Except for the letter that has been lost, the Derringer still belongs to a Meade County resident, and the dice to another Meade County citizen living in Louisville.

Friends came to his aid and secretly hid him, and provided him with medical aid and attention. His wound was not only painful, but the loss of blood brought him to death's door, and at one point he almost arose and entered. There was a hue and cry throughout Brandenburg, calling for his capture and trial. Frank James was guilty of not being able to show a quality he never had and could not display—cowardice. Those soldiers intent on abuse, did not know that there was no such thing as physical fear within Frank James.[202]

This was not the only time Frank James was in Brandenburg. Sometime in 1869, Frank was back in town, and he brought his brother Jesse and another man along with him. It was their intention to stay in Ashcraft's Hotel that night and board the steamer *Morning Star* the next day. Things didn't work out as they had planned. Some of the soldiers in town heard of Frank coming back, and, thinking the men were horse thieves, planned to capture them. When the soldiers came in, Jesse was having his boots blackened. A young Negro shoeshine boy named Tabby Jackson was blacking Jesse's boots when the soldiers and the James began firing. Tabby dove under the shoeshine stand and did not come out until the smoke cleared. Frank and Jesse got away, and were reportedly staying in some caves near Garnettsville. Frank was reported to have been wounded in the jaw.[203]

Another version of this story states that Frank and Jesse were staying in Brandenburg, and had just gotten their boots polished by Tabby. As the men mounted their horses, they flipped a $5.00 gold piece to Tabby, and fired their pistols in the air, making him dive under the stand. They yelled, "You just shined the boots of Frank and Jesse

James." Either of these stories could be true. Years later, when Tabby was an old man, working as a prescription delivery man and sweeping out the old drugstore, and long past the incident having happened, people who knew him would say, "Frank and Jesse's coming." And Tabby would look worried, and everyone would laugh.[204] There are other stories about the James, one which I have heard repeated many times in various forms, but none more so than the way it was told to me, my wife Fran, and my mother Virginia, in that long day we spent with James Wakefield in 1993. It may be that since the story is a good one often told, that it could have happened more than once. For whatever reason, the story is related as it was told to me by James Wakefield.

Jesse and Frank and the Widow

One day in the vicinity of Taylorsville, in Spencer County, the James boys heard of a widow who was going to suffer an eviction by the Spencer County sheriff. The amount owed was about $600. Frank and Jesse, touched by the story of the widow's plight, rode to her house, and handed her the amount needed to pay off the mortgage and taxes she owed. They told her to pay strict attention to what they were instructing her to do. She should not let the sheriff have the money until she had a receipt for it in her hand, the mortgage marked paid, and the deed to the land in her possession. The sheriff was due to be there at noon the next day to move her out.

Sure enough, as soon as the sun was directly overhead, along came the sheriff riding slowly up the farm lane. When he got there, she counted out his money, and the sheriff, happy he did not have to evict, wrote her a receipt, marked the mortgage paid, and presented her with the deed to the land. He placed the money in his coat and proceeded back to Taylorsville, when shortly he was met at the gate by two men with masks over their faces, and they robbed him of the $600 and whatever other cash he had. It was of course Frank and Jesse James.[205]

These stories, and others about how the James boys would have the fireman on a locomotive they were robbing, shovel off coal, for the poor people in the winter, helped create the Robin Hood like stature of these men. When others like John Edwards wrote so highly of them, and published their activities as gallant, striking a blow for the Confederacy and such, it perpetuated the myth. There is no doubt that Frank and Jesse were good to their friends, and loyal to those who helped them. It is also true that they were cold-blooded men who would kill without hesitation.

Chapter 20

Notes: Concerning Guerrillas

There are some interesting things to note about guerrillas—their "guerrilla locks" for example. Many, if not most, of the guerrillas wore their hair long. Edwards writes of Mundy as having long black hair flowing like the mane of a horse from under his hat. Marion wore his hair long, as did One-armed Berry, Billy Magruder, and others. There was probably some convention about the neck and shoulder length hair that many of the guerrillas sported. It may have been a means of doing something that teenagers do today. That is, to show their individuality by dressing and wearing their clothes and hair just like all of their friends. They conform in their non-conformity. There could well have been other reasons that many of these men had long hair. It was not easy for a guerrilla being hunted by the law to ride into town, hitch his horse, stroll into a barber shop and take a seat in the chair. Still, in a time when most hair was cut at home by the mothers or fathers of the children, there would have been opportunity to get a haircut. I think upon reflection the fact that many guerrillas wore their hair long, may have caused Sue Mundy to have been often misidentified.

There was a thing called "the mark", or the act of "putting the mark on a man". This referred to shooting someone in the middle of the forehead between the eyes so that when the body was found it had the mark of the guerrilla soldier. Edwards describes the killing of 22 Union militia when Quantrill and his men, dressed in blue, came upon the approaching Federal column. He ordered his guerrillas to ride by the side of each man in the Federal column, and engage him in conversation. On a pre-arranged signal, they were to "blow their brains out." Quantrill gave the signal promptly, shooting the militia man assigned to him through the middle of the forehead, and where upon their horses twenty-two confident men laughed and talked in comrade fashion, a second before, nothing remained of the unconscious detachment, literally exterminated, save a few who struggled in agony upon the ground.[206] This frequently was the way the guerrillas executed their captives. Richard Taylor writes in his well-researched historic novel, "Sue Mundy," that Sam Berry avenged his sister's killing by the Home Guards, in this same manner, tying the hands of his captives, giving them some sort of questioning, and then shooting each in the forehead right between the eyes…and each of the guardsmen fell, each forehead bored by a single shot.[207] The mention of this kind of shooting seems to be consistent with a number of old accounts.

Riding under the "Black Flag," and taking the "Black Oath," are something the guerrillas were supposed to do, thus, setting themselves apart from Confederate soldiers that fought under the red, white, and blue, "Stars and Bars." Although, there are some factual references to these legends, they were certainly not the norm for guerrilla fighters. The exception may apply to some of Quantrill's earlier practices. Carl W. Briehan writes in his book "Quantrill and his Civil War Guerrillas," that Quantrill did possess a black flag. It is described as a three-foot by five-foot flag of black quilted alpaca, with QUANTRELL in bright colors stitched in the center. Briehan states that the flag was probably not used extensively, and was rumored to have been made by a Missouri woman named Annie Fickle. The flag was supposed to be affixed to an eight-foot pole.[208]

Briehan also states that J. Frank Dalton said that in the early stages of the war that Quantrill demanded a "black oath" of his men, but as the war waged on there was less time for these dramatics. Dalton, as well as Allen Parmer, said there never was a black flag.

The Black Oath, according to Dalton and Briehan, was sworn to in the name of God and the Devil, one to punish and one to reward. The affiant pledged to consecrate heart, brain, body, mind, and limbs, to devote my life to obedience of my superiors. That, the affiant, will exert every possible means to in his power for the extermination of Federals, Jayhawkers, and their abettors. The affiant will show no mercy, but strike with an avenging arm, so long as breath remains. He further pledged not to betray a comrade, and will submit to all tortures, and to suffer the most horrible death, rather than reveal a single secret of this organization. The remaining portion of the oath spelled out what would happen to the affiant if he broke his solemn vow. Among these things was to pray to God and the Devil to tear out my heart and roast it flames; his head be split open and his brains scattered all over the earth, his body be torn up, and his bowels ripped out, and that his limbs will be broken by stones, and cut off by inches. And lastly, the affiant will go to hell where this punishment will be administered for eternity, in the name of God and the Devil. Amen.[209] There is no evidence I have found, of Quantrill being a Mason, but he had to be aware that being in the Masonic Order might save his life during battle, as it did for many soldiers from the north or the south when they were come upon by other Masons. This oath, which I have abbreviated, is similar to several oaths I have read that were sworn to by Masons, save the invocation to the Devil.

Hats worn by guerrillas were often decorated with metal emblems, badges, or pins, such as the crescent moon on Sue Mundy's hat. Bryant was known to sport a small Confederate flag sewn to his, and Bill Marion adorned his hat with Polk leaves, white Pheasant feathers, and Ostrich plumes. Other guerrillas used chicken feathers, Ostrich plumes, ribbons, and evergreen leaves. Marion had specially cobbled high riding boots he wore, and some guerrillas had tailored clothing made for them in red, black, and gray cloth, with gold braid and buttons. Even Ed Terrell, the guerrilla hunter, had an all-red suit of clothes made for him. Interestingly, a parallel practice is to be found with Baron Manfred Von Richthofen "The Red Baron" of WW I, who had his airplane painted all-red, so his enemies could identify him.[210] Perhaps the guerrillas used their hats and clothing, in the same way, to make them more identifiable to their enemies or perhaps to let their compatriots know their whereabouts, if they were in a fight. It seems to me that the deadly game they played required a bit of the theatrical. They not only had to act the part, but they also needed to look the part, and in one way or another, they left their mark.

Chapter 21

Lucy Hamilton and Catty Rhodes

I thought hard about including the following two stories in my book, because one started years before the Civil War, and the other occurred during and extended after the war, and they have little to directly relate to the guerrilla war about which I have written; however, they make tenuous connections in a sort of back-handed way, to two groups of the most unlikely people to connect, slaves and those fighting to preserve the institution of slavery while at the same time, trying to do what is right.

Lucy Hamilton

In 2008 I wrote an article in the *Meade County Messenger* about Lucy Hamilton, a slave girl who was hanged in Brandenburg, Kentucky for the murder of her master's son. The proceedings began on Tuesday November 3, 1846, and concluded with her execution June 1, 1848. The story of Lucy made the newspapers and was witnessed by thousands of slaves and their owners who brought their slaves to show them what would happen to them if they harmed their masters. This execution happened about four years before Harriet Beecher Stowe's book "Uncle Tom's Cabin" debuted. That book, like Lucy's death, fanned the flames of the abolitionist movement.

On Tuesday November 3rd, Lucy and Peter Hamilton, of color, the property of Lewis Hamilton, were indicted for murder. Lucy stabbed William Hamilton to death with a butcher knife. On the day after the indictment, the charge against Peter was discharged. This was likely done for two reasons, firstly Lucy stabbed William, and secondly, he was more valuable as property. A good field hand was simply worth more money. Lucy was pregnant. When the next Thursday came, two days later, Lucy was brought from the jail, and a jury was empaneled. After hearing the evidence, Henry P. Byrum, a juror, withdrew and the jury was discharged. Mr. John Helm was appointed by the court to defend Lucy, and Lewis Hamilton was ordered by the court to pay costs of $10.00 to Helm. On May 4, 1847, Lucy, who pled not guilty, threw herself on the mercy of the court, but was found guilty of the murder of William Hamilton. Friday next, of that the court session, and upon Lucy's suggestion, to the satisfaction of the court, all further proceedings of the prosecution were suspended. At the August term of the court further proceedings in this case were postponed, on account of the tender age of the child that Lucy had delivered, and with a view of not endangering the life of the newborn.

The honorable A.H. Churchill was the judge, and William Alexander was the prosecuting attorney. Churchill resigned rather than pass sentence on Lucy. The talk around the neighborhood was that Lucy was raped, and that the infant was fathered by William Hamilton. To date, so that Lucy could live to deliver her child, one juror and one judge had resigned their post to make that possible. Governor Owsley appointed Samuel Carpenter in his stead, and on May 1, 1848, Lucy was sentenced to be hanged on June 1, 1848, between the hours of 9 o'clock in the morning, and 3'oclock in the afternoon. It was ordered that the sheriff take the condemned to a gallows previously erected on some public road leading from the town of Brandenburg, not nearer than one half mile, nor farther than three miles from the said town, and hang her by the neck until she be dead. The court valued Lucy at $500.00 and ordered that Lewis Hamilton be paid that amount upon execution of the sentence. The $500.00 came from the treasury of the State of Kentucky.

Thomas J. Gough was the sheriff, and Leonard P. Buchman was the acting deputy sheriff who carried out the execution, as directed by the court. Lucy had been kept in the old log jail, about 100 yards from the newer brick building. Jailer Thomas Mill's wife, Aunt Peggy, dressed Lucy for the last time and assisted her to the ox-cart where she was seated upon her coffin. The place of execution was a black-jack oak tree on the farm of William Saunders. Lucy carried her child, who was born in prison, in the slow ride to the gallows. The ride was about 20 minutes, and several thousand people were there to see the hanging[211]. When the officers came to the tree, the child was taken from her arms, and they were tied, the noose was adjusted about her neck, and a rope was tied around her skirt below the knees, for reasons of modesty. Lucy stood on her coffin, and the oxen were driven away. Lucy died.

The location of her place of execution was across the street from the old fairgrounds, which is now the location of the Meade County High School. The descendants of that black jack oak still stand in the yard of a house there. Interestingly, a descendant of the Richardson's disagreed with the history of the event, as I wrote it, and stated that only a handful of people were at the hanging. Ridenour states there were thousands and that it was one of the events that buttressed the abolition movement.

Catty Rhodes

On Wednesday October 24, 2007, an article I wrote about Catty Rhodes appeared in the *Meade County Messenger*. The idea for the article was given to me by my friends, Peggy and Larry Greenwell. Peggy told me the story after Larry had asked her to take a photograph of a wood line, on Fackler Road. They were on a field trip taking photographs of old houses and buildings that were likely to be torn down or succumb to the ravages of the weather, when Larry stopped the car and said take a picture here. Peggy asked why? And Larry replied, "That's Catty's springs." And there the story began.

Sometime in 1860 or 1862, a mulatto baby named Sarah Catherine was born into slavery under the ownership of Edward Rhodes, postmaster of Payneville, Kentucky. Catty, as she was called, lived in Payneville most of her life, and attended St. Mary Magdalene of Pazzi Church. The Rhodes were Catholic and attended services at St Mary's Church, where they took Catty on Sundays and holy days of obligation. Catty did not sit in a pew, but rather in the back of the church on a chair. Other slaves attending are not recorded.

No one today can say with certainty who was Catty's father, but a goodly number of slaves named on the slave schedules at that time were listed as mulatto, and Catty was either fathered by another mulatto, or her father could have been white. In the various censuses her race has been listed as white, black, mulatto, and colored. Her name is inconsistently spelled as well. She is listed as Caddie, Catty, Cattie, Catherine, and Sarah C. Rhodes. Catty's life was a riddle. She negotiated between two worlds neither family nor friend, neither slave nor free. As Catty got older, when other Negroes came around to visit, she was made to go upstairs and stay out of sight. She was discouraged from fraternizing with Negroes, and she was occasionally treated harshly.

In the 1880's, Catty's job was carrying water from the springs, on Fackler Road, to the Rhodes' home a half-mile from the spring. She may have carried the water in buckets or loaded on a horse and sledge, but she made so many trips that over time the series of three springs came to bear her name. They continue to be called that by the old folks today. The Rhodes family had seven slaves, and when the war ended Catty was between three and five years old. After slavery ended in 1867, Catty and others like her were not really free, being untrained in anything but what she did as a slave. Slaves possessed little if any education because laws forbade slaves to read and write, making job opportunities almost nonexistent. And so Catty stayed with the Rhodes family.

In the 1870 census Catty was now thought to be eight years old, but may have been ten, and was listed as white living in Meade County with Priscilla Rhodes. We know she lived with the Rhodes family through the 1890's taking care of, at different times, Edward, Tommy, and later Priscilla's daughter, Mary. She was missing from the census until 1900, where she is listed as black, and about 40 years old. Interestingly, she is listed in the 1910 census as 40. How nice it would be not to age in ten years! In 1920 she is listed as living in the home of Tommy Rhodes, her name is Catherine Rhodes, and her race is Mu, and her age remained listed as 40. In 1920, she is listed as Sarah C. Rhodes, mulatto, and is now aged 60, probably a more accurate age. By this time Catty was living with and caring for Mary Rhodes, the daughter of Priscilla, who had no children of her own.

Catherine Rhodes, Edward Rhodes' youngest daughter, married Samuel Burch in Meade County in 1876. The Burch family had five children and the middle child was Bob Burch. Bob married Mary Cashman and they had six children. After their sixth child, Myra, Mary Burch caught pneumonia and died January 6, 1925. When Mary died, her husband Bob was left with six children to care for and a farm to work. Since Mary died, Catty, once again needing someone to care for, moved in with that family and helped raise the children, until Bob Burch remarried in 1929. In 1928 Catty became a wealthy woman when Mary left $1000.00 in her will to Catty, who had taken care of Mary. Catty who always cared for others, moved into Brandenburg in 1930, and took a domestic job with the Guy Hardin family. While in Brandenburg Catty would attend Catholic Church and often visited with Bob Burch's family. She simply loved his children. Bob Burch would fetch Catty from Brandenburg, and drive her home. When Catty visited the Burch family, the children would tease her while she pretended to get mad when she really wasn't. They would all have a good time visiting, laughing and enjoying each other's company. Mrs. Mildred Burch recalled her as a good old soul. At some point it is believed she moved to Guston, and it was rumored she had a boyfriend. By this time she would likely have been about 70. In February of 1950, a notice appeared in the *Meade County Messenger:*

> *"Aged Colored Woman Taken To Hospital"*
> *Catty Rhodes, colored, was taken to the Red Cross Hospital sast Sunday. The aged woman is blind and has been bedfast for weeks.*[212]

According to Virginia M. Fischer, my mother and a registered nurse, the Red Cross Hospital was the only hospital that treated Negro patients during the 1940's and 1950's. To be so well thought of, so important, or loved, that the newspaper announced her hospitalization, speaks to the fact that she touched many peoples' lives. Catty Rhodes died in 1950. Her age was believed to be 91 years. Bob Burch signed her death certificate, and she is buried in the St Mary's Cemetery in Payneville. Larry, Peggy, Phillip Burch, a descendent of Bob Burch, and I visited the grave of Catty Rhodes, a woman born into slavery and servitude, who dedicated her entire life to helping other people and by so doing, improved the lives of the people of Meade County and Brandenburg. We found her grave mirrored her life. It is marked by a sturdy plain and simple stone, like the person she was. The grave was devoid of decoration, and ironically, like her name, race, and date of birth, the dates on the stone are a riddle. The birth date is in error by about ten years. Our community should remember her, and I believe it would make Catty smile to get flowers on the next decoration-day, and I am sure she will.

The story of Lucy Hamilton is one where Lucy fought back when she was likely raped and paid for it with her life. It was the juror and judge who desisted in continuing their sworn duty thus allowing the baby to be born, and gave some possible but improbable chance for clemency. All of that ultimately resulted in the death of Lucy, and the probable enslavement of her child. There seems to me, though, that a social wedge was driven between the legality of slavery, and the inhumanity with which Lucy had been subjected. It was not right, but there was only so much people could legally do. The situation with Catty Rhodes was in some way similar. There is no doubt that her father was white, or of mixed blood. Catty was in many ways treated like family, and considering her peculiar treatment, she may have been family. She lived in the big house, she was churched, and was allowed only to associate with white people, but she had to sit in the back of the church because of her color. She spent her entire life serving other people and doing menial work, almost masquerading as a slave. Because of her color, and because of her rearing, she walked alone, between two Worlds, not accepted as an equal in either the black or white society. In some ways, admittedly tenuous and aslant, these two women share the lives of the Confederate guerrillas. The guerrillas came into their situation not always of their choosing. Bill Marion and Quantrill chose to be guerrillas, but Jerome Clarke and Henry Magruder were soldiers without companies or officers, banding together with others of like mind to continue to fight. Still others like Sam Berry came into the war for reasons of vengeance for wrongs real and perceived committed by his Union favoring neighbors or the Federal Home Guard militias. Like Lucy and Catty, they were trapped by the deeds they had done, the life they chose, or that life fate chose for them. They reacted as men should, with courage and resolve, and were immortalized by their story.

Afterword

I have been reading about and interested in the guerrillas that fought behind the Union lines, since I first entered college in 1963. The study was interrupted many times by the things that always seem to divert a person from whatever direction their interests take them, such as making a living, going to school, and raising a family for example, but, my interest in this topic never waned, and to it I always returned.

When I began amassing material toward a book sometime in 1995, I began with the intention of telling the stories of "stone cold killers." But the more I learned about them, the more I think I understood them. Their bloody gunfights, ambuscades, robberies, burning of trains and buildings as well as their shooting of Union soldiers was all done in an effort to hurt the Union army and its war efforts, and extend the life of the Confederacy. What else could you expect Confederate guerrillas to do? They could have given up, laid down their arms, and knuckled under the tyrannical rule of Stephen Burbridge or fight. I cannot fault them for choosing the former over the latter. In doing so, I remain critical of their lack of good sense and cavalier attitude they exhibited in the killing of unarmed soldiers such as Edward Caldwell in 1865. I do not think they were wrong in their killing of Union soldiers, after all, they were at war; but, the circumstances within which some of the soldiers were killed were in my opinion, extenuating enough that by their actions, the guerrillas hurt their own cause. The David Henry and Caldwell murders, for that's what they were, created bad press, and were rightly criticized by even the people who favored the South.

These men, with all of their faults and occasional bad judgment, were no worse than their Union counterparts, Bridgewater, Terrell, and further to the west, Jim Lane. No men were braver, no men fought harder or with more resolve, than did these, scruffy, long-haired, battle-scarred veterans. It is easy to be critical of them now, because they lost. The victors always get to write the history of the wars, and it always becomes politically correct to turn the losers into villains, but in some small way, this work may give a measure of vindication for these soldiers, and for what they fought. They battled, not under a black flag, but rather under the Confederate Battle Flag, and were authorized by the Confederacy to do so under the 1862 Partisan Ranger Act. They were originally soldiers not outlaws.

Robert E. Lee did not have medals or ribbons awarded to the Confederate soldiers. He thought that any who wore the butternut or gray were heroes. After the war however, the Daughters of Confederate Veterans created a medal entitled "The Southern Cross of Honor." I was happy to find it awarded posthumously to Captain William "Billy" Shacklett, and to William Clarke Quantrill. My wife, Fran, had gotten in touch with the Arch Diocese and was sent a map of the currently named, St. John's Cemetery, where part of Quantrill remains are still buried. The Director told her that he was informed that a marker was on his grave, although everything I have read has stated it was unmarked and anonymous. Sunday, January 27, 2013, we took the map and walked directly to the grave. There is a flat, granite marker on the grave, placed horizontally and flush with the ground. This message and the Southern Cross of Honor are engraved in the stone. Quantrill fancied himself a poet, and as I read it, I wondered if he wrote this inscription:

IN MEMORY
COL. WILLIAM CLARKE QUANTRILL
JULY 31 ST. 1837 – JUNE 6 TH 1865

HERE'S A SIGH TO THOSE WHO LOVE ME
AND A SMILE TO THOSE WHO HATE
AND WHATEVER SKY'S ABOVE ME
HERE'S A HEART FOR EVERY FATE

I have an old friend named Jeff Caulfield, who sent me a poem about his great-great-grandfather, Jessie "Doc" Shacklett, a Meade County Rebel who rode with John Hunt Morgan, and who died at the Confederate Veterans Home in Peewee Valley, Kentucky, on July 16, 1905. He is buried there, in the Confederate Cemetery. Jeff and I made an extended visit to a number of Civil War guerrilla raid sites in Meade County, and spent quite a bit of time at the Old Meadeville Cemetery, where many of his and Jessie's relatives are buried. The next day after his visit Jeff wrote a poem and sent it to me. I received it about three months later, and I opened it just after I had written the last word in the last chapter in this book. It was likely coincidence, but it seemed providential. I print it here for your enjoyment, and it expresses my feelings about these guerrillas better than I could ever express:

"The Good Old Boys in Gray"
By Jeff Caufield

Down in the valley, where my Great Gran Pappy lay
He rests with his brothers, who wore the tattered gray.

'T was generations ago, which seems so far away,
They fought for the Southland, and didn't fight for pay.

They believed in their families, their God and their farms,
They fought for their freedom, and against the government's harm.

They sacrificed their all, those good ole boys in gray.
I only wish they were still here to help us fight today.

Now, their grand ole flag is slandered
Tho it's stained by their sacred blood
And the government's evil, comes on us like a flood.

Don't accuse those good ole boys, of fightin' for the wrong
'T was their love of God and family that made 'em so very strong.

Their hearts were pure, their deeds were brave
'T was only freedom that they craved.

Dedicated to Jesse D. Shacklett-Southern Cross of Honor
And W. K. Shacklett-Southern Cross of Honor

Jessie "Doc" Shacklett, like many Kentucky Confederates, was a brave and honorable man, who just happened to be on the losing side. He was wounded in battle. In his private life, he worked as a blacksmith, farmer, and wagon maker, was Town Marshall of Brandenburg, Sheriff of Meade County, and Judge of the Elizabethtown, Kentucky, Police Court. He once fined a repeat offender, in a most unusual way. The man stood before the court many times before, and he was now there accused of stealing a can of peas, Doc had him open the can and count the peas. When the man was finished counting, he was sentenced to serve one day in jail for every pea in the can! Captain Marion would have been proud of Jessie's justice. If the South had won the war, and the Confederacy had written the story, what prominent place in history would all of those courageous, gloriously dangerous, and sometimes hard-hearted and cruel, guerrilla fighters have commanded?

ENDNOTES

1. R. Berry Lewis, Kentucky Archaeology: (Lexington: 1996),4- 5
2. Ibid. 17-18
3. Ibid. 19
4. Ibid 4
5. Johnston, Col. J. Stoddard and Col. John C. Moore, Kentucky and Missouri: Confederate Military History, Volume IX, (United States: Blue and Gray Press.) , 22-23
6. Ibid. 26-27
7. Ibid 26-27
8. Ibid 28-29
9. Ibid 30-32
10. Virgil Carrington Jones, Gray Ghosts and Rebel Raiders, (St. Simons Island, Ga., Mockingbird Books, Inc., 1956) 9
11. Ibid. 10
12. Harrison, Lowell H. and James C. Klotter, A New History of Kentucky, (Lexington, The University of Kentucky Press, 1997) 167-169
13. Ibid. 192-193
14. 24, Bryan Bush, Louisville in the Civil War, Kentucky's Civil War 1861-1865 Volume V, 2008-2009 Edition
15. Louisville Daily Journal, September 9, 1861
16. Ibid. June 5, 1861
17. Ibid. June 5, 1861
18. Ibid. September 16, 1861
19. Ibid. September 16, 1861
20. Ibid. September 16, 1861
21. Ibid. October 25, 1861
22. Ibid. April 5, 1862
23. Ibid. May 1, 1862
24. Ibid. 73

25. Elizabeth Stith, The Hill Grove Community, Memories of Meade County, 1792 to 1992, the Celebration, (The Kentucky Bicentennial Commission, 1992) 178

26. George L. Ridenour, Early Times in Meade County Kentucky, (Louisville, Kentucky, Western Recorder 1929, Utica, Kentucky, McDowell Publications, 1977) 23

27. Ibid. 30

28. Ibid. 30

29. Meade County Messenger, January 8, 1908

30. Ibid. January 8, 1908

31. Watson, Thomas Shelby, with Perry A. Brantley, Confederate Guerrilla Sue Mundy: A Biography of Kentucky Soldier Jerome Clarke (Jefferson: McFarland & Co. Publishers, 2008) 43-44

32. Watson, Thomas Shelby, with Perry A. Brantley, Confederate Guerrilla Sue Mundy": A biography of Kentucky Soldier Jerome Clarke, (Jefferson, North Carolina: McFarland & Co. rewritten 2013) 44

33. Dee Alexander Brown, Morgans Raiders (New York: Konecky & Koenecky, 1959) 87

34. Ibid. 89

35. Ibid. 175

36. Ibid. 178

37. Henry C. Magruder, Three Years In The Saddle, The Life And Confession of Henry C. Magruder, the Original Sue Mundy (Louisville, Major Cyrus Wilson, 1865) 24

38. Compiled by Rita Adkisson Thompson, Rambling Remarks of William Miller Boling (Meade County: 1972) 16

39. The Methodist Men's Club, The Brandenburg Story (Brandenburg: July 13, 1963) 13-14

40. Meade County Kentucky Newspaper abstracts 1906-1908 compiled by Carolyn Wimp, published by

Ancestral Trails Historical Society Inc. Vine Groove, Kentucky 2007 169-170

41. Ibid. 169

42. Carl W. Breihan, Quantrill and his Civil War Guerrillas (New York: Promontory Press, 1959) 153

43. Louisville Daily Journal, January 19, 1865

44. Ibid. January, 24, 1865

45. Ibid. April 10th, 1865

46. Louisville Daily Democrat, April 15, 1865
47. Richard Taylor, Sue Mundy A Novel Of The Civil War, (The University of Kentucky Press, Lexington, Kentucky 2006) 272-273
48. Thomas Shelby Watson with Perry A. Brantley, Confederate Guerrilla Sue Mundy (McFarland & Company Inc. Publishers, Jefferson North Carolina, and London 2008) 66-67
49. Louisville Daily Democrat, April 19, 1865
50. John N. Edwards, Noted Guerrillas or the Warfare on the Border (Bryan Brand and Company, St. Louis, Mo. 1877) 417
51. Ibid. 426-427
52. Gerald Fischer, Captain Bill Marion, His loyalty, daring, and Bravery in Meade and Breckenridge Counties (The Meade County Messenger", March 11, 2009
53. Information taken from Lewis Collins, History of Kentucky, and W. H. Perin, J. H. Battle and G. C. Kniffen Kentucky: A History of the State, (Breckenridge County, Kentucky History and Biographies, Mountain Press, signal Mountain, Tennessee 2002) 17-18
54. John N. Edwards, Noted Guerrillas or the Warfare Of The Border (Bryan Brand and Company, St. Louis Mo. 1877) 421
55. Henry C. Magruder, Three Years In The Saddle The Life And Confession Of Henry C. Magruder The Original Sue Mundy, The Scourge Of Kentucky, (Maj. Cyrus J. Wilson, Louisville, Kentucky, 1865) 24-25
56. Louisville Daily Journal, March 6, 1865
57. Henry C. Magruder, The original Sue Mundy, the Scourge of Kentucky, Maj. Cyrus Wilson, Louisville, Ky., 1865) 58-59
58. Ibid 59
59. Ibid. 57-58
60. Thomas Shelby Watson with Perry A. Brantley (Confederate Guerrilla Sue Mundy, McFarland and Company, Inc. Publishers, Jefferson North Carolina and London, 2008) 110-111
61. Ibid. 196
62. J.B. Nation, Major Walker Taylor, C. S. A. www.math.hawaii.edu~articlejb/walker.pdf
63. Hancock Clarion, September 2, 1893
64. Louisville Daily Journal, April 8, 1865
65. Louisville Daily Journal, May 26, 1865
66. Louisville Daily Journal, March 4, 1865
67. Louisville Daily Journal, March 9, 1865

68. Louisville Daily Journal, March 25, 1865

69. Louisville Daily Democrat, March 18, 1865

70. Louisville Daily Democrat, March 18, 1865

71. Carolyn Wimp, Meade County Newspaper Abstracts 1906-1908 (Ancestral Trails Historical Society, Vine Grove, Kentucky 2007) 170

72. Louisville Daily Journal, March 25, 1865

73. bIid. April 1, 1865

74. Nelson County Families and their Place in History, 2012, 310-311

75. Horowitz, Lester V., The Longest Raid of the Civil War,(Farmcourt Publishing, Inc., Cincinnati, Ohio, 2001) 47

76. "Surrender of Sue Mundy", Louisville Courier Journal, January 27, 1939

77. Thomas Shelby Watson with Perry Brantley, Confederate Guerrilla Sue Mundy (McFarland & Company Publishers, Jefferson North Carolina and London, 2008) 164

78. Ibid. 166

79. James Louis Head, The Atonement Of John Brooks (Heritage Press, Dandridge, Tennessee) 131-132

80. Louisville Daily Journal March 16, 1865

81. James Louis Head, The Atonement Of John Brooks (Dandridge, Tennessee: Heritage Press, 2001) 146

82. Louisville Daily Journal, July 16, 1864

83. James Louis Head, The Atonement Of John Brooks" (Dandridge, Tennessee: Heritage Press, 2001) 148

84. Louisville Daily Journal, August 12, 1864

85. Louisville Daily Journal, August 31, 1864

86. Louisville Daily Journal, Aug. 31, 1864

87. James Louis Head, The Atonement Of John Brooks (Heritage Press, Dandridge, Tennessee, 2001) 173

88. James Louis Head, The Atonement Of John Brooks (Heritage Press, Dandridge, Tennessee, 2001) 43

89. Edited by William J. Davis, The Partisan Rangers of the Confederate States Army (George G. Fetter Company, Louisville, Kentucky 1904) 104

90. Edited by William J. Davis, The Partisan Rangers of the Confederate States Army (Geo. G. Fetter Company, Louisville, Kentucky, 1904) 106-107

91. John N. Edwards, Noted Guerrillas or the Warfare on the Border (Bryan Brand and Company, St. Louis, Missouri, 1877) 31

92. Shelby Foote, The Civil War, A Narrative, Fort Sumter to Perryville (Random House, New York 1958) 558

93. Ibid.558

94. Carl W. Breihan, Quantrill and his Civil War Guerrillas (Promontory Press, New York City, 1959) 17

95. Ibid. 17

96. Ibid. 18

97. John N. Edwards, Noted Guerrillas or The Warfare on the Border (Bryan, Brand, and Company, St Louis, Missouri 1877) 382-383

98. Ibid. 383-384

99. Ted P. Yeatman, Frank and Jessie James, , the Story Behind the Legend (Fall River Press, New York, 2000) 60

100. John N. Edwards, Noted Guerrillas or the Warfare on the Border (Bryan, Brand, and Company, St. Louis Missouri, 1877) 399-404

101. Ibid. 407-408

102. Ibid. 409

103. Ibid. 413

104. Ibid. 414

105. Louisville Daily Journal Feb. 2, 1865

106. Louisville Daily Journal, February 4, 1865

107. Louisville Daily Democrat, February 4, 1865

108. Louisville Daily Journal, February 5, 1865

109. Ibid. February 10th, 1865

110. Thomas Shelby Watson with Perry A. Brantley, Confederate Guerrilla Sue Mundy (McFarland Press, Jefferson North Carolina & London 2007) 132

111. Ted P. Yeatman, Frank And Jesse James, The Story Behind The Legend (Fall River Press, New York, 2000) 69-70

112. Ibid 70

113. Louisville Daily Journal, January 24, 1865

114. Ted P. Yeatman, Frank And Jesse James, The Story Behind The Legend, (Fall River Press, New York, 2000) 70

115. Thomas Shelby Watson with Perry A. Brantley, Confederate Guerrilla Sue Mundy (McFarland Press, Jefferson North Carolina & London, 2008) 127

116. The Elizabethtown News, May 19, 1904

117. Louisville Daily Journal, April 29, 1865

118. Louisville Daily Democrat, April 29, 1865

119. Thomas Shelby Watson with Perry Brantley, Confederate Guerrilla Sue Mundy (McFarland and Co. Publishers, Jefferson, North Carolina & London, 2008) 200

120. Louisville Daily Journal April 30th, 1865

121. Ibid May 1, 1865

122. Louisville Daily Journal, April 16, 1865

123. Louisville Daily Journal, April 17, 1865

124. Louisville Daily Democrat, April 17, 1865

125. Ibid. April 18th

126. Louisville Daily Journal, May 2, 1865

127. Personal interview with, Horace Brown, Great-Great-Grandson of Joseph Hughes, 2009

128. Thomas Shelby Watson with Perry Brantley, Confederate Guerrilla Sue Mundy (McFarland and Company Inc, Publishers, Jefferson, North Carolina, and London 2008) 182

129. Ibid. 181

130. Personal interview with James Wakefield, summer, 1993

131. Ibid

132. John N. Edwards, Noted Guerrillas, or Warfare on the Border (Bryan, and Brand & Company, St. Louis, Missouri 1877) 438

133. John N. Edwards, Noted Guerrillas, or Warfare on the Border (Bryan Brand and Company, St. Louis, Missouri, 1877) 428-433

134. Louisville Daily Democrat, May 13th, 1865

135. Louisville Daily Journal, May 20th, 1865

136. Louisville Daily Journal, May 21, 1865

137. Ibid. May 26, 1865

138. Louisville Daily Democrat, June 1, 1865

139. Personal Interview with James Wakefield, summer 1995

140. Thomas Shelby Watson with Perry A. Brantley, Confederate Guerrilla Sue Mundy (McFarland and

Company Publishers, Jefferson, North Carolina & London 2008) 185

141. Carl W. Briehan, Quantrill and his civil war guerrillas (Promontory Press, New York City 1959) 165

142. Find A Grave Memorial, Cemetery Records Online, cemetery.us.org, 1/15/13, Bio by: David Greyfield

143. Carl W. Briehan, Quantrill and his civil war raiders (Promontory Press, New York 1959) 24

144. Ted P. Yeatman, Frank and Jesse James, The Story Behind The Legend (Fall River River Press, New York, 2000) 78

145. Thomas Shelby Watson, with Perry A. Brantley, Confederate Guerrilla Sue Mundy (McFarland and Company Publishers, Jefferson, North Carolina & London, 2008) 189

146. John N. Edwards, Noted Guerrillas, Or Warfare On The Border (Bryan, Brand, & Company, St. Louis, Missouri 1877) 443

147. Louisville Daily Journal, June 15, 1865

148. John N. Edwards, Noted Guerrillas, Or Warfare On The Border (Bryan, Brand, and Company, St. Louis, Missouri 1877) 444

149. Louisville Daily Journal, June 6, 1865

150. Louisville Daily Democrat, June 6, 1865

151. Louisville Daily Journal, June 15, 1865

152. Louisville Daily Democrat, June 26, 1865

153. Louisville Daily Journal, August 27, 1865

154. Ibid. October 27, 1865

155. Louisville Daily Journal, November 4, 1865

156. Thomas S. Watson, Confederate Guerrilla Sue Mundy (McFarland & Company, Jefferson, N.C.) 191

157. Louisville Daily Democrat, November 7, 1865

158. Louisville, Daily Journal, December 4, 1865

159. Louisville Daily Democrat, December 11th, 1865

160. Thomas Shelby Watson with Perry A. Brantley, Confederate Guerrilla Sue Mundy (McFarland & Company Publishers, Jefferson, North Carolina, and London 2008) 71

161. Louisville Daily Journal, December 22, 1865

162. Richard Taylor, Sue Mundy (University Press of Kentucky, 2006) 346

163. Louisville Daily Journal, January 7, 1865

164. Louisville Daily Democrat, January 7, 1865

165. Thomas Shelby Watson with Perry A. Brantley, Confederate Guerrilla Sue Mundy (McFarland and Company Publishers, Jefferson, North Carolina, and London 2008) 112-113

166. Louisville Daily Journal, January 11th, 1864

167. Louisville Daily Journal, January 19, 1865

168. Louisville Daily Democrat, January20th, 1865

169. Louisville Daily Journal, January 26, 1865

170. Shelby Record, February 21, 1913

171. Henry C. Magruder, Three Years in the Saddle, The life and Confession of Henry C. Magruder (Maj. Cyrus Wilson, Publisher, Louisville, Kentucky 1865) 54

172. Louisville Daily Journal, October 20th, 1865

173. Ibid October 21, 1865

174. Ibid October 14, 1865

175. Richard Taylor, Sue Mundy, University of Kentucky Press,Lexington, Kentucky, 2006) viii

176. Marie Coleman and Laura Young Brown, The History of Meade County, Kentucky 1824-1991 (McDowell Publications, Utica, Kentucky, 1991) 303

177. Louisville Daily Journal, March 6, 1865

178. Louisville Daily Journal, August 3rd, 1865

179. Dee Brown, Morgan's Raiders (Konecky & Konecky, New York, New York 1959) 240

180. Ibid. 242

181. Lester V. Horowitz, The Longest Raid of the Civil War (Farmcourt Publishing Inc. Cincinnati, Ohio 2001) 362

182. Lester V. Horowitz, The Longest Raid of the Civil War (Farmcourt Publishing Inc., Cincinnati, Ohio 2001) 364

183. Bryan S. Bush, Butcher Burbridge (Acclaim Press, Morley Missouri 2008) 109

184. Ibid. 156

185. Bryan S. Bush, Butcher Burbridge (Acclaim Press, Morley Missouri 2008) 167

186. Ibid 34-35

187. Ibid. 35-36

188. Mary Josephine Jones, The Civil War in Hardin County Kentucky (Mary Josephine Jones, 1999) 52

189. Louisville Daily Journal, August 14, 1864

190. Ibid. August 19, 1864

191. Ted P. Yeatman, Frank and Jesse James The History Behind The Legend (Fall River Press, New York, New York 2000) 80

192. John N. Edwards, Noted Guerrillas, or Warfare On The Border (Bryan, Brand & Company, St. Louis, Missouri, 1877) 446

193. Ibid. 446

194. Ted P. Yeatman, Frank and Jesse James, The History Behind The Legend (Fall River Press, New York, New York 2000) 102

195. Ibid. 93

196. Ibid. 219

197. Ted P. Yeatman, Frank and Jesse James, The History Behind The Legend (Fall River Press, New York, New York, 2000) 83

198. Ibid. 85

199. Ibid. 86

200. G. Fischer, Meade County Kentucky History and Families (Acclaim Press, Morley, Missouri, 2012) 20

201. Gerald Fischer, Meade County Messenger, January 3rd 2008

202. John N. Edwards, Noted Guerrillas, Or Warfare On The Border (Bryan, Brand, and Company, St. Louis, Missouri 1877) 448- 449

203. Mark Ford (editor) R. M. Guibert, J. E. Troyan, J. Smiley Collins, (Minister), The Brandenburg Story, (Methodist Men's Club, Brandenburg Kentucky, July 13th, 1963) 27

204. Gerald Fischer, Meade County Messenger, January 3, 2008

205. James Wakefield, Personal Interview, 1993

206. John N. Edwards, Noted Guerrillas, Or Warfare On The Border (Bryan, Brand, and Company, St. Louis, Missouri, 1877) 132-133

207. Richard Taylor, Sue Mundy (The University of Kentucky Press, Lexington, Kentucky, 2006) 165

208. Carl W. Briehan, Quantrill and his civil war guerrillas (Promontory Press, New York, New York 1959) 44

209. Ibid. 43-44

210. P.J. Carisella and James W. Ryan, Who Killed the Red Baron (Fawcett Publications, Greenwich, Connecticut, 1969) 72

211. George L. Ridenour, Early Times in Meade County Kentucky (Western Recorder, Louisville, Kentucky, 1920) 76-78

212. Meade County Messenger, February, 1950

References

Books

Briehan, Carl, *Quantrill and his civil war guerrillas*. New York, New York: Promontory Press, 1959

Briggs, Richard, *West Point and the Civil War*. West Point Kentucky: Tops Books, 1993

Bush, Bryan, *Butcher Burbridge*. Morley, Missouri: Acclaim Press, 2008

Bush, Bryan, *Louisville and the Civil War*. Charleston, South Carolina, London: Published by The History Press, 2008

Brown, Dee, *Morgan's Raiders*. New York, New York: Knoecky & Knoecky, 1959

Carisella, P. J. with James W. Ryan, *Who Killed the Red Baron*. Greenwich, Connecticut: Fawcett Publications, 1969

Coleman, Marie and Laura Young Brown, *The History of Meade County, Kentucky 1824-1991*. Utica, Kentucky: McDowell Publications, 1991

Collins, Lewis and W. H. Perin, J. H. Battle and G. C. Kniffin, *Breckenridge County, Kentucky History and Biographies*, Information taken from History of Kentucky and Kentucky: A History of the State. Signal Mountain, Tennessee, 2002

Edwards, John, *Noted Guerrillas, or Warfare on the Border*. St. Louis, Missouri: Bryan, Brand & Company, 1877

Foote, Shelby, *The Civil War a Narrative, Vol. Fort Sumter to Perryville*. New York, New York, and Toronto, Canada: Random House, 1986

Ford, Mark (Editor), *The Brandenburg Story*. Brandenburg, Kentucky: Methodist Men's Club, 1963

Head, James Lewis, *The Atonement of John Brooks*. Dandridge, Tennessee: Heritage Press, 2001

Johnston, Col. Stoddard, & Col. John C. Moore, *Confederate Military History, Vol. IX*. Seacaucus, New Jersey: Blue and Gray Press, (Original Printing) 1899

Jones, Mary, *The Civil War In Hardin County, Kentucky*. Hardin County, Kentucky: Mary Josephine Jones, 1995, reissue, 2006

Jones, Virgil, *Gray Ghosts and Rebel Raiders*. St. Simmons Island, Georgia: Mockingbird Books, 1956

Harrison, Lowell and James C. Klotter, *A New History of Kentucky*. Lexington, Kentucky: The University of Kentucky Press, 1997

Horrowitz, Lester, *The Longest Raid*. Cincinnati, Ohio: Farmcourt Publishing, Inc. 2001

Lewis, Berry, *Kentucky Archaeology*. Lexington, Kentucky: University of Kentucky Press, 1996

Magruder, Henry, *Three Years in the Saddle, the Life and Confession of Henry C. Magruder*. Louisville, Kentucky: Cyrus J. Wilson, Publisher, 1865

Scott, Alice Bondurant, *The Doe Run Settlements*, Utica, Kentucky, McDowell Publications, 1996

Stith, Elizabeth, *Memories of Meade County, 1792-1992*. Meade County, Kentucky: The Meade County Bicentenial Commission, Meade County Fiscal Court, 1992

Taylor, Richard, *Sue Mundy*. Lexington, Kentucky: University of Kentucky Press, 2006

Thompson, Rita Adkisson, *Rambling Remarks of William Miller Boling*, Compiled by, R. A. Thompson, Meade County, Kentucky: R. A. Thompson, 1972

Bennett, Verda, Robert Cogswell, Fred E. Coy, Gerald Fischer, Cindy Henning, Charles Hockensmith, Robert Prather, and numerous other co-authors, *Meade County, Kentucky History and Families*, Morely, Missouri, Acclaim Press, 2012

Walden, Geoffrey R., *Remembering Kentucky's Confederates*. Charleston South Carolina: Arcadia Publishing, 2008

Watson, Thomas with Perry A. Brantley, *Confederate Guerrilla Sue Mundy*. Jefferson, North Carolina and London: McFarland and Company Publishers, 2008

Watson, Thomas Shelby "Bob" Watson, *Silent Riders*. Louisville, Kentucky: WAKY Radio, Documentary Series, 1970

Wimp, Carolyn, Compiled Breckenridge County Newspaper Abstracts 1893-1896. Vine Grove, Kentucky: Ancestral Trails Historical Society, 2003

Wimp, Carolyn, compiled Meade County, Kentucky Newspaper Abstracts 1906-1908

Vine Grove, Kentucky: Ancestral Trails Historical Society, 2001

Wright, Stephen, *Kentucky Soldiers and Their Regiments in the Civil War*, Abstracted From the Pages of Contemporary Newspapers, Vol. I, II, III, IV, V. Utica, Kentucky:

McDowell Publications, 2009

Wright, Stephen, *On Trial For Their Lives Volume 1*, Hodgenville, Kentucky: Steven L. Wright, 2012

Articles

Abner, Rhonda, "Was Rome Clarke really "Sue Mundy," or merely the victim of an editor's deadly prank?" American Civil War, January 1994

Allison, Young E., "Sue Mundy," An Account of the Terrible Kentucky Guerrilla of Civil War Times, The Register, Kentucky Historical Society, October 1959

Board, G. H., "Surrender of Sue Mundy," Louisville Courier Journal, Friday January 27, 1939

Fischer, Gerald W., "Meade County and the Civil War," Meade County, Kentucky History and Families, Acclaim Press Morley, Missouri 2012

Fischer, Gerald W., "Fairness of Sue Mundy's Trial in question," News Standard February 8, 2012

Newspapers

Courier Journal
Elizabethtown News
Louisville Daily Democrat
Louisville Daily Journal
News Standard
Meade County Messenger
Shelby County Record
Shelby County Sentinel

Acknowledgments

Since I retired as a teacher, I have been very fortunate to receive assistance from many people. Inevitably, I know I will probably miss someone who has helped over the years with this book and its contents. I will make every attempt to mention everyone that has been influential or contributed in the preparation of this book, including those writers, from whom I have drawn facts. In places where information I have researched differs with those writers, who dwarf me in their accomplishments, I simply put it out there for what it is, something different. Much of my information has come from old newspaper articles and compiled abstracts, church histories, bicentennial commemorative books, historical records, family documents and papers, books written many years ago, and recently written books on this admittedly limited area of study.

I would first and foremost like to thank the libraries that have helped me so much. Margaret Benham, Rachael Bealze, and Cindy Henning of the Meade County Public Library, and all of their staff, Deborah Magan of the Shelby County Public Library, and her staff, and the staff of the Louisville Free Public Library and all of the many people who were so helpful to us in researching the old files. I want to thank Sue Shacklett Cummings and Charlotte Fackler, former owners and editor of *The Meade County News Standard*. Former Editor Sandra Stone, owner Rena Singleton, and reporters Vickie Carwile, and Larry See, of *The Meade County Messenger*. I would also be remiss if I did not thank Steve Robbins, host of the popular Meade County, radio talk show "Edgewise", and WMMG Radio Station. Thanks to Mr. Kenny Popp of the cemetery record division, of the Archdiocese of Louisville, for help with locating Quantrill's grave. County Judge Executive Craycraft, who permitted me to copy the courthouse photograph collection, and County Judge Executive Lynn who added Jessie Doc Shacklett's name to the Civil War Veterans Plaque, also deserve thanks. I wish to thank Charles Hayes Publisher and Editor Elisha Richardson, of *The Kentucky Explorer Magazine, and* the Editors of *Good Old Days.*

I especially wish to thank my friend Steve Straney, a knowledgeable Meade County historian, who tramped the backwoods of Meade County, Kentucky with me, searching out the old sites, while relating to me the stories his grandfather told. Thanks Steve.

Peggy and Larry Greenwell deserve special thanks for guiding me to many places and telling me the old stories. Peggy, an artist, historian, and genealogist, co-authored several articles with me in that process.

Shirley Brown, a gifted genealogist, has helped with my research and I thank her. I also want to give special thanks to Jess and Frances Scott for their assistance in researching the Shumate School, and Billy Shacklett, and providing me their collection of photographs. Thanks to Carol Logsdon of the Brandernburg Area Chamber of Commerce, and Debra Masterson for allowing the use of her photographs. And thanks to Alice Bondurant Scott for meeting with me and writing her book "The Doe Run Settlements." I thank Mark Henderson for sharing his Grandfather John Cox's story and family papers about the Sue Mundy capture and for letting me hold Sue Mundy's pistol. That is a thrill I will never forget. I cannot forget to thank Ronnie Hall for allowing me to hold Tom Hall's muzzle loading shotgun he carried during the Civil War, which was an equally thrilling event.

Thanks to all of my extended family at the Meade County Historical and Archaeological Preservation Society has helped me in ways many may not know. Bill and Joanne Whalen, Rice Dugan, Rick Brown, Fred Coy, Andy and Beth Woolfolk, Jon Whitfield, and Beverly Furnival, who encouraged me to complete the book, after she started and completed one of her own, deserve special thanks. I also wish to thank Beverly for her masterful editing of the book. Many land owners have assisted us with information or permission allowing us to explore historic sites, and I thank them: Mr. Bucky Board, Tom and Ronnie Hall, Mr. and Mrs. Edwin Kurtz, Herb and Jan Pollock. Two friendships I made are Dan and Sabrina Redenius. Dan is the former caretaker of the Meadeville Cemetery, and of course, James Wakefield and Hobart Coomes. James and Hobart told me the old stories as only they knew them. The Hobart Coomes children deserve thanks for arranging for me to interview Hobart, and write his story of "The Coomes Cabin

Raid." The staff and people of the Medco Nursing Homes graciously provided us private space to speak with Mr. Coomes, thanks to them. Thanks also to Horace Brown, a wonderful wildlife photographer who contacted me and allowed me to interview him about Quantrill's raid on his great-great-grandfather's farm.

I also want to thank the authors I most admire, Mr. Steven Wright, who not only has written a comprehensive five volume set of contemporary Civil War newspaper abstracts, and his newest book "On Trial for Their Lives," concerning the court-martial of Sue Mundy, Henry Magruder, and Henry Metcalf, but also for providing background research and information concerning William Davison, Stanley Young, William Marsh, and the 12th Kentucky Cavalry. Mr. Tom Shelby Watson, author of "Silent Riders, and "Confederate Guerrilla Sue Mundy," with Perry Brantley, Virgil Carrington Jones, Shelby Foote, Ted Yeatman, Richard Taylor, a great Meade County Historian, author, and teacher, Dr. Marshall Myers, noted Civil War author, Bryan Bush, and Robert Prather, who not only is a good author, but was also instrumental in the publishing of our Meade County, Kentucky History and Families Book, and finally Eddie Price. I give special thanks to Jeff Caufield for allowing me the honor of publishing his poem in my book. Thanks Jeff, to you and your great-great-grandfather Shacklett, for his service. Thanks also to Jerry Williams.

Lastly, I want to thank my wife Fran for all of her help in organizing and assembling photographing, and proofing this material. She put up with long drives through the countryside, to strange and apparently empty places to photograph sites where various events occurred, and to cemeteries long ago gone to weeds. I also owe her thanks for researching the genealogy of many of the people mentioned in the book, and most of all, thanks for helping me wend my way through the tangle of computer mazes within which I found myself hopelessly lost, and for the dismal moods in which they put me. Thank you, Fran, for your help and more especially for not killing me.

—*Gerald W. Fischer*

About the Author

Gerald Fischer was born in Kentucky in January of 1945. He acquired an Associate in Arts degree in Anthropology in 1977 and in 1981 a Bachelor of Arts in Anthropology and History from the University of Louisville. In 2002 he graduated with honors from Catherine Spalding University with a Master of Arts in Teaching. He taught school in Florida and at St. Simon and Jude Catholic School in Louisville.

Fischer coauthored the "Meade County, Kentucky – History & Families Book", writes for the *Meade County Messenger*, the former *Meade County News Standard*, and *The Kentucky Explorer* magazine. He has authored numerous articles on the Civil War and guerrilla activity in Kentucky. Currently, he writes a Meade County Area Chamber of Commerce history blog entitled "Fischer's Feature's."

While doing archaeology and presenting papers at the University of Louisville, and Eastern and Western Kentucky Universities, he made presentations on historical and archaeological topics to schools, colleges, historical and archaeological societies. A member of the Falls of the Ohio Archaeological Society, he was first President of the Meade County Archaeological Society, the Meade County Historical and Archaeological Preservation Society (MCHAPS), past Vice President of the Kentucky Archaeological Association, and Activities Director of the Louisville Archaeological Society. He is currently Vice President of MCHAPS. Fischer has been interviewed on talk radio shows, television, and in 2013 was interviewed on the History Channel's "Unearthing America."

Frances and Gerald Fischer have two daughters, six grandchildren, and six great-grandchildren. They reside in a cabin on their farm in Meade County, Kentucky, with their two dogs and cat.

INDEX

E

F

G

H

I

J

K

L